Home Recording Studio

Build It Like the Pros

by
Rod Gervais

THOMSON
™
COURSE TECHNOLOGY
Professional ■ Technical ■ Reference

Publisher and General Manager, Thomson Course Technology PTR: Stacy L. Hiquet

Associate Director of Marketing: Sarah O'Donnell

Manager of Editorial Services: Heather Talbot

Marketing Manager: Mark Hughes

Executive Editor: Mike Lawson

Marketing Coordinator: Jordan Casey

Project Editor & Copy Editor: Marta Justak

Thomson Course Technology PTR Editorial Services Coordinator: Elizabeth Furbish

Cover Designer & Interior Layout Tech: Stephen Ramirez

Indexer: Sharon Shock

Proofreader: Steve Honeywell

Important: Thomson Course Technology PTR cannot provide software support. Please contact the
appropriate software manufacturer's technical support line or Web site for assistance.

Thomson Course Technology PTR and the author have attempted throughout this book to distinguish proprietary trademarks
from descriptive terms by following the capitalization style used by the manufacturer.

Information contained in this book has been obtained by Thomson Course Technology PTR from sources believed to be reliable.
However, because of the possibility of human or mechanical error by our sources, Thomson Course Technology PTR, or others,
the Publisher does not guarantee the accuracy, adequacy, or completeness of any information and is not responsible for any
errors or omissions or the results obtained from use of such information. Readers should be particularly aware of the fact that
the Internet is an ever-changing entity. Some facts may have changed since this book went to press.

Educational facilities, companies, and organizations interested in multiple copies or licensing of this book should contact
the publisher for quantity discount information. Training manuals, CD-ROMs, and portions of this book are
also available individually or can be tailored for specific needs.

ISBN: 1-59863-034-2
Library of Congress Catalog Card Number: 2005929806

Printed in the United States of America
06 07 08 09 10 PH 10 9 8 7 6 5 4 3 2

Thomson Course Technology PTR, a division of Thomson Learning Inc.
25 Thomson Place
Boston, MA 02210
http://www.courseptr.com

To my Mother and Father

You raised us to believe that the only limitations existing in our lives were those that we set upon ourselves. For this (and for not drowning me when I was 13), my everlasting thanks and love.

Acknowledgments

I wish to acknowledge the following people for their assistance with this book:

Mike Lawson at ArtistPro, my everlasting thanks for the opportunity you gave me. I hope this book is everything you envisioned.

My editor, Marta Justak, who had to endure my lack of experience as an author and who gently guided me through the process with the patience of a saint. You took a process that could have been difficult (to say the least) and made it painless.

Stephen Ramirez, layout wizard. Steve worked tirelessly on the layout of this book and designed the cover, all this while being driven crazy (I'm sure) trying to explain his needs to an author who didn't have a clue. Steve, it's beautiful. Thank you for your patience and attention to detail.

Eric Desart, even with everything else going on in your life, you found time to help me understand what I needed as I worked my way through this. My best to you and yours.

Wes Lachot, without you I could not possibly have achieved this. Your contributions and comments were truly needed. Again, you prove to me what a true friend you are.

Doug Plumb of Acousti Soft Inc., for the time you devoted to helping me understand your software. You provide an invaluable tool for the people looking to achieve what this book is trying to guide them to, and I hope that they understand your gift to the field of acoustic analysis.

Brian Ravnaas, for your contributions to both the book and my education in general.

Jeff D. Szymanski, PE, special thanks for your assistance and contributions to various chapters throughout the book. You've helped me see certain areas of acoustics in a different light.

And finally, last but certainly not least, to my brother Marc, thanks for the time and effort you devoted to review this book, and the moral support you provided throughout this process. Without you, I certainly would have gone crazy at times and lost it.

About the Author

Rod Gervais is a multi-disciplined engineer who is located in northeast Connecticut. He is a member of the Acoustical Society of America, the Audio Engineering Society, and the National Fire Protection Association. His background in construction is wide ranging, from national museums to recording and movie studios. It was his involvement in recording studio construction that first fired his need for knowledge in the field of acoustics, a fire that still burns today. His quest for knowledge is a never-ending part of his life.

Rod is also an accomplished musician, with over 40 years' experience in percussion, as well as playing guitar, bass guitar, and keyboards. His musical experience runs the gamut from classical to jazz, although the musical love of his life is the blues.

It is this combination of the analytical engineer coupled with the artistic musician that has led him to write this book—one more step on his journey through life.

Contents

Introduction

If you've bought this book then you must be a musician who wants a home studio. It's been my dream for years, and is still an ongoing, evolving project for me.

With the advent of today's gear, a musician can set up a home recording studio capable of 24-track digital recording for pennies compared to the cost of the same 10 years ago.

I've been blessed in my career with some fantastic projects, one of which you'll see inside this book. There are pictures of the "A" room at Power Station New England in Sonalysts Studios, which is located in Waterford, CT. Constructing this studio, which was designed by the world-famous record producer Tony Bongiovi, was one of the highlights of my career. It was the project that brought me (eventually) to the realization that home recording studios were an idea worth pursuing.

There are, of course, limitations. For example, the size and shape of your room will mean a lot. Professional studios tend to have large rooms for tracking and mixing. This gives them a natural ambiance. You cannot compete with that when you look at the acoustics found inside of an 8'x10' home studio.

In the same way, you won't produce the same music with a chain of gear that includes a $1,000 mixing board compared to a $600,000 board, or with $400 compressors compared to $4,500 compressors.

But what you can do is to set up a space. Then treat it, "learn it," and have fun doing what you enjoy doing most—making music that you can capture and reproduce with good to professional quality, depending on your gear and your talent.

Do I believe that home studios will ever do away with professional studios? No.

Do I believe that I will produce the same quality within my home studio that I would get in the "A" room I constructed? No...well, maybe, perhaps. A lot depends on the quality of gear and talent—some great recordings have been made in some very bad rooms (acoustically speaking). From my perspective, where you take this after construction is totally up to you.

One of the challenges that we face as musicians is the fact that we have family and neighbors who want to live their lives without having to constantly hear our music. For some strange reason, they want to be able to hear the TV or have a conversation without having our music constantly in the room they're in.

It also works in the other direction.

We want peace and quiet when we record.

We don't want to hear the dog barking in the middle of a song that was a perfect take. We don't need to hear the garage door opening when we're tracking vocals. We don't want to hear cars drive by as we record a violin passage.

This book is going to teach you (among other things) how to construct your rooms with sound isolation techniques used by the professionals in the construction industry. I'll show you how to take this one step beyond anything you've seen in books covering standard construction techniques.

I'll teach you how to design and understand your room—how to treat it, wire it, and condition it—all this while using widely available materials. No sense in showing you how to do it if you can't buy the materials it takes to get it done.

If you're handy with tools, you can build it yourself and save tens of thousands of dollars over what you would pay to have it done by professional contractors, yet you will achieve the same results.

If you're a putz when it comes to working with your hands—for example, if you can't tell the difference between a circular saw and a router—then you will have this book at hand with clear concise details of exactly what has to be done in order to use it for the purposes of specifying and inspecting the work of your contractors.

One note here about contractors and sound isolation. Unless contractors have years and years of studio experience, they do not understand sound isolating construction. Typically, contractors think they do, and for the purpose of building walls with STC ratings for hotels, offices, and apartment buildings, they can get the job done pretty well.

But when you talk about isolating a recording studio or a movie studio—places where the least sound can break an otherwise perfect audio take—they just can't get it done.

It isn't their fault, simply because it isn't their specialty. They just have no idea of what happens in the construction of anything requiring the degree of isolation that a recording studio does.

That's where this book will come into play. It will show you what they don't know. You will be able to sit with your contractors and walk through exactly what you expect of them. You will then be able to perform inspections and verify that they are indeed doing exactly what you paid them for.

There's nothing worse than spending a ton of money and having to settle for less than you need (and paid for) when it's all said and done.

I'm here to see to it that this doesn't happen to you.

By the way, because one of the goals of this book is to save you from having to learn a lot of math to get the job done, I've put some tools online for your use. These tools were put together by Brian Ravnaas, Jeff D. Szymanski PE, and me, specifically to accompany this book and make your life easier. The gents who assisted me in this effort are two of the brightest minds in the field of acoustics today. I hope you'll appreciate their efforts; I know that I do.

Please go to the Thomson Web site at www.courseptr.com/downloads or my Web site, http://www.rodssoundsolutions.com/ and visit the "Outside the Box" page. There you'll find a wide variety of useful tools to help you on your quest.

Enjoy!

CHAPTER 1

Getting Started

So…you want to build a home recording studio? Well, join the club.

Due to the recent advances in technology in the field of electronics, building a home recording studio is now more of a reality than it was 15 years ago. For example, 15 years ago, setting up a home studio to record 24 tracks at once would have been unthinkable for most people. The cost of the gear alone would have made it almost impossible to do, unless someone had some serious money to burn for a hobby. Today though, the unthinkable has become the affordable.

A Variety of Equipment Options

Just look at current gear costs for a moment. For an investment of well under four grand, you can have a 24-track board designed by Malcolm Toft of Toft Audio Designs®, which has the same technology used on the Trident Boards he designed back in the '70s and '80s. And even better yet, it's constructed directly under Malcolm's watchful eye. That price is amazing when you think about the fact that you would spend upwards of $27,000 for a used 32-track Trident Console. Heck, even the 80B input modules cost $950 a pop used—*if you can find them.*

Plus, you can have top-of-the-line tube gear produced by companies like Manley® in Chino California or Sebatron in Australia, and EveAnna Manley and Sebatron themselves are leading the way to innovative designs, while directly overseeing the construction of the gear they're selling you.

Then you have thousands of options for affordable solid-state gear, including effects boxes, compressors, limiters, pre-amps, amplifiers, etc.

Companies like Joemeek®, Tascam, PreSonus, M-Audio, and more all give you a wide variety of options for your recording needs.

All of this creates an affordable cost for starting your own home recording studio.

The Room's Design

Most of you reading this book probably have a fair idea of how to use this gear—after all, you're musicians. However, what you lack is the knowledge that it takes to build a room in which you can use this gear effectively.

Don't get me wrong—you can set up in any old room of your house (or apartment) and play around with your gear. Maybe you can even make some halfway decent sounding demo CDs if you run back and forth 10 or 12 times to your car so that you get the levels corrected. But, without a decent room, you'll never be able to sit down and really make anything you'll be truly proud of and excited to have other people hear.

The gear is only part of the equation when it comes to recording and mixing; the other part is the room(s) you do it in. The picture you see on page 3 of this book is a world-class recording studio I had the pleasure of "gently guiding" from a hole in the ground to final finishes. Designed by acoustical genius Tony Bongiovi, it was the first recording studio I ever worked on, and it was the beginning of my love and appreciation for everything special that it takes to make a recording studio.

Some Background on Tony Bongiovi

Tony Bongiovi is the president and co-founder of Bongiovi Entertainment and has built a "solid gold" reputation as an engineer and record producer, amassing more than 50 gold and platinum albums since beginning his historical career at the famous Motown label of the late 1960s. His production discography includes such artists as Jimi Hendrix, Bon Jovi, Talking Heads, The Ramones, Ozzy Osbourne, Aerosmith, Gloria Gaynor, and The Scorpions. He co-produced the biggest selling pop instrumental single of all time, "Theme from Star Wars" by MECO.

Tony conceived, created, and operated Power Station Studios, the New York based mega-studio that remains the gold standard in the recording industry, and whose client list reads like a who's who of the music industry.

Designing and constructing a recording studio is not like any other construction you might do. If you begin with a blank piece of paper and an empty piece of land, designing (and constructing) a home is easy. You decide the type of home you want, the total square footage you can afford, and then you make it all fit.

If you have to shift a wall 6" to fit some furniture in—no problem. If a bedroom ends up being 10'x10'—no problem. You only have to worry about the house being functional, but never have to concern yourself with how it will sound. Yes, I said "sound," because sound is a function of room size. You'll learn more about this later.

On the other hand, with a recording studio, not only do you need to concern yourself with its function, but you also have to concern yourself with its sound. That same 10'x10' bedroom that isn't a problem for sleeping or reading in is a problem for recording in. And if it had 10' ceilings, it would be even worse.

Next, you have to be concerned about what function you will be performing in the room—because function drives design. For example, if you are going to have a dedicated control room, then you want the room to be perfectly symmetrical. Whereas, for a dedicated tracking room, asymmetrical would be ideal. With a combination tracking/control room, settle for symmetry; otherwise, the control room part of the equation won't work.

Take a look at the figures below. These very different rooms in Studio "A" have different needs and therefore different finishes, shapes, and sizes.

Figure 1.1
Main Room.

In the Main Room of the facility, you want to be able to record it all, whether it's a full band or just a vocal. At ground level, you want it to be fairly dead—mics at that level capture just the instruments. The higher you place the mic in the room, the more lively it gets. By the time you reach the "coffin" you see in the ceiling, it sounds as if you recorded in a nightclub. A combination of close micing and room mics for ambiance make for great recording in this room.

All of these needs (and effects) were considered by Tony as he worked his way through the design of this studio in his mind, but were never perfectly executed until this particular studio was constructed, which is why *this* studio did not require "tuning" upon completion of the work.

Notice how the board spacing tightens up (the space between boards gets smaller) as you climb higher into the room. This creates a greater ratio of board surface to airspace between the boards (and whatever is behind the boards). The more square feet of exposed board (per square foot of wall surface) you have, the more the mid and higher frequencies are reflected (and bass captured).

Also, as the room rises, note how it closes down until it finally reaches the smaller volume of the coffin. This effectively creates a gradually greater reverberant field as you rise into the room. That's why mics placed in the coffin capture the feeling that you recorded live in some nightclub—that exciting, vibrant, feel of the club scene.

I can't tell you any more about this than I have. The items discussed here are all visible on the surface, and anyone who is an expert in acoustics would be able to see and understand them. But there is much more behind the boards that make this work as well—from the designed construction of the walls to their geometry in relation to the geometry of the finished surface. All of this works together hand in hand to create a room like this.

Figure 1.2
Percussion/Rhythm Room.

In the Percussion/Rhythm Room, you see just the opposite. The spacing is wide and very open between boards. This lowers the ratio of mid/high frequencies reflected back into the space. Cymbals will have a faster decay in this room, while the low frequency thump of the bass drum will be accentuated. Bass guitar recorded in this room is clear and concise once again, with all of this carefully controlled by what you see, as well as what you don't. By the way, modal issues aren't a problem in this space because of the way it opens into the main room. There is an isolation assembly for this room, but it uses glass partitions that allow just enough isolation not to cause problems in the Main Room, without creating modal issues in this room. As you will see, that's quite a juggling act.

Figure 1.3
String Room.

The String Room is designed to record a grand piano, full string section, or a single violin. This design begins with a slightly tighter board spacing at floor level, which becomes increasingly tighter higher in the room. It's a relatively small space with a tall ceiling. Oh, one thing to remember as you work your way through your studio, don't be afraid to get real creative. In the original Studio "A," there was no chance for what happened here, so it did not exist in the original. But in this studio, the wall you see on the left side of the picture was adjacent to the building exterior, with just enough room for an air-lock entrance. It's a great place for vans to back up and enter directly into the room. But there were no doors in the original, so we put some in and made them invisible. If you look carefully, you can see the edges of a pair of 3' doors by the corner of the two walls, with the surface finish applied over them.

Figure 1.3a
String Room.

Figure 1.3a gives you a different view of this room (looking into the Main Room), with the isolation panels in the closed position. There are three sets of these movable partitions that separate this room from both the Main and Rhythm Rooms and the Rhythm Room from the Main Room.

Figure 1.4
Vocal Booth.

In the Vocal Booth, you see some very different construction. Acoustic ceilings come into play. It still has wood-finished walls and floors, but in this room, you want to deaden it more than in the other rooms. You don't want a very reverberant room—you just want to capture the vocals. Adding acoustically absorbent materials to the ceiling helps a lot with this cause. Low frequency issues aren't really a problem with vocal booths, as long as they are used as vocal booths. Note how the walls in this room are out of parallel, which helps stop issues with flutter echo and comb filtering. You'll learn more about that later in the book.

Figure 1.5
Control Room.

Finally, the Control Room—once again the design is very different from any of the other spaces in the studio. This room is symmetrical, whereas the tracking rooms are not. Symmetry, in a Control Room is critical to proper stereo imaging. As you viewed in the Vocal Booth, the Control Room has a soft absorbent ceiling for acoustic control. Note how the ceiling is splayed from a low point over the board to high points at the front and back of the room. Again, this helps to alleviate problems with comb filtering and flutter echo at the engineer's location.

This room is designed to approach the acoustics found in a typical living room, but without the acoustic anomalies that would normally exist there. If you look at the rear wall of this room (Figure 1.5a), you'll see that this is also laid out in a symmetrical manner, with plenty of soft fabrics (and what's behind them) to help tame down early reflections and modal issues within the space. Plenty of space is provided for rack gear and patch bays on this wall. Front to back—left to right—perfect symmetry equates to perfect stereo imaging.

Figure 1.5a
Rear wall of Control Room.

Looking through this pro studio gives you a feel for what is involved in studio design and construction, but unless you have some serious money to invest, you aren't going to go to this extreme in your home studio. Let's take a quick look at the challenges facing you in your quest.

Sound Isolation

You can't forget the issue of sound isolation, which is possibly one of the most important aspects to consider when designing a home studio, and even high-end residential construction is generally not good enough to satisfy those needs.

In any house I design, we generally put sound-batt insulation in every sleeping area and bathroom. We also use resilient channel with sound-batt insulation for the master bedroom. This will generally make it so that you can't listen to conversations taking place in those rooms, which represents decent sound isolation for a home.

What Is a Sound Batt?

Sound-batt insulation is a lightweight, fluffy fiberglass insulation placed inside wall cavities to help stop the passage of conversations from one room to the next. This material is less dense than standard fiberglass insulation used to keep a building's climate from being affected by outside conditions.

But that doesn't even *begin* to produce the isolation required for a recording studio.

It's one thing to ask a teenager to turn down his stereo because it's too loud. It's another thing altogether to have to turn down a band that you're recording because the baby can't sleep. Or to have someone drop a dish on the floor above you and have the resultant sound destroy an otherwise perfect take in a recording session.

No—standard isolation techniques simply will not suffice in a studio environment.

If you live in a condo, an apartment building, or some other environment where your ability to modify the existing structure is severely limited, you're probably thinking that buying this book was a waste of money because you won't be able to do what you need to create your studio. Actually, this may or may not be true. You may not be able to soundproof your room, but there are plenty of treatments you can use to improve its sound that are nondestructive in nature. You can either build or purchase room treatments and install them in your space to deal with modal and non-modal issues (more about them in the second chapter). Then, perhaps you can develop a schedule with your neighbors, such as times when they won't be around, when you can work with your band to record. Maybe you can record with headphones on and everyone DI (direct in), including electronic drums (*ouch*—as a drummer not my first choice, but it would beat the heck out of not playing at all) in order to record. Then you could mix down afterwards, at a lower volume—at times when no one else is going to be bothered.

If this is the case, then you probably want to go directly to the second chapter, then to the eighth, and finish the book from there. Those are chapters you need for treating the room itself—the rest of the book pertains to sound isolation construction techniques.

If not, then keep reading.

What Sets This Book Apart from All the Rest

This book is going to show you how to get it done: how to determine the best use of that space you have, how to isolate yourself from the remaining space in your home (and the outside world at the same time), and how to treat it so that not only does your music sound right, but the room does as well.

Now, there are other books on the market that you can buy that will show you all of this, but there is a difference between this book and those books. Acoustics (whether for sound isolation, room modes, or room treatments) is all about math. It is not necessarily intuitive, and that (for a lot of people) is a problem.

EASY EXPLANATIONS

Not everyone gets along with higher math—for some people it's like speaking Latin. When they see equations on a page, they start having flashbacks to high school trig classes with teachers they didn't especially like and frustrations they don't want to revisit. Their sight begins to blur, their heart starts beating faster, they get faint, and they long for a drug to calm them down.

Well, don't worry, because with this book you don't have to deal with math at all. You'll get straightforward, easy explanations about how to make it from point "A" to point "B." I'll break down some of the math into its simplest forms for you, and I'll also provide you with the tools to get the job done without the need to understand the math that's involved.

THIRTY YEARS OF CONSTRUCTION EXPERTISE

Another thing that will set this book apart from others is that the people who wrote those other books—although they are some of the brightest and best in the world of recording studios and acoustics—are not necessarily experts in construction itself. With this book, I bring you over 30 years of construction experience, so ideas that don't really work won't be in here. Also, I'll give you some construction techniques that aren't found on paper anywhere else, but have proven themselves to be useful for me over the years.

There's no magic with any of this, regardless of what you might have heard about egg crates. There are, however, some formulas for success that (if you follow them very closely) will give you a home recording studio you can be proud of—one that will give back to you what you expect for your investment of time and money.

One thing I do want to make very clear to you is this: If you don't get it—read it again and again—and then once more until you do get it. Do not stumble blindly forward thinking that you can slip a sheet of drywall in a location where this book says you don't want it. Don't think that leaving a sheet of drywall in a location where the book recommends that you "take it out," is *not* going to make much of a difference. If you're going to bake a cake, then leaving out key ingredients is not going to get you there, and adding ingredients willy-nilly isn't going to get it done either. Follow the recipe or don't bother with the baking.

When Things Go Wrong

Two years ago I joined a Web site called www.recording.org (highly recommended, by the way, for those of you interested in advice for recording techniques from some of the pros in the industry), and shortly thereafter I was asked to help moderate their acoustic forum. In the last two years, you would not believe the number of times that people have come to the site and asked for advice, only to return later and complain that their rooms did not have any real isolation value. They are totally frustrated, have spent a lot of money building their rooms, and they are not much better off than before they started. They just can't understand it.

So we (the other moderators and I) spend a lot of time going over with them exactly what they did in the construction of their rooms, just to find out that along the way they decided that it would not make a big difference if they just left the existing drywall on the exterior wall in place (or ceiling if they built in a basement). Well, they were wrong. They were told to remove it—but they couldn't see how it could hurt—so they ignored us.

Now they have a finished room—spent thousands of dollars to build a room within a room—and they can only fix the problem by removing finishes to get at that old drywall and remove it. Pulling out that old sheet can mean the difference of 10 or 20dB of isolation, and now it also means thousands of dollars in re-work for the owner.

It's not only what you have in the construction, but also where you put it, that makes the difference between an assembly working or not working.

THE DEVIL IS IN THE DETAILS

We have had people come to us with the same complaints over and over again—for example, they've spent time reviewing their work and looking at pictures, just to find out that what they installed as resilient channel wasn't resilient channel at all, but was hat channel.

Once again, after spending thousands of dollars for materials and labor, the answer is the same—to rip it all down and start over. Had they paid attention in the first place, none of this would be necessary, but they didn't and now it's going to cost them.

One important point—please don't trust your contractors to know the difference between isolating and non-isolating materials, because the vast majority of them don't. In one of the cases with hat sections being substituted for resilient channel, the substitution was done by a contractor hired for the project—whose contract specifically stated RC-2, and who argued with the homeowner afterwards that there "really wasn't any difference." Well, I have a surprise for him—there really is.

A hat channel is simply designed as a framing member, generally used to frame suspended ceilings in commercial work. It is a cold rolled steel member without any isolating slots cut into its legs. RC-2 is specifically designed and tested to create isolation between a structural assembly and the wall surface, which is usually drywall. The isolating slots cut into its legs make all the difference. It's just that simple. That's one of the reasons that you will find illustrations in this book detailing the proper members, and the proper manner in which to install those products to get the results you're paying for.

What Is a Member?

"Member" is an all-inclusive term, which can apply to any part of any assembly. For example, a stud is a member used to frame a wall. A joist is a member used to frame a ceiling or a floor.

Another point I want to make is this: If you don't find a recommendation for a particular product in this book, then it's probably because it's not the most cost effective way to go.

There are a lot of isolation products on the market that will get the job done, but when you set them down side by side with standard construction and do a square foot analysis on the isolation received versus using standard construction with drywall (as one example), there is no way that they can compare.

It isn't that their claims of isolation value are false—they aren't—it's just that they are so expensive that they cannot compete with standard materials. Remember that the basics are mass, mass, and more mass, and some of the cheapest mass you can buy is standard 5/8" fire-code drywall.

The last thing I want to touch base on (before moving to the next chapter) is quality control.

Assuring Quality Control Protection

In the construction industry, we would typically have a project manager who buys out the project and makes the administrative decisions required to bring a project to a successful end. We would also have a project superintendent who manages the day-to-day scheduling and on-site supervision necessary to verify that the work has been completed and is installed correctly.

DOING THE JOB YOURSELF

The project superintendent is the on-site quality control inspector. It is his responsibility to make certain that everything is done according to plans and specifications in each step of the project. In the case of your home studio, you are probably going to be taking on that role.

If you want to do all of the work yourself, make it easier by taking it one step at a time and referring back to the book as you move along. But, if you hire contractors to do the work for you, it will be much harder for you to follow the progression of the work between your daily job and the performance of their contracts. Work can easily get buried before you ever have a chance to see it, and this is a recipe for disaster if your contractor decides to "cut a few corners."

Remember that what is outlined in this book does not reflect standard construction practices for 99% of the work that these contractors will ever perform, so they might get the attitude that it is "overkill" and not really required in order for them to get the job done "right." However, what's outlined in this book is what's really required to attain the extra degree of isolation required for a studio environment.

HIRING THE JOB OUT

Thus, it's up to you to do one of two things to protect yourself:

The first possibility is to find someone who knows construction, i.e., a trusted friend. Spend some time going over the requirements in this book with him/her, making certain that they understand exactly what needs to be done. Then have them do inspections for you along the way to ensure that the contractor is doing the work properly.

The only other possibility is for you to specify in your contract with the subcontractor some work limits that will allow you to perform the proper inspections.

For example, if they could install two layers of drywall in one day, they might decide that the caulking of the first layer is overkill, and not bother to do it at all. You would never know this unless you began destructive testing of the work, such as removing the caulk and backer rod from the second layer to see the first layer. You could specify (in your contract documents) that the second (third, fourth, etc.) layer of drywall could not be installed prior to inspection of the completed first layer.

If they had someone they could call for inspections, they could schedule this inspection so that their work would move along seamlessly. However, in the case of having to wait for you to inspect at the end of the day, they will probably charge you a premium for this. Pay the premium; otherwise, you might get only part of what you are paying for.

The same goes for treatments behind the wall prior to the first sheet. Although you can count on your building inspector to ensure that the electrical wiring is correct , he can only insist on adherence to the code and nothing beyond that. Thus, you could pay for certain things and not have them in the end.

So, if you are going to contract out part (or all) of the work on your studio, make absolutely certain that you outline all of the steps where inspections will be required. Insert clauses requiring removal of materials (at no cost to you) to allow for inspections, for any work that is covered up prior to your inspection *and* acceptance of the work in place.

Trust me when I tell you that you will pay extra to do work as outlined in this book compared to standard construction techniques, but if you follow the techniques outlined, you will achieve your goals for creating a home studio you can be proud of.

CHAPTER 2

Modes, Nodes, and Other Terms of Confusion

Understanding how sound works within an enclosed space helps determine how to properly design recording studios. You pick up the best speakers you can afford—special amplifiers—all made specifically for recording studio environments, all designed to avoid adding color to your mix. Then you place them inside of a room that colors the sound anyway. Room modes can lead to uneven levels in frequency and longer sound decays than normal. In a critical listening room, like the control room in your studio, you need to hear exactly what's coming out of those speakers. You don't want to have the levels affected by anything other than how you set them on the board. But the room you're in can do just that—make some notes louder, some softer, and some go away completely. Understanding what causes this discrepancy, and how to avoid (or at least minimize) it, is an important part of designing a room in which you will enjoy working. Let's look at how all of this works together.

All frequencies act in waves; however, low frequencies tend to be less directional than higher frequencies. If you think about your setup on a stage, you'll see that this is true. No matter where you are on the stage, including sitting behind a set of drums, you can feel the bass even if you don't hear it. That's because the bass frequencies get into the stage (the building), and they envelope everything around them.

Unless you have monitors, you won't be able to hear the vocals, the keyboard, or the lead guitar. The drummer especially suffers from this problem. Let's look at how this affects us in a room. Let's take a brief look at sound itself.

Sound

Sound is made up of a series of tones (frequencies), which contain amplitude (volume). There is a third variable, velocity (the speed of sound), but for the purposes of small rooms and this book, we won't worry about calculating this. We will use the conventional speed of 1,130fps (feet per second) for any calculations we might make.

AMPLITUDE

Amplitude refers to the difference between the maximum and minimum pressures within a sound wave. Pressure fluctuations in these waves are symmetrical about the current atmospheric pressure. In order to keep things simple, we will use a reference value of zero and show maximum pressure as a positive value above zero and the minimum as a negative (see Figure 2.1).

Figure 2.1
A typical sound wave.

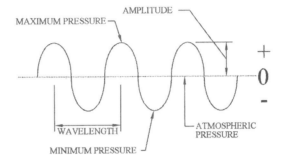

FREQUENCY

Frequency refers to the number of waves (pressure peaks) that travel a distance in one second. For example, low E on a four-string bass is 41.2 Hz (based on A440 tuning) and thus has 41.2 waves traveling 1,130 feet in one second, while a 1 kHz (1,000 Hz) sound would have 1,000 waves traveling 1,130 feet in that same second.

WAVELENGTH

Wavelength refers to the physical distance between successive pressure maxima and is thus dependent on the speed of sound in the medium divided by the frequency of the wave. The equation for this is:

$$\lambda = V/f\,^{1}$$

Where:

λ = wavelength (feet)

V = velocity (Speed of Sound)

f = frequency (Hz)

Thus, the 41.2 Hz frequency has a wavelength (distance between peaks) of 27.43 feet (8.37m) rounded to two decimal places 1130/41.2 = 27.43, while a 1 kHz frequency has a wavelength of 1.13 feet.(0.344m) 1130/1000 = 1.13.

Room Modes

Every room, including even the most professional studio, has what are called "room modes." Let's begin with an understanding of what our real concern is here, which is frequencies from 200 Hz and below. (I know Everest says 300, but I think 200 is a more reasonable cutoff, since this is roughly G below middle C. Middle C is certainly a midrange note in my book—and frequencies above this can easily be absorbed with fiberglass.) For now, let's walk through what creates room problems acoustically. We'll deal with how to treat them in Chapter 10.

A room mode is created by a room dimension coinciding with a particular frequency's distance of travel. This sounds quite simple, but in reality gets a little more involved if you are really going to understand it. All rooms have a unique distribution of low frequency standing waves, also known as "modes." Modes are resonances of a room governed directly by the dimensions of a room. The math for figuring out the modes of a room is[2]:

$$f = \left(\frac{c}{2}\right) * \sqrt{\left[\left(\frac{n_x}{L_x}\right)^2 + \left(\frac{n_y}{L_y}\right)^2 + \left(\frac{n_z}{L_z}\right)^2\right]}$$

Where:

f = resonant frequency in Hz

c = 1130 ft/sec or 344 m/s (speed of sound in air)

nx, ny, nz = room mode numbers≥0

Lx, Ly, Lz = room dimensions in feet or m

The reason that we need to know this is due to what can happen when room dimensions are the same as wavelengths (also 1/2 wavelengths, 1/4 wavelengths, etc.). As mentioned previously, one of the goals of recording is to capture the song being played as truly as you possibly can. Once this is completed, you want to mix the final product down, while hearing the mix reflect exactly what is coming out of the speakers on your system (hopefully, an accurate reproduction of what you recorded). Room modes can affect the amplitude (volume) (see Figure 2.1) of a note by increasing or decreasing it.

MODAL WAVES

This phenomenon occurs when a room dimension coincides with the wavelength, and the distance of travel is not great enough to allow the wave to naturally decay to the point that the incidence of it crossing itself (head-on) is neither constructive nor destructive.

A constructive action boosts the amplitude of a wave, while a destructive action will reduce that amplitude. Destructive areas within a wave are referred to as *nodes*. Nodes are areas where the sound decreases in amplitude. Constructive areas are referred to as *antinodes*. Antinodes are found between nodes and are the locations where the sound increases in amplitude. All of this becomes more problematic the smaller and more reverberant the room is. A room that is dead (anechoic) will suffer this to a lesser degree. However, due to the fact that it will have no natural reverb or life within it, it will end up being a very boring room. Take a look at Figure 2.2 for a moment.

Figure 2.2
Tangential modal wave in excited state.

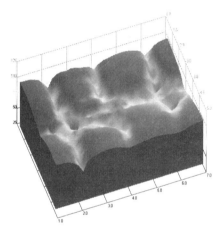

When a tangential mode (more on this in a little while) is excited in a room, the resonant standing wave is "set up" and the resulting pressure distribution will be like Figure 2.2. The dark gray shades in the contour in Figure 2.2 are areas where sound pressure is at a maximum. The lighter areas in the "troughs" of the contour are areas of minimum pressure. This contour correlates directly to what is heard when this particular room is excited by a frequency near the {3,1,0} tangential mode. In the case of this room, the dimensions are roughly 6m x 4m x 2.8m, and the frequency in question is roughly 96 Hz. This response is dependent on the location of the loudspeakers. The loudspeakers for this model were placed very near a wall. If the speakers were located instead in or near the "trough" areas (nodes), the dark areas (antinodes) would not be as "hot" with sound energy because the loudspeaker would be unable to excite this particular mode. Likewise, if a listener were seated in or near the "trough" areas, their perception would be that bass in the 96 Hz range is "thin" or somehow lacking. The frequency in Figure 2.2 roughly corresponds to G2 on the musical scale, or G an octave and a half below middle C. Mixing songs where this note is frequently played by a guitarist or bassist (in a room with these dimensions) may sound "thin." Not knowing that this is a room problem, the person mixing may overcompensate by boosting the low frequency EQ in this range. Consequently, the mix would not translate well, and would probably sound "muddy" or even distorted on the low end when played back on another system. Let's back up and look at our 41.2 Hz example for a moment. The wavelength is 27.43. If the room length, width, or height is that same dimension, the sound pressure within the room will create a standing wave. If the listener were walking around the room, there would be a series of peaks and nulls, which would correspond to the wave itself. Depending on the position of the listener in relation to the wavelength, he might hear a peak, a null, or normal amplitude in the tone.

Where this begins to get a little more involved (like we needed that) is that frequencies that are harmonics of a prime frequency related to a room dimension can also be excited. Any whole number multiple of the frequency will also be a problem. So if 55 Hz is a problem, then 110 is a problem, 165, 220, 275, etc. This corresponds to 1/2 of the room length, 1/3 of the room length, 1/4 of the room length, 1/5 of the room length, etc.

By the same token, constructing a room with a dimension of 13.72' (1/2 of the room dimension above) will provide exactly the right conditions for all of those frequencies to still get excited, causing the same problem.

If you haven't thought about all of this before now, you're probably wondering why any of this matters to you. The answer is that standing waves, or any wave that acts like a standing wave (more on that in a moment), can affect the amount of a particular frequency that you add (or subtract) during mixdown, due to it sounding louder or softer than it really is in the mix. It can also cause various musical parts of an instrument being played to vary in amplitude if you used a room mic for ambiance.

One of the ways of attempting to deal with this problem when recording in small rooms is to close mic the instrument or amplifier. When doing this, you can lower instrument volumes, which at least helps to take some of the room out of the equation. However, if your mic sits in a null, nothing can help you to capture a note that isn't heard. In the control room, you do not have that option. There you generally want to lie back, set your mix levels, and generate the sound you would hear if you took this to another room to play it back. You can always wear headphones (to take the control room out of the equation), but this is not the preferred method of mixing down a recording.

Suppose for a moment that your listening position was in a location where that same E (41.2 Hz) we've been discussing here had a peak of 6dB. (We'll look at exactly how we get this 6dB peak in a moment.) Because the room is artificially amplifying this sound in your mixing spot, you would naturally lower the levels until the mix sounded right. But when you walked out of that room and began to play this in another location—one that this phenomenon did not exist in—you would suddenly find that your mix had holes in it where the bass belonged. A 6dB cut would sound like the bottom just fell out. In reverse, should you be sitting in a null, the mix would end up being bass heavy. The design goal for a mixing room is to be able to hear exactly what's coming out of your speakers without the room affecting the outcome.

Now to understand this all in greater depth. A manner I have found to aid people in viewing this initially is to compare a mode to a series of colliding balls, also known as Newton's Cradle (see Figure 2.2). We've all seen this one time or another.

It's a case of an outer ball (or multiple of balls) being swung so that they impact an adjacent ball—with the result being an equal number of balls on the opposite side being propelled at (apparently) the same speed and distance—with this repeating from side to side once set into motion. The balls in the middle never seem to move. They are actually being placed in a state of compression, transferring this energy to an adjacent ball, at which point they are in a state of rest until they are again compressed and do the same in reverse.

Figure 2.2a
Here is an example of Newton's Cradle.

Now picture a wall sitting on either side of those central balls—with the walls moving in and out (to impart the energy), instead of having those outside balls in motion. To the viewer (in either case), those balls in the middle don't move. If you could physically see the excited mode of a room, you would be amazed to be seeing virtually the same thing. The wave doesn't move—it just sits there and grows in level.

In the case of the balls, you have impact, compression, transfer of energy, and then a period at rest. In the case of the room mode, you have a spring effect , thus you have, compression—tension—compression—tension, with no point of rest.

With sound then, you have a source point sending a wave, which strikes a boundary, and the signal is returned towards the source. While this is taking place—at the exact point in time as the original signal is being returned—a second signal is being sent by the speaker. They meet in the middle of the room and pass one another. We now have two waves passing perfectly in sync in opposite directions from one another. This is the point where the wave becomes standing. The points of pressure and velocity become essentially locked in place and do not move. They simply begin to build within the space.

At the initial intersection of one another, the amplitude is increased or decreased by 6dB, depending on the particular location of the listener within the space. But if the duration of the tone generated is long enough, this can grow quite dramatically. It isn't unusual during room testing to see peaks and nulls of much greater than 20dB.

OK, before you say anything, let me clarify. "*This would be the case if the speaker were perfectly flush with the face of the wall. But if he isn't, how would this still work?*" (You were thinking that, weren't you?) Remember when I said earlier that bass frequencies traveled in waves? I explained that they permeate that which is around them, for example, build up within a space like waves spread out in a pond if you threw a rock into the water. Well, that's exactly what they do. So, even if the speakers aren't at the edge of the room, you can still create a standing wave by exciting a room mode. It doesn't matter whether the completion of the cycle occurs at the edge of the room or 1' from that edge. When the source meets itself head on, it will create a standing wave. I do want to point out to you that a mode is able to be excited to a greater extent from the room boundaries, and because of this, you can minimize the level of this phenomenon by proper speaker placement. However, regardless of where a source begins, if its dimension relates to a room dimension, it can generate a standing wave.

NON-MODAL WAVES

Although technically only a room mode creates a standing wave, I like to use the term non-modal waves to describe a phenomenon that is similar to a room mode, but has different causes. Whereas a standing wave is related directly to room dimensions, non-modal waves can be related to the distance of a speaker to a surface, an instrument to a surface, etc. Let's look at a few examples of non-modal standing waves.

Back Wall Interference

Back wall interference is probably as significant an issue as modal standing waves. In this case, where the listener is located, between the speaker and the interfering boundary, becomes important. As the listener moves forwards and backwards, he will hear nulls at different frequencies. In this case, as the listener moves forward in the room, the effect of this interference on the various frequencies will become less apparent. When we look at room design, we will examine speaker placement and seating positions to minimize this problem.

So, now we have room modes, nodes, antinodes, non-modal standing waves, speaker placement, listener location—all of these problematic issues to contend with. Could it get any more challenging?

Yes, it could, and it does. In addition to all of this, you can have nulls created by something called "speaker boundary interference response."

SBIR

SBIR (speaker boundary interference response) is the coupling of the listener and the loudspeakers to reflections from the wall behind the speaker (the speaker is sitting between the boundary and the listener, in this case). This problem again exists primarily with low frequencies. It is a combination of the interference (both constructive and destructive) from the loudspeaker's direct sound and reflections from the room boundaries that can cause severe peaks and nulls. In this case, though, the effect is constant in nature, and you can learn to adjust for this fairly easily in your mix.

Other Reflective Problems

You also have reflected sounds that can destroy the stereo imagery of your recording. Although these effects are easier to deal with than the modal issues that plague small rooms, they will have to be dealt with nonetheless.

FLUTTER ECHO

Flutter echo is a distinctive ringing sound caused by echoes bouncing back and forth between hard, parallel surfaces following a percussive sound, such as a handclap.

To minimize flutter echoes, which can plague even a studio having a perfect T60 across the band, certain precautions can be taken. If you're building from scratch, facing walls can be made out of parallel by at least 1 in 10 (6%), but if this isn't possible, some form of mid/high absorber can be applied to one or both walls to reduce the problem. Figure 2.3 indicates causes of flutter echo.

Figure 2.3
Flutter echo.

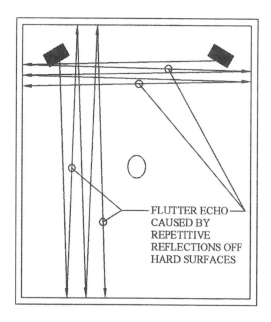

FLUTTER ECHO
CAUSED BY
REPETITIVE
REFLECTIONS OFF
HARD SURFACES

COMB FILTERING

Another form of acoustic distortion introduced by room reflections is comb filtering. Comb filtering is due to interferences that exist between a direct sound and the reflected sound from the same source. In Control Rooms, you are primarily concerned with the interaction between direct sounds and their first-order (i.e., single-bounce) reflections. These reflections cause time delays because the reflected path length between your ear and the source is longer than the direct sound path. Thus, when the direct sound is combined with the reflected sound, you'll experience notching and peaks referred to as comb filtering. The term "comb filtering" comes from the plot that this data provides, which resembles a comb. Figure 2.4 indicates the cause of comb filtering. Figure 2.4a is a graphical representation of the comb filtering effect.

Figure 2.4
The cause of comb filtering.

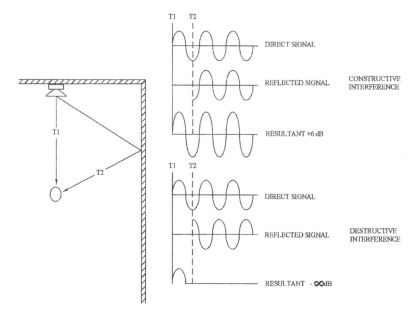

Figure 2.4a
Comb filter plot indicating peaks
and dips in amplitude.

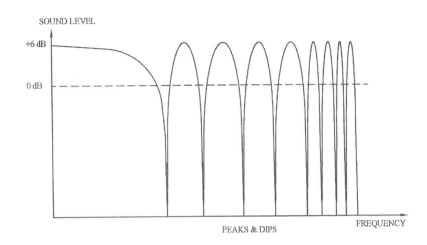

EARLY REFLECTIONS AND STEREO IMAGING

You can also have the stereo image destroyed by early reflections from the wrong speaker. This takes place when a sound from one speaker bounces off a side wall and enters the ear a split second after the direct sound from that ear's speaker. Because the delay is only a split second, the mind does not differentiate between the two sources. It tricks the brain into believing the sound came from the speaker located on that side of the room. The occurrence of this destroys proper stereo imaging. For example, your left ear believes that it hears (from the left speaker) sounds that are actually emanating from the right speaker. This makes it impossible for you to properly mix a true stereo image of your recording. Figure 2.5 shows you the cause of this early reflection issue.

Figure 2.5
Early reflection destroying a stereo
image.

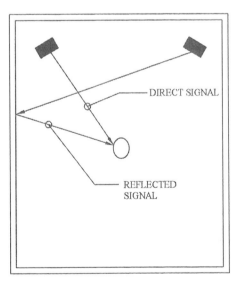

Because of the fact that this problem exists within the mid to high frequency range, it is another quirk that can be handled fairly easy. You will treat this by creating a reflection free zone within the room.

Mode Analysis

"Rod, I used one of the 'best' room ratios to design my room, I paid attention to detail, everything is constructed, and I ran a test on my room, but the modes are not what were predicted with mode analysis. What did I do wrong?"

It is possible that you could properly design a room, completely test it after construction, never make a mistake, and yet have different results with nodes and antinodes than you expected based on an analysis with a room mode calculator.

I have never seen this completely explained anywhere, but when I think about it, at least one contributing factor comes to mind. I want you to know that this is my own conclusion based on my understanding of this subject, which has not been proven by any tests I know of to date. But the conclusion is perfectly logical to me, so I offer it for your consideration. At some point in time, I am going to have to develop a construction model for this and have it tested.

I believe that part of the reason for this is due to the fact that a modal analysis of any space makes certain assumptions of that space. One is that the room is rectangular in shape. Another is that the modal boundaries are an infinitely rigid dense material that sound is incapable of escaping from. Although the math works from the perspective of calculating the effects (if these infinitely dense walls really existed in our room) in the vast majority of cases, this is not anywhere near reality, especially with small home studios.

We all construct walls that sound escapes from. In fact, we might build a wall that has a center frequency, which allows sound at that frequency to strike a boundary directly on the other side of the wall, and then re-enter the room through that same wall.

Let's take a look at a basement studio for a moment. Suppose that you have a basement with a wall-to-wall dimension of 36'-7 3/8". Within this space, you construct a "room within a room" studio, with the walls 1" clear from the face of foundation wall, 2x4 construction with drywall over that, and when completed the walls have a center frequency of 30.87 Hz (which just happens to coincide with the low B string on a five-string bass guitar). In this case, a note from that B string would (as I pointed out earlier) pass through the wall "like a knife going through hot butter" and be reflected off the outer boundary back into the room. Because your concrete walls are 36'-7 3/8" from one another, which coincides with the wavelength of that B string, you could have a room mode you didn't account for if you base the mode analysis strictly on the room itself.

Now understand, I am neither suggesting that you ignore room modes during design, nor do I suggest that an analysis of room modes never makes sense. Nothing could be farther from the truth. I am simply explaining to you that there is much more to this than analysis, math, and acoustic theories. You should understand that when it comes to the predictive models in the acoustic world, once constructed things do not always behave exactly as predicted. Testing after the fact is always required to verify the treatments you will require within the space.

This is one of the reasons that many thousands of dollars are spent testing isolating assemblies, room treatments, etc. The math involved is a good thing because it gives you a fairly good idea of whether you're headed in the right direction. However, the only way you can ever know with any degree of certainty whether your predictions were correct or not is to perform tests. So begin with the best you can, build it the best that it can be built, and then test for actual conditions before you begin any room treatments.

Room Sizes

By the way, all of this becomes more problematical the smaller the room becomes. Modal activity in relatively large rooms might be small due to the natural decay rate of waves. As rooms become smaller, the amplitude of the wave has less decay time during its travel and thus exhibits greater constructive/destructive interference. Let's look at these rooms a little more closely.

LARGE ROOMS

For home studios, I would describe large rooms as rooms with minimum lengths of around 30'+/-, widths of 20'+/-. and average room heights of not less than 12'—or combinations thereof equaling greater than 5,000 c.f. (cubic feet). In large rooms, there is generally enough travel distance so that sound has a chance to decay to the point that constructive/destructive actions in the room are beginning to minimize. What effect there is ends up being fairly easy to manage from a treatment point of view. In addition, large rooms have the advantage of being able to institute designs, including splayed walls, which, if the splay is large enough, can create a modal zone that spans multiple frequencies in any given wall dimension. You can construct a room with acoustic qualities rivaling most professional studios if you can provide this much volume in your room.

MEDIUM ROOMS

Medium sized rooms—and by this I mean rooms of 2,000 to 5,000 cf in size—tend to exhibit more modal activities, but are generally large enough that some care can be taken to alleviate problems relating to modes without having to go to extremes.

SMALL ROOMS

Small rooms, however, (rooms less than 2,000 c.f. in area) become more and more problematical as you decrease the room area. And in some small rooms there can be dimensions that cause even more problems than you might expect.

Occasionally, I have people come and ask how to deal with rooms that are cubed dimensionally, for example, 8'x 8'x 8' or 10'³. I tell them that these rooms are to be avoided like the plague. Not only are they small in area (512 c.f. to 1,000 c.f.), but also they have exactly the same modes in all three dimensions—a modal nightmare that will drive you crazy. The only advice I can give them if they can't make physical changes to the room dimensions is to either find a new room or make the room completely dead.

You should know that there are also problems inherent with making rooms completely dead. The first is a matter of human comfort. We are not accustomed to existing in an environment that is without any amount of reverb, and thus we tend to tire quite quickly when confronted with working in this environment. The next is that one tends to overcompensate for the lack of natural reverb by adding too much artificial reverb into the mix.

Having said that, I would like to clarify one thing—you could learn to compensate for this. You can learn to compensate for a mode, non-modal standing waves, and any other acoustic anomaly that might exist in a room. If you truly pay attention to what goes on in your mix and learn your room, you can make the adjustments necessary to mix right, even if your room is wrong. It's been done before, and some real great music has come out of some really bad rooms. But, if you do this as a hobby—if you don't do this day in and day out—you may never really "get it," and even if you do—it will still never sound "perfect" to you while you're in the room, even if it sounds great when you finally play it outside. Besides, that all sounds (to me) like a little bit too much work, and I don't know about you, but I do this for fun. Better if we can make rooms that minimize these problems.

Types of Room Modes

All of our work so far has been to focus on sound moving side-to-side, front to back, or top to bottom. However, this is only one type of room mode. There are actually three types of room modes: axial modes, tangential modes, and oblique modes.

AXIAL MODES
The first mode is the axial mode, which is exactly the concept we have been discussing above. This mode is based on the simple dimensions of walls opposite one another and the dimension of the floor to ceiling.

Figure 2.6
Axial modes in a room.

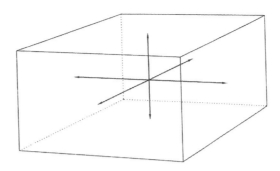

Take a look at Figure 2.6, which is an example of axial modes in a simple rectangular room. The activity is focused on any two surfaces only. Understand that this is not an either/or situation. You will have modal activity from all of these surfaces. That's why it's so important to make certain that your room ratios are such that they reinforce modes in multiple directions.

TANGENTIAL MODES

Tangential modes are formed by the relationship of any four surfaces within a room. When the travel distance formed by the four surfaces coincides with a frequency wavelength, the tangential mode can become excited. Tangential modes require two times the power of an axial mode to produce the same change in amplitude (pressure level). In Figure 2.7, you see an example of a tangential mode in a rectangular room. In this case, you see one modal activity in play (for clarity's sake), which includes only the four walls, but it could just as easily be any two walls with the ceiling and floor in play as well.

Figure 2.7
Tangential modes in a room.

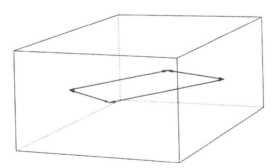

OBLIQUE MODES

Oblique modes are formed by the relationship of all six surfaces within the room. When a travel distance formed by those six surfaces coincides with a frequency wavelength, the oblique mode can become excited. Oblique modes require four times the power of an axial mode to produce the same change in amplitude (sound pressure).

Figure 2.8 indicates the sound travel required to produce an oblique mode. As shown, this mode becomes excited when the travel of the sound takes all six surfaces into account. Because of the power requirements of

Figure 2.8
Oblique modes in a room.

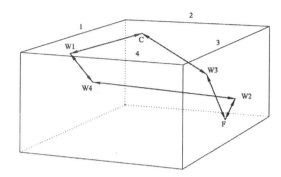

Figures 2.6 through 2.8 are simplified, to say the least. They are intended to help you understand the manner in which these modes work, but they are also slightly deceptive in that they paint the picture of a very tight sound wave. A laser beam, with properly placed mirrors, would travel as shown above, but sounds waves, especially low frequency sound waves are not that directional. As discussed in the beginning of this chapter, LF waves are very broad and tend to permeate the room. Thus, although ray tracing (as shown above) can help to understand how this works, in general, it is not completely representative of LF modal behavior.

In properly designed large and medium sized rooms, I do not become overly concerned with oblique and tangential modes. Because mixing is generally done around 85dB (this is about the maximum sound level that can be used without tiring one's self out quickly), the decay rate of the sound should allow for very little amplitude interference. This is due to the distance of travel within the space. Treatment of what interference exists is relatively easily handled. But small rooms are a different story. In small rooms, I would recommend that any modal analysis includes all three modes.

For the purpose of small room design, there have been numerous studies of the effects that room ratios have in relation to modal activity. Next, we will look at some of the outcomes of those studies.

Room Ratios

In order to design rooms in which these types of problems can be minimized, a series of known good ratios have been established over the years specifically for small room designs.

Some of the more popular ratios are as follows:

(In all cases, 1 is equal to ceiling height, and walls are represented as a ratio relating to the ceiling height; thus, Height x Width x Length)

	H W L
L. W. Sepmeyer: [3]	1: 1.14: 1.39
	1: 1.28: 1.54
	1: 1.60: 2.33
M. M. Louden: [4]	1: 1.40: 1.90
	1: 1.30: 1.90
	1: 1.50: 2.10

I would note that the orders listed above are (top to bottom) the first to third best ratios in both cases. There are many other ratios that can be found, but those listed first best by both Sepmeyer and Louden are two of the more widely used in professional studios worldwide.

MODE CALCULATORS

I want to touch on the subject of mode calculators for a moment. There are literally hundreds of these on the Internet. Some are much better than others. Personally, I don't use them. The reality is (especially in small rooms) that in the end you are going to have to treat your room to make it right. If you use known room ratios to begin with, then you are that much further ahead of the game. If you do not have the space to do that—for example, if you have such a small space that you just can't afford to give up any real-estate to make these adjustments—then just build your room and deal with what treatments you have to in the end. I say this because although running a mode calculator is easy, understanding it is altogether different. You could be building your room for a long time before you figure out what it's about.

However, should you decide to get into it, should you decide to calculate room modes beforehand, don't get nervous if you use the ratios listed here (or some other of the famous room ratios) when you check your room modes. When you do, you'll see a lot of excited modes. This is to be expected in small rooms. One of the things that makes these rooms work is that when you have enough modes excited, things tend to smooth out. If you could create a room in which all frequencies were modes—and all were excited equally— then for all intents and purposes, the modes would not exist.

To make it easier for you to identify frequencies with distance, I have included a frequency chart on the following pages.

Frequency Charts

These tables were created using $A_4 = 440$ Hz

Speed of sound = 1130 ft/s

("Middle C" is C_4)

Note	Frequency (Hz)	Wavelength (cm)	Wavelength (ft)
C0	16.35	2100	69.11
C#0/Db0	17.32	1990	65.24
D0	18.35	1870	61.58
D#0/Eb0	19.45	1770	58.10
E0	20.6	1670	54.85
F0	21.83	1580	51.76
F#0/Gb0	23.12	1490	48.88
G0	24.5	1400	46.12
G#0/Ab0	25.96	1320	43.53
A0	27.5	1250	41.09
A#0/Bb0	29.14	1180	38.78
B0	30.87	1110	36.61
C1	32.7	1050	34.56
C#1/Db1	34.65	996	32.61
D1	36.71	940	30.78
D#1/Eb1	38.89	887	29.06
E1	41.2	837	27.43
F1	43.65	790	25.89
F#1/Gb1	46.25	746	24.43
G1	49	704	23.06
G#1/Ab1	51.91	665	21.77
A1	55	627	20.55
A#1/Bb1	58.27	592	19.39
B1	61.74	559	18.30
C2	65.41	527	17.28
C#2/Db2	69.3	498	16.31
D2	73.42	470	15.39
D#2/Eb2	77.78	444	14.53
E2	82.41	419	13.71
F2	87.31	395	12.94
F#2/Gb2	92.5	373	12.22
G2	98	352	11.53
G#2/Ab2	103.83	332	10.88
A2	110	314	10.27
A#2/Bb2	116.54	296	9.70
B2	123.47	279	9.15
C3	130.81	264	8.64
C#3/Db3	138.59	249	8.15
D3	146.83	235	7.70
D#3/Eb3	155.56	222	7.26

Note	Frequency (Hz)	Wavelength (cm)	Wavelength (ft)
E3	164.81	209	6.86
F3	174.61	198	6.47
F#3/Gb3	185	186	6.11
G3	196	176	5.77
G#3/Ab3	207.65	166	5.44
A3	220	157	5.14
A#3/Bb3	233.08	148	4.85
B3	246.94	140	4.58
C4	261.63	132	4.32
C#4/Db4	277.18	124	4.08
D4	293.66	117	3.85
D#4/Eb4	311.13	111	3.63
E4	329.63	105	3.43
F4	349.23	98.8	3.24
F#4/Gb4	369.99	93.2	3.05
G4	392	88	2.88
G#4/Ab4	415.3	83.1	2.72
A4	440	78.4	2.57
A#4/Bb4	466.16	74	2.42
B4	493.88	69.9	2.29
C5	523.25	65.9	2.16
C#5/Db5	554.37	62.2	2.04
D5	587.33	58.7	1.92
D#5/Eb5	622.25	55.4	1.82
E5	659.26	52.3	1.71
F5	698.46	49.4	1.62
F#5/Gb5	739.99	46.6	1.53
G5	783.99	44	1.44
G#5/Ab5	830.61	41.5	1.36
A5	880	39.2	1.28
A#5/Bb5	932.33	37	1.21
B5	987.77	34.9	1.14
C6	1046.5	33	1.08
C#6/Db6	1108.73	31.1	1.02
D6	1174.66	29.4	0.96
D#6/Eb6	1244.51	27.7	0.91
E6	1318.51	26.2	0.86
F6	1396.91	24.7	0.81
F#6/Gb6	1479.98	23.3	0.76
G6	1567.98	22	0.72
G#6/Ab6	1661.22	20.8	0.68

Note	Frequency (Hz)	Wavelength (cm)	Wavelength (ft)
A6	1760	19.6	0.64
A#6/Bb6	1864.66	18.5	0.61
B6	1975.53	17.5	0.57
C7	2093	16.5	0.54
C#7/Db7	2217.46	15.6	0.51
D7	2349.32	14.7	0.48
D#7/Eb7	2489.02	13.9	0.45
E7	2637.02	13.1	0.43
F7	2793.83	12.3	0.40
F#7/Gb7	2959.96	11.7	0.38
G7	3135.96	11	0.36
G#7/Ab7	3322.44	10.4	0.34
A7	3520	9.8	0.32
A#7/Bb7	3729.31	9.3	0.30
B7	3951.07	8.7	0.29
C8	4186.01	8.2	0.27
C#8/Db8	4434.92	7.8	0.25
D8	4698.64	7.3	0.24
D#8/Eb8	4978.03	6.9	0.23

Now let's head into the next chapter and learn a bit about sound isolating construction techniques.

Endnotes

[1] Source Unknown

[2] A New Criterion for the Distribution of Normal Room Modes*, Oscar Juan Bonello, J. Audio Eng. Soc., Vol. 29, No. 9, 1981 September

[3] Computed Frequency and Angular Distribution of the Normal Modes of Vibration in Rectangular Rooms. Journal of Acoustic Society of America Volume 37 No. 3, pages 413-423 (1965)

[4] Dimension-ratios of Rectangular Rooms With Good Distribution of Eigentones. Acustica, Volume 24, pages 101-104. (1971)

CHAPTER 3

Isolation Techniques—
Understanding the Concepts

First, please don't get too hung up on the term "STC ratings." An STC (Sound Transmission Class) rating is a single number rating used to compare different assemblies, based on the reduction in noise levels that the assembly provides. Partition sound transmission losses are measured by using ASTM E 90 "Standard Test Method for Laboratory Measurement of Airborne Sound Transmission Loss of Building Partitions and Elements" and are calculated using ASTM E 413 "Classification for Rating Sound Insulation."

The higher the STC rating, the better the sound isolation value of the assembly will be. However, STC ratings were really designed and intended for the frequencies dealing with human speech not for music. There is no standard (that I know of) that is specifically designed for recording studios. So although we will deal with STC for initially choosing an assembly to start with, we will leave it behind as we try to deal with isolating the frequencies below those that the STC ratings deal with.

Second, forget about building "soundproof" rooms—they don't exist. Any assembly will let sound through—it just depends on the volume and frequency of the sound. What you are really going to build are sound isolating walls, ceilings, and floor assemblies, which affect the amount of sound able to travel through the assembly when completed. The challenge when designing a home studio is to figure out what you need to isolate yourself from (or whom you need to isolate from you), what the offending sound levels are, what the frequency ranges are, and just how much of that sound needs to be affected to get the job done right. For example, if you will only be playing an acoustic violin within the space, you live alone in the middle of the woods, 400' from your nearest neighbor, 500' from the road, and in a no-fly zone—then you can get away with standard construction techniques without worrying about outside noise bothering you (or you bothering anyone else). The only thing you will have to do is treat your space acoustically.

However, if you have neighbors 10' from your house, who play rap music outside in nice weather at 110dB with the speakers pointed towards your room, then you have your work cut out for you to isolate yourself from that noise source.

Determining what you need to keep out (or in—once constructed, isolation works the same in both directions) is as simple as obtaining a sound level meter and gathering data on the sound levels. Take some readings within the space you plan to use when the noise levels outside are at their worst. Alternatively, (if you live in a quiet area), get some musicians inside your space and let them jam. Take some readings outside your house, both within 3' of the house and then near your property lines. Take some readings throughout the house. Make sure to take notes along the way, because this data will help you decide exactly how much isolation you need. It will also let you know where your areas of concern are within the house.

Sound level meters are measuring devices for sound pressure levels. These devices are as inexpensive as $40 for non-recording meters to several thousands of dollars for professional data gathering devices. I would point out that the $40 meters generally do not read below 50dB, but if readings before any construction are below that level, you are in pretty good shape anyway. The Radio Shack, Digital-Display Sound-Level Meter (Model33-2055) is a good buy for $49.99.

If you aren't comfortable with your ability to gather the data, you can always hire a local acoustician (acoustic engineer) to come over and take some readings for you. The overall cost of a few hours of readings (by a professional) should not cost you as much as a decent quality meter would.

We will discuss in more detail what you require, based on those readings in Chapters 4 and 5 when you learn about isolated assemblies. For now, let's focus on what you need to get the quality of the work that's going to be required to meet your needs.

For the purpose of constructing sound isolating assemblies, certain conditions need to be met. Acousticians pay close attention to three areas when designing assemblies for isolation.

You need to understand the following areas:

▶ Mass

▶ Airtight construction

▶ Flanking paths

Let's examine each of these items in detail.

Mass, Mass, and More Mass

Forget the myths you've heard over the Internet. Forget what your friends tell you. There aren't any magic beans you can buy that will stop your sound from bothering your family or neighbors. It takes airtight construction, decoupling from structure, and mass to keep sound within (or out of) your room(s). Every doubling of mass increases isolation by an additional 6dB. This is known as the *Mass Law*. Although the Mass Law strictly applies to non-rigid (limp) assemblies, it can be used as an approximate guide to determine the amount of isolation possible—especially if you have a good idea what the wall design you're using is capable of before beginning construction.

Decibels

Let's take a moment to understand the decibel (dB) and how it works relating to the sounds you hear. The decibel is (strictly speaking) a way to compare power levels, where the two levels may be measured in watts, milliwatts, microwatts, or kilowatts. To make it clear, picture a simple speaker cabinet containing one speaker. Assume an output of the speaker of 100 watts. Adding a second speaker adjacent with the first and set to the same 100 watt output will be an increase of 3dB, which is an increase of 50%. In order to take the next step, you will have to place two more speakers with the first pair. Now you have four speakers, all with 100 watts of output and an increase of 6dB from the original signal. So 6dB is a doubling of SPL (sound pressure level). However, the human ear does not perceive this as double in volume. The next step is to add four more speakers to the stack. A total of eight speakers, with 800 watts of output, for a net increase of 9dB. Now you're almost there. The human ear hears a doubling in volume at roughly 10dB. For the purpose of discussion in this book, 6dB will be referenced as either double or one-half as loud.

Unfortunately, it also holds true that for roughly every octave drop in pitch, sound isolation is halved. Thus, although sound isolation for higher frequencies is relatively easy to obtain, isolation for lower frequencies is much more difficult to achieve.

To truly understand this, you would need to look at (and understand) how mass, stiffness, and damping come together to affect an assembly. Plus, you need to understand that panel resonance is affected at lower frequencies and coincidence at higher frequencies.

At lower frequencies (roughly 10–20 Hz), sound transmission tends to depend mostly on how stiff the assembly is. Lucky for us, this frequency range is well below that of the music we are dealing with, so it shouldn't to be a problem for most home studios. As frequencies rise, resonance begins to control transmission. Every assembly essentially creates a panel that will have its own center frequency. This is called the *resonant frequency,* and it consists of a fundamental frequency (having the greatest effect), and multiples of this fundamental called *harmonics.*

Picture a tuned drumhead. Connect a guitar tuner to a microphone and set the mic over your drum. When you strike the head, you can see the frequency the head is tuned to. (This is easier if the snares are off by the way). That is the resonant frequency of that drumhead. A wall, floor, or ceiling assembly is much the same as that drumhead. A resonant frequency will pass through a wall like a hot knife through butter. For this reason, it would be a fairly perfect world if we could create assemblies with resonant frequencies below 10 Hz. (Remember that we do not often use that frequency in most music.)

Frequencies above the resonant frequency are the ones controlled most by Mass Law. Those are the frequencies that we can handle strictly by adding mass to our system. While doing that, again remember that the doubling of mass increases isolation by (roughly) 6dB.

That leaves us with understanding coincidence. For every frequency above a certain critical frequency, there is an angle of incidence for which the wavelength of a bending wave can become equal to the wavelength of an impacting sound. This condition is known as *coincidence*

When coincidence occurs, it allows an easy transfer of sound from one side of a panel to the opposite side. This shows up as a big "dip" at the critical frequency. In thin materials like glass, coincidence frequencies begin somewhere between 1,000 and 4,000 Hz. What's interesting to note is that speech frequencies begin in this same region. Above the critical frequency, stiffness begins to play an important role again. See how easy that was?

It's not really that difficult, because (in the end) unless you plan to become an acoustic engineer, understanding all the little details about how this works is not as important as understanding exactly how to construct your room. There is a belief among a lot of people posting on the Internet that constructing walls with materials that have different densities, or the same densities with a different thickness, will increase sound isolation.

I see people posting all the time that they have superior walls because they installed one layer of 1/2" gypsum board over one layer of 5/8" gypsum board over one layer of 5/8" medium density fiber board. They believe that the wall is superior because each of the materials has a different TL value. Although I might understand their thought process, I cannot find any hard data to support that this is a better wall than it would be if they used the equivalent mass of standard 5/8" gypsum board. I always ask them how they tested their walls, and what the actual TL value of the final product was at the various frequencies we're all interested in. The responses were pretty much always the same: "I didn't actually have it tested, but when I stand outside and the music is blaring inside, I can hardly hear it, so it must be better."

Actually, what they heard outside, or in another room of the house, does not indicate the value of the assembly over standard construction techniques. Only laboratory testing of an assembly will give you accurate answers. Without that, it's nothing more than guesswork. I will never suggest that you spend your hard-earned money on construction when the outcome is not based on laboratory-tested assemblies. Rather, I would have you plan your construction based on the extensive testing that has been performed in certified laboratories. Expand on that by simply adding mass to the wall to increase isolation. "Tested, tried, and true" is my motto, and I stand behind that because it's the only way I can assure you of the outcome you desire.

Airtight Construction

Simply put, where air goes—sound goes.

Some of the biggest problems I've seen over the years with sound transmissions from room to room have to do with a contractor's failure to pay attention to air paths created during construction between rooms. Contractors install walls designed (and tested) to provide STC ratings of 54, and when the job is finished, they have actual STC values as low as 34.

For example, think about the small cracks that exist at the bottom of walls formed between the bottom plate and the floor, which are generally ignored when finishing the rooms. A 1/16" crack located at the bottom of a wall 10' long is the equivalent of a hole through the wall 7 1/2" square in area. That's a hole in the wall 2 1/2" wide by 3" high. I am sure you can see why this would seriously reduce sound isolation room to room.

Similar weak spots exist with electrical boxes that penetrate the wall surface, the physical joints between the wallboard in the body of the wall in base sheets of drywall, as well as with the corners of the room where wallboards meet together. Yet these areas that I mention are the most commonly ignored items during construction, with no money allocated in the construction budget for proper treatment. It is important that your contractors (or you if you intend for this to be a DIY project) understand and pay close attention to duplicating the exact construction details I outline in this book. Otherwise, you may as well throw your money in the wind—it will be an easier way to lose money. After all, construction is a lot of hard work if you have nothing of value in hand when it's all done.

Eliminate Transmissions Through the Building Structure

This is another area that acousticians pay close attention to—and most people, including the "experts" doing the actual work in the construction industry, are not even aware it exists. Sound traveling through the structure of the building itself follows what are called *flanking paths*. An example of this can be seen if you take a wood stud, place your ear to one end, and have someone tap lightly on the other end with a hammer. You will hear the sound quite clearly through the stud itself—much more loudly than you would by just listening to that same tap in the room. Sound transmissions travel very well through the structure of a building, so disconnecting your studio from the rest of the building is very important if you want to isolate yourself from people walking around above you, the TV playing, or if your wife is trying to sleep while you're recording your band. Other sources of flanking sounds can be water pipes, drainage and sewer pipes, and ductwork for HVAC systems. Anything that interconnects different parts of the building with your studio space can create pathways for sound to travel through.

If you are in the process of designing a new building, care should be taken to design isolation into the structure. If your studio will be within an existing building, you can minimize the effects of flanking paths by isolating your room from the existing structure.

I'm not going to bury you in math or confuse you with the complex analysis that an acoustic engineer performs when working on room designs. If that's what you're looking for, there are already some excellent books on the market. I have no interest in duplicating their work or competing with them. Instead, I'm going to show you the practical side of this industry—how to achieve what you want most and give you the ability to make your music in peace. In the process, I am also going to let you know where not to waste your time and money. Sometimes, you just can't get from A to B no matter how hard you may want to.

What to Avoid

It amazes me the number of times people have posted on sites that they have completed work on their studio and did not achieve the level of isolation they either expected or required. They ask how they can increase the level of isolation, to which I respond by asking them to explain exactly what they constructed, in as much detail as they can give. It usually takes me a while to get to the bottom of it, but I find that they had some "great ideas" to improve wall, floor, or ceiling assemblies. For example, they figured that they could gain more isolation by adding sheets of drywall within the cavity of a double wall assembly. Their logic was: "Heck, if two sheets on each side were good, then putting two sheets in the middle must be better." Unfortunately, reality is just the opposite. Not only is it important that you have the right materials, but it is equally important that you put them in the right place. We'll look at what those "right places" are in the next chapter.

CHAPTER 4

Floor, Wall, and Ceiling Construction Details

Physically constructing a home studio isn't as simple as just buying a lot of wood and putting it together. There's a lot of thought and planning that has to go into this project in order for it to come out right. Deciding what you need and how to construct it in a manner that achieves your goal is probably more work than the actual work itself. In this chapter, we'll examine the options you have for various construction types as well as the pros and cons of those techniques. By the end of this chapter, you should be well prepared to make the decisions you need to proceed with design.

Floor Construction

In more cases than not in a home recording studio, you'll be trying to fit your room(s) within existing spaces. Hopefully, these spaces will be located on concrete slabs. I say this because it is much easier to achieve adequate isolation on concrete slabs than on elevated wooden decks. We'll spend a little bit of time looking at the "why's" of that later in this section.

SIMPLE CONCRETE SLABS

Simple concrete slabs are what you would typically see in your basement or garage. They are generally 4 to 5" thick and probably don't have much in the way of reinforcing within the slab itself—that's if they have any reinforcing at all. The slab is poured above compacted earth, usually above a vapor barrier.

If a room within a room is constructed on an existing simple slab (as you might see in a garage with wood framed exterior walls), sound can be transmitted through the slab and surrounding foundation into adjacent spaces. However, this sound transmission will probably be minimal compared to what loss you will have with ceiling and wall assemblies, depending on the building structure.

In the case of a full basement (walls buried below grade), the sound could also be transmitted through the slab into the foundation wall and then into the structure above. However, I would point out that for the most part, earth is a fairly good damping material, and generally you can obtain the isolation you require by simply constructing your space above that existing slab.

ISOLATED CONCRETE SLABS

Isolated concrete slabs are those that are poured on earth, but only to the outside face of the walls for the room that sits on them. These are excellent slabs for studio design and that's how we constructed the slabs for Power Station New England. After pouring the main slab for the first room, a separate slab was poured adjacent to, but not touching, the first slab. The space between the two slabs was treated with an expansion joint material and then caulked to seal out moisture.

Figure 4.1 indicates typical details used for isolated slab construction. Note the use of the haunch at the slab edge. This is created to provide adequate bearing for the room walls, which will sit on top of the slab in that location. There is a school of thought that a simple slab can be turned into an isolated slab simply by saw-cutting the slab in between the party walls of separate rooms. I don't suggest this method due to the fact that a simple slab is not designed to carry a room load on its edge. It is very possible that the slab could crack and settle along the edge, causing problems with room finishes down the road. This is the sort of thing that you may not experience until after all of the load superimposed on the slab is in place. It's a pain in the neck to finish your room, be fairly happy with your product, and suddenly have a wall on one corner settle 1/4" or more. The best scenario would be to remove the existing slab at least enough to install a proper haunch at the wall edge and then use a bonding agent to join the new to the old. If the existing slab has reinforcing in it, all the better, because you can remove the concrete without destroying the reinforcing and use it to help tie the new to the existing.

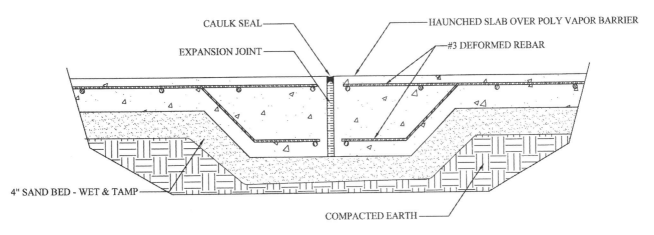

CAULK SEAL — HAUNCHED SLAB OVER POLY VAPOR BARRIER

EXPANSION JOINT — #3 DEFORMED REBAR

4" SAND BED - WET & TAMP

COMPACTED EARTH

Figure 4.1   Here is a typical isolated slab.

Figure 4.2 indicates the detail for adding bearing capacity to your existing slab. Note how the new slab/haunch pours slightly under the existing slab. This is referred to as *underpinning,* which helps to ensure that the two members act as one. You do not want the sections to act independently from one another.

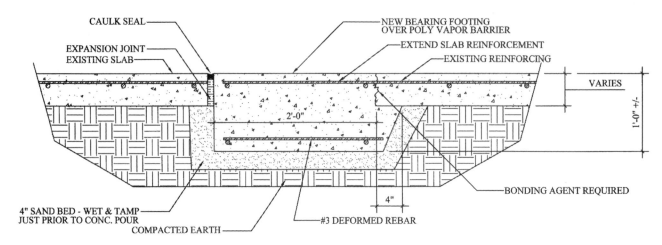

CAULK SEAL

NEW BEARING FOOTING
OVER POLY VAPOR BARRIER

EXPANSION JOINT
EXISTING SLAB

EXTEND SLAB REINFORCEMENT

EXISTING REINFORCING

VARIES

1'-0" +/-

2'-0"

BONDING AGENT REQUIRED

4"

4" SAND BED - WET & TAMP
JUST PRIOR TO CONC. POUR

#3 DEFORMED REBAR

COMPACTED EARTH

Figure 4.2   Here you can see added bearing at the slab.

By the way, just so you understand completely, this is not easy work. First, you really want to know if the slab has some reinforcing you can use to tie the old and new together. This requires the use of a jackhammer to open up a section of slab or special equipment to perform testing of the slab. Both pneumatic and electric jackhammers are readily available at all local equipment rental centers. Electric ones will not provide the same working speed as pneumatic, but are easier to work with, due to the ease of running cable versus 1 1/4" hose and the tendency to weigh less. The testing equipment is generally not available for rental purposes and would require you to hire a consultant to test it—or the purchase of the equipment, which is not inexpensive. Chances are that you will use the hammer. If you do find rebar or reinforcing wire installed within the slab, then the entire work must be done with that same jackhammer. As I mentioned earlier, it's a lot of work.

Locate the outside face of your room wall and snap a chalk line. At this point, saw-cut through the entire slab thickness. Use your jackhammer to carefully remove enough concrete to determine whether slab reinforcing exists. If it does, then locate a line about 2' inside of your room from the existing line. At this location, you will want to adjust your saw to cut only 1/2" deep into the concrete. This will provide a professional looking joint to finish your new concrete to. Jackhammer out all the concrete into small pieces, which can be removed without removing the reinforcing. Save as much of the reinforcing as you possibly can. You will then have to bend that up along the face of the concrete in order to excavate for your new bearing point. Figure 4.3 indicates the condition that should exist at this point.

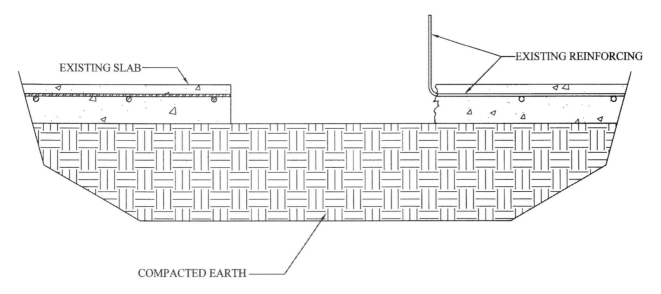

Figure 4.3   Slab preparation should look like this.

Excavate for your new concrete, making certain to remove at least 4" of material underneath the existing slab for bearing, then install your expansion joint (a couple of pieces of expansive foam typically used for "sill seal" is perfect for this purpose), and bend the rebar down into place. Pour your new haunch, using the existing concrete surface as your screed. When it's cured, you can clean the edge and caulk.

If you find no rebar in your slab, then you can just saw-cut the concrete in the second location full depth and remove the concrete in larger sections. In this case, when you excavate, you should make certain to underpin the existing slab a minimum of 8". Figure 4.4 indicates a section through the finished product in this condition.

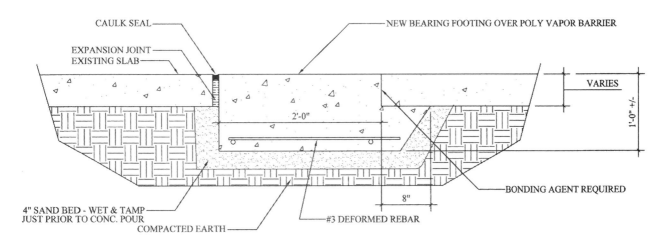

Figure 4.4   An example of slab preparation, minus reinforcement.

Prior to pouring your concrete haunch, you will want to cover the edge of the existing concrete with a bonding agent made for that purpose. Sika Corporation© manufacturers a product called *SikaDur Hi Mod®*[1], which is an excellent bonding agent that I have had great success with in the past. Simply follow the manufacturer's instructions for a fail-safe installation.

FLOATING CONCRETE SLABS

Floating (also referred to as elevated or isolated) concrete slabs are also excellent products for sound isolation, if designed and constructed properly. They are also very expensive, a tremendous amount of work, and on the low end of recommendations I would make for a home studio. I will include information here, but unless you are very serious about spending the time, effort, and money to obtain nothing shy of professional results in your home studio, I would not suggest that you bother including them for consideration. The slabs must be designed for a center frequency of no greater than 10 Hz, and they only really make sense if you are going to achieve the same results with your wall and ceiling assemblies as you do with your slab. For this purpose, picture seven layers of drywall on your wall and ceiling assemblies.

Figure 4.5 is one product manufactured by Mason Industries for the purpose of constructing an elevated concrete slab.

Figure 4.5
To construct an elevated concrete slap, you can us the Mason jack-up floor slab system.

This is a lift slab product, utilizing a neoprene puck as the spring in the system. With this product, you can pour a new slab directly over an existing slab (thus saving on the bottom formwork required to pour an elevated slab in place.). Figure 4.6 is another member of the Mason Industries family. It's an FS Spring Jack, which utilizes a coil spring instead of the neoprene isolator. Both systems will work very well when the slab is properly designed, but for the purposes of examples in this book, we will use the neoprene puck system.

Figure 4.6
An example of spring jack floor mounts.

There's something you need to understand if you plan on using this method of construction. Lightweight concrete weighs as much as 115 pcf (pounds per cubic foot). The spacing of the supports for this particular system can be as great as 54" on center. That translates to 20.25 s.f. (square feet) per support, which, with a 6" thick slab, would be 1,164 pounds per support. That's just for the slab. In addition to this, you will have the load imposed by the new walls and ceiling. It's quite possible that a simple slab would not be able to take this loading; for example, that you could have cracking and settlement of the existing slab which would destroy your new work. We typically pour reinforced concrete with a series of mini haunches to carry pin loads like this in new construction. It is very important that you contact a structural engineer to assess your existing structure if you plan to use this method as a part of your studio design.

I promised you I would not bury you in math in this book, and I intend to keep that promise. There are calculations that need to be performed to design your slab to the required 10 Hz center frequency, but I'm not giving them to you. It is so much easier for you to contact the manufacturer directly, and they will happily perform those calculations as a part of their service in selling their product to you. You will be required to provide them with detailed information about your construction, so it isn't as if you can decide today that you want this without planning your entire studio at the same time.

The design of these slabs is based on the slab weight itself, the weight of all walls and ceiling loads (including finishes), and the weight of equipment to be placed permanently within the room. (This is what makes up your actual and superimposed dead loads.) Then you have to figure out what your live loads will be. This should be a fairly accurate assessment of people and gear that will be brought into the space.

Floating slab isolation is based on a Mass Spring Mass (MSM) system. The first Mass being the element the slab will be supported by. The spring is (in this case) the Dupont Neoprene pad sitting below the lift mechanism. The second Mass is the elevated slab itself. The reason for identifying all of the imposed loads properly is due to the fact that for a MSM system to operate properly, you must load the spring just enough to fully engage it. Overloading (overcompressing) the spring will cause the system to fail because the sound will transmit directly through the spring. Underloading (thus undercompressing) will cause the same effect. It's the combination of the mass and the air gap that provides your isolation. You do not want the spring to create a flanking path of its own.

The air gap is an important factor to take into consideration when using this system. For example, tests performed at the Riverbank Laboratories in Geneva, Illinois proved that pouring a 4" slab over an original 6" slab only increased isolation from STC 54 to 57. Adding a 2" sealed airspace raises the STC to 79. Doubling the airspace to 4" increased this to STC 82.

A Comment on the Value of Air Spaces
Theoretically, a doubling of air space would add 5 STC to an assembly, but other things also affect the outcome. In this case, resonance takes over, so the effect is closer to 3.

In reality, if you have a slab with a resonant frequency of 10 Hz and an STC rating of 79, you will be stretching it to achieve this with the remainder of your room construction.

After your design is finalized, you'll lay out your grid, install your edge forming, and place the lifts on the intersecting points (see Figure 4.7). The spacing at the slab edge will often be closer than the spacing in the field (center) of the slab. This is due to the load that will be imposed on the slab edge by the walls and ceiling.

Figure 4.7
Placement of isolation materials should look like this illustration.

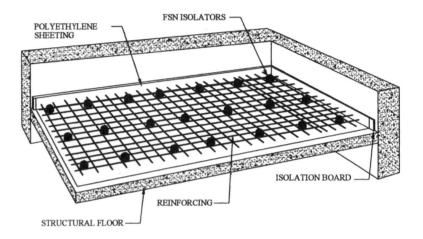

Rebar is then installed and supported by the hooks you see on the lifts. You need to make certain to tie your rebar together using "tie wire," which can be purchased in rolls at any lumberyard. A couple of turns around the rebar, where two bars intersect, and a few twists of the wire together to lock it into place, and you're all set. This will ensure that the rebar stays put when you place the concrete. It won't do you any good if it's lying on the bottom of the slab when the pour is complete.

Edge forming isn't all that difficult in this case. You can do this with 2x6 or 2x8 framing lumber for the sides (depending on your slab thickness) with 2x4 framing to lock them into place. The tops should be straight and true; then they can be tied in with 2x4 braces. You can use a builder's dumpy level or a laser (both are available in any tool rental company) to strike a level line completely around the slab. Mark the sides of the forms and then use a 6- or 8-penny finish nail to mark the finish height of your slab. These are easier to pour than trying to use a line that gets covered with concrete and becomes invisible. Just tap them about 3/4" into the form to lock them securely into place.

A lot of people say that floor finish depends on floor covering, or that if you plan on covering it up you don't have to be too fussy. They're wrong. The better the quality of finish you provide to the floor, the flatter the floor will be in the end. And flat is important if you want to put down wood flooring and not have it make funny noises. I'm not going to try to teach you here how to pour and finish a concrete slab. If you don't know that already, you would be much better off paying someone experienced to do the work for you. Figure 4.8 shows the conditions expected during the concrete pour. Make sure to install the rubber plugs prior to the pour, which ensures that no concrete can enter the threaded chamber of the slab lift.

Figure 4.8
This illustrates a concrete pour in progress.

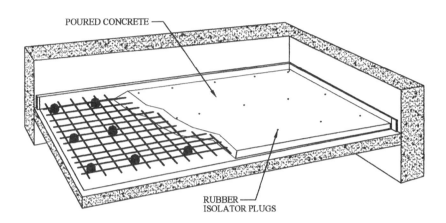

One trick you can use to help you along is to rent a laser level. You can set this to your finish slab height and use it to maintain the proper screed height as you go along. We don't generally use pipe screeds anymore in the industry; this equipment is the only way to go. If you do this yourself, make sure to set the instrument to a fine setting (1/8"). This will help ensure a flat surface when you're finished.

You are going to have to let your concrete fully cure before you begin to lift the slab. Don't even consider lifting the slab for the first 28 days. Twenty-eight days is typically the point where concrete will cure to its designed strength. In order to ensure that the concrete cures properly, you will want to flood it with water after finishing and then cover it with a layer of poly. Be certain to check it at least once a week (or sooner) to make sure it stays wet; this is an important part of the curing process. There are also curing compounds you can use for this purpose, but the least expensive manner is simple water.

After the concrete finishes curing, remove the forms, lift the slab, and you're ready to begin work on the studio walls. Figure 4.9 shows a slab in the elevated position before any additional work is in place.

Figure 4.9
Here is an isolated slab in its jacked up position.

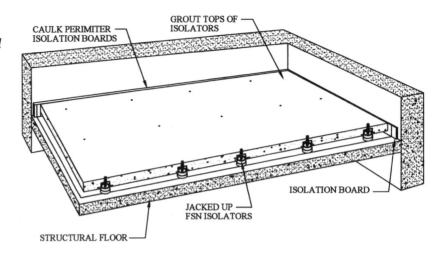

For the actual results you might expect with this system, we provide the following data from tests performed for Mason Industries.

Description of Test Specimen

The test specimen consisted of a 4-inch thick reinforced concrete slab, with an average weight of 50 lb. per square foot, supported on a grid of Mason Industries Type FSN-1336 and 1337 mountings with Type EAFM neoprene elements. The mountings are spaced on 24-inch centers, supporting the 4-inch thick "floating slab" 2 inches above a 5-1/2lb. per square foot elevated composite concrete slab. The floating slab was finished in the studio with a layer of 1/8-inch linoleum flooring. The floating slab was isolated along its perimeter with Type 34AFG-10, 3/4-inch thick, 10 lb. density fiberglass boards. The test surface area was 1054 square feet.

TEST METHODS

A) Impact Test

The test method used in obtaining the data is in accordance with ISO (International Standards Organization) Recommendation R-140-1960, "Field and Laboratory Measurement of Airborne and Impact Sound Transmission." The data obtained were corrected to a reference room-absorption of 10 square meters. In accordance with the R-140-1960 Standard Recommendations, the absorption of the receiving room was measured by recording the acoustical decay rate.

Test equipment consisted of the Bruel & Kjaer Tapping Machine Type 3204, which was placed at two positions on the test floor. Sound pressure levels were measured in one-third octave bands in the receiving room by using the General Radio Noise and Vibration Analyzer Type 156A, and corrected for ambient noise levels in the receiving room. Test results represent the arithmetic average of the two positions measured. These positions are indicated with "X" marks on drawings Z-1075-1.

B) Airborne Sound Transmission Loss Test
The test was conducted in full conformity with Section 6 of American Society for Testing and Materials Designations E 336-71, "Standard Recommended Practice for Measurement of Airborne Sound Insulation in Buildings."

Acoustical test signals of pre-recorded 1/3 octave band random noise were generated in the source room with loudspeakers placed in such manners as to generate a diffused sound field. Four loudspeakers were used consisting of two 8-inch diameter acoustically suspended speakers, and two horn speakers.

Test frequencies were 1/3 octave band frequencies between 100 and 5,000 Hz inclusive. Sound pressure levels were measured in the receiving room in 1/3 octaves by using the General Radio Noise and Vibration Analyzer Type 1564A, and corrected for ambient noise levels in the receiving room. The data obtained were corrected to a reference room-absorption of 10 square meters. In accordance with the ASTM E336-71 Test Standard, the absorption of the receiving room was measured by recording the acoustical decay rate.

TEST CONFIGURATION
The test specimen separates the 25th floor TV Studio and elevator equipment room on the 24th floor. For the Impact Test, the receiving room was the elevator equipment room. Measurements were made in the elevator equipment room in the late evening hours with all elevator equipment as well as ventilation equipment shut down in order to permit measurable sound pressure levels tied to the Tapping Machine.

For the Airborne Sound Transmission Test, the elevator equipment room was used as the source room and the TV Studio was used as the receiving room so as to minimize the amount of time elevator equipment was shut down. Partitions around the TV Studio were partially supported on the test specimen floor as shown on Mason Industries drawing Z-1076. Furthermore, the ceiling over the TV studio consisted of a resiliently suspended gypboard ceiling with a layer of 4-inch thick glass fiber blanket laid over the top.

TEST RESULTS

A) Impact Noise Rating (INR)
Sound pressure levels at 1/3 octave intervals, normalized to 10 square meters, are indicated in the following table:

Center Frequency (Hz) In One-Third Octave Bands	Sound Pressure Levels (dB) Normalized to Ao = 10 M sq
100	51
125	49
160	48
200	48
250	47
315	42
400	36
500	34
630	28
800	29
1000	28
1250	24
1600	24
2000 2500 3150	*
Impact Noise Rating	INR + 24

*Note: * Denotes sound pressure levels due to Tapping Machine being below ambient noise levels for those frequencies indicated.*

B) Field Sound Transmission Class

Sound transmission loss values are tabulated below at the eighteen standard test frequencies.

Center Frequency (Hz) In One-Third Octave Bands	Sound Pressure Levels (dB) Normalized to Ao = 10 M sq
100	47
125	48
160	50
200	54
250	60
315	66
400	71
500	79
630	85
800	90
1000	95
1250	92
1600	92
2000 2500 3150 4000 5000	*
Field Sound Transmission Class	FSTC - 71

*Note: * Denotes transmitted sound pressure levels being below the ambient noise levels for those frequencies indicated.* " [2]

One of the things I like about this test data is that it gives us a chance to look at the difference between laboratory tests and real-world field conditions. The expected Impact Noise Rating (INR), based on lab testing, was INR + 17, which in the field test yielded a result of INR + 24, a fairly significant increase in isolation. This was attributed to 1/8" linoleum flooring placed on the field specimen versus a bare concrete slab in the lab. Also, part of the increase was apparently due to the supporting slab itself, which was a rigid structural slab (in the real world) compared to the precast "T" section concrete panels used in the laboratory tests. The impact rating could obviously go in either direction, based on field versus lab structural differences.

The difference in STC rating was as follows:

Laboratory STC rating was 79 vs. FSTC rating of 71. (The F in FSTC stands for Field, i.e., the Real World).

Once again, this is a very significant difference. An 8dB reduction in field application (although not surprising to me) means that the noise making it through to the other side is more than two times louder than expected by lab results. The apparent reasons for this were that the walls surrounding the studio were capable of less sound attenuation than the slab itself. The partitions in the studio were drywall vs. masonry partitions used in the lab. Also, a single layer of gypsum was installed in the ceiling of the studio. This was not capable of matching the double layer used in the lab. The walls in the studio were constructed to the underside of the structure above. The single layer drywall ceiling (coupled with the wall assembly's attachment to structure) allowed sound to travel through the building structure outside of the TV studio and then into it. This is an example of flanking noise affecting your total sound isolation.

The third item had to do with something I've mentioned earlier in discussion here, and that has to do with the quality of work performed in the field by the professionals in the construction industry. In lab tests performed by a bona fide laboratory, the construction is as perfect as can be done. Care is taken to provide properly installed and sealed assemblies. In the real world (the world in which your construction will take place), the contractor has a vested interest in getting in and getting out of the project. It isn't that they don't really care about the finished product, but they don't necessarily devote the attention to detail that takes place in that laboratory. Many times the person who bids the work never even sees the job. The workers in the field never receive the information they need to understand exactly what steps need to be taken, or the order they need to be taken in.

In addition, they see some of what we (the owners and engineers) place importance on (which is that same care taken in the labs), as being less than necessary for a "decent job." They do not understand the importance—they think it's overkill—and they think that the small difference in quality won't mean a whole lot at the end of it all. They could not be more wrong.

One other point I will make here before moving on is that the test result you see only relates to a floor-to-floor separation and not room-to-room. I can guarantee that the wall and ceiling construction used for this studio would not come anywhere near the STC 71 reported here floor to floor, and thus the money for the floating slab would have been wasted if that were a concern.

In the case of this TV studio, apparently their biggest challenge was noise being transmitted from the elevator machine room into the studio. In their case, it paid off. In your case, however, it's going to be a concern for you with your neighbors and family. So unless you plan on going the full route, meaning that unless you plan on building a "bomb shelter" to record in, don't waste your money by taking this path. You can get some fabulous results with a floating room on a floating slab if you need them, but you have to make it all work as a whole—one piece won't get it done by itself.

FLOATING WOOD DECKS

I will spend just a moment with you discussing these decks. This is only because I hope to save you some money and aggravation. I wish I had a dime for every time I've seen someone ask on an Internet site how to calculate the spacing of pucks for a floating wood deck. I know immediately that they do not have a clue what they're building. Someone, somewhere, just told them that they needed to float a deck in order to get real isolation, and they listened.

Reality is that you can't get isolation for a recording studio with a simple elevated wood deck. Period.

Elevated wooden decks are great for impact noise, so they'll work well in dance studios, bowling alleys, condos, etc., but they do not have enough mass to properly isolate a recording studio. The frequencies of the bass drum and bass guitar are too low to be handled with a deck of this nature.

Comment from Mason Industries Regarding Wood Framed Floating Floors

This is another bit of information from the Mason Industry site:

"It is often necessary to provide a wooden floating floor rather than the heavier concrete construction with wood topping. Cost or weight restrictions may be the factor. In older buildings, it is often necessary to improve on existing floors with a lightweight impact noise resistant construction. A resiliently supported wooden floor will reduce the rumbling noise of a bowling ball, the click, click of a woman's heels and that portion of a typical noise generated by a piano that travels down the piano legs and into the structure. It will offer only minor reduction of airborne sound, as there is insufficient mass in the surface. In some applications on stages or in rehearsal rooms, the primary purpose is relief and comfort for the dancers. Landing on concrete or hard mounted wood surfaces is very damaging to a dancer's feet and legs."[3]

Another problem with isolated wood decks (and this again relates to the lack of mass) is that the resonant frequency of the deck itself may create problems. As I pointed out with the elevated concrete decks above, the resonant frequency of the deck needs to be around 10 Hz. With concrete, achieving that frequency is a matter of proper design; with a wood frame deck, it's a matter of being so close to impossible that it isn't worth the effort or expense.

For example, I recently came in contact with someone who owns a professional studio, with some of their rooms rented for space for practice, and others for tracking and control rooms. They were inquiring about the density of the insulation they should use in these already-built isolating decks they constructed. I explained to them the problems they were going to experience, but they apparently did not believe me. They completed their construction (based on "expert advice" they received from others) and then came back to let me know about the problems they were having with these "drumheads" they built. Frequencies between 200 and 400 Hz were being amplified by the deck construction, and they wanted to know what they could do to solve the problem, My answer to them was to either remove the decking and fill the frame completely with dry sand or remove the decks in their entirety.

Seeing as this is a (roughly) 3,000 s.f. facility, that translates to a lot of wasted materials and labor any way you look at it. All of the decks were filled with mineral wool and then multiple layers of decking plus finished floors. Picture the cost of that construction and now add to it the cost of removing those finished floors and decks—pull out that mineral wool (throw it away because it isn't going to do you any good now)—now bring sand in and begin finishing these spaces all over again.

So please, I don't care what your friends tell you. I don't care what some "expert" on the Internet tells you. Save your money. It's too precious to just throw away.

SAND-FILLED WOODEN DECKS
Unlike elevated wood decks, sand-filled decks can be of some benefit. One benefit is the creation of a pathway below the floor to route low voltage wiring (through the use of PVC conduits). It's a big advantage if the LV wiring can be separated from line voltage cable runs (plugs, lighting, etc.).

You can also gain some small benefit from an isolation point of view, which is due to the ability of the sand to damp sound vibrations.

However, this is a very heavy assembly (sand alone weighs roughly 100 pcf) and (as in the case of concrete slabs) will require your structural engineer to confirm that you can safely install this on your existing structure.

Wall Construction

Wall construction is not really all that involved, provided you pay attention to details. Your biggest challenge is to determine what level of isolation you need, the amount of mass you need to handle that, and then to make certain to put everything in the right location.

The right location. Think about that for a moment. There *is* actually a right location for materials.

Look at Figure 4.10 for a moment.

Note that the wall assembly third from the left has an STC rating of 40dB. It is constructed using two separate wall frames with four layers of drywall total, and with insulation installed in the cavities of both walls. The drywall is installed on both faces of each wall assembly.

If we remove one inside layer, note how the STC rating raises from 40 to 50. Remove the second layer, and it raises another 7dB of isolation to 57. Now take those two layers and install them over the two faces of the outside wall, and you add another 6dB of isolation for a total of STC 63.

This is a 23dB increase in isolation using exactly the same materials in different locations!

That's an amazing increase in isolation, and it didn't cost a single additional penny to gain it.

This appears to fly directly in the face of what I told you earlier— that each doubling of mass adds roughly 6dB of isolation to your wall. However, the reason for this has nothing to do with the amount of mass and everything to do with the location of that mass.

Consider that each different location of the drywall constitutes a leaf. In the case of the STC 40 wall assembly, you have two walls with one layer on each wall face, thus, a four-leaf system. You count the leafs thus: Mass, Air, Mass, Air, Mass, Air, Mass. Each area of mass (drywall) equals one leaf. When you remove one inner face, it becomes a three-leaf system, and then a two-leaf system when you remove the last inside face of drywall. A two-leaf system with 1/2 the mass of the four-leaf system will provide almost eight times greater isolation. It is at that point that the doubling of the mass becomes what I told you earlier. Note the 6dB increase from the STC 57 to 63 when the mass is doubled and put in the correct location.

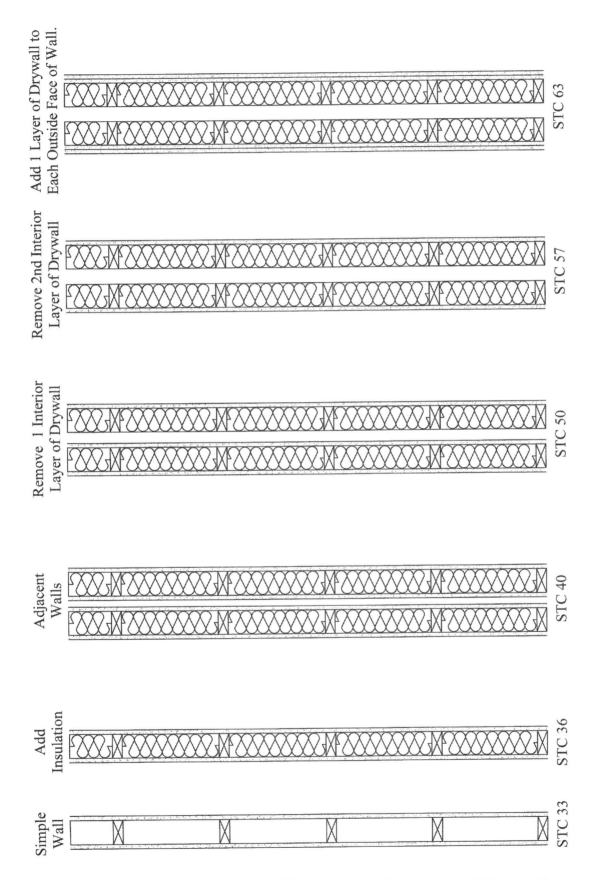

Figure 4.10   This shows you some different walls and their associated STC ratings.[4, 5]

So get a picture firmly in your mind—two-leaf wall systems are good—two-leaf wall systems are your friends. Three- and four-leaf wall systems are evil devious fiends that suck up the money in your wallets and give you less than nothing in return.

So when you build, strive for two-leaf wall systems and nothing else. These wall assemblies are Mass Air Mass (MAM) Systems. With MAM systems, the air between the leaf walls becomes the spring. Thus, sound pressure builds up with the space striking the wall surface and causing it to deflect inward. This compresses the air within the space, which causes the outer surface to deflect outward. The compressed air becomes the spring. The transfer of sound is its vibrational energy traveling through the spring from one layer to the other. If this energy rested within the frequency range of the wall assembly, it would cause a fairly significant lowering of the TL (transmission loss) of the assembly.

EXISTING WALLS

Existing walls are going to be your biggest challenge. The exterior walls are probably a long way away from being airtight. Interior walls might be running parallel with a corridor, and perhaps that corridor is already only 36" wide, which means you can't add more mass to the corridor wall without creating a violation of the building code by creating a corridor whose width is too narrow. Maybe your building is in a basement and has to contend with windows, perhaps large gaps between the foundation and the plate that carries the deck framing. Or you are using an existing bedroom that the building official requires to remain as is, with the egress windows intact.

In all these cases, there are solutions to your problems. In the case of the concrete foundation, you can fill those cracks between the plate and concrete with mineral wool. Just pack it well to make certain you have good density and then caulk the joint between the two with acoustic caulk.

Figure 4.11 indicates both the original condition of the foundation and the finished seal.

In the case of that corridor wall, you can remove the drywall on your room side and install additional mass within the wall cavity itself, which will go a long way towards helping your isolation.

We will look at the actual construction of these assemblies in chapter 10. For now, let's look at the various types of wall assemblies and their possible benefits or drawbacks.

Figure 4.11
Sound leak at existing slab—before and after seal.

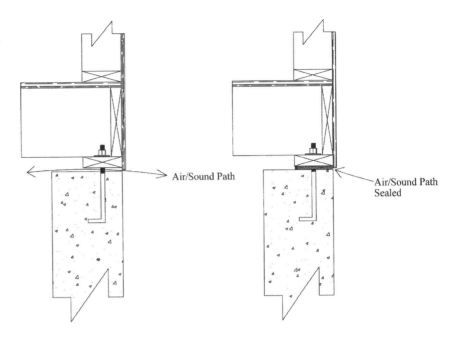

WOOD WALLS

Wood is one of my personal favorites when it comes to studio construction. There's just something beautiful about a properly framed wood wall. In the days where I used to swing a hammer, we had a saying about wood framing, "It should be so pretty you don't have to cover it up."

Let's focus on the options.

SINGLE WALL CONSTRUCTION

Single wall construction is what you're used to seeing in your home. It's a simple wall—typically a single 2x4 or 2x6 plate—with studs ranging from 16"to 24" on center (oc). It probably has double top plates and usually a layer of 1/2" gypsum board mounted on each of the faces.

You already know it's not a good isolator, or you wouldn't be reading this book.

RESILIENT CHANNEL/RISC ASSEMBLIES

Take that same wall and add resilient channel to one side of it. This decouples the layer of gypsum on that face from the framing behind it. With that same layer of 1/2" gypsum, you just increased your isolation from somewhere between 3 and 5dB.

There are many different types of resilient channels on the market today, as well as materials you might mistake for resilient channels, i.e., hat channels or Z channels. RC-1 is a single-leg channel primarily used for walls. RC-2 is a double-legged channel primarily used for ceilings.

Figure 4.12 is a picture of various types of resilient channels. I have also included a section of hat channel. Note that hat channel does not have any holes or slots along its "leg." The slots and holes are one of the main reasons that the members isolate in the manner they do. Without them, isolation is nil.

Figure 4.12
Resilient channels.

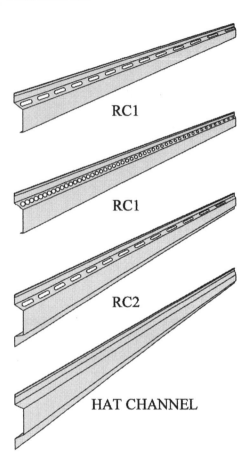

RC1

RC1

RC2

HAT CHANNEL

You can use either RC-1 or RC-2 for walls and ceilings; however, RC-1 used on a ceiling will not support the same load as the RC-2.

Figure 4.13 shows RC-1 installed properly on 2x4 framing. Note that the flange is installed in the bottom position. It is important that these products be installed correctly to ensure they isolate properly.

Make certain to be very careful that you do not use the hat channel or standard Z channel instead of RC, because the net effect will be no gain in isolation with a lot of added material and labor costs. And, amazingly, there are a lot of drywall contractors out there who can't tell the difference between the two. Whatever you decide to purchase, make sure to ask for (and receive) the technical data as a part of the purchase. This will ensure that you're getting the right material.

Figure 4.13
Resilient channel installation method.

RISC 1 clips (resilient sound isolation clips) are another excellent way to decouple drywall from a structure (see Figure 4.14). These products use a rubber isolator to decouple the clip from the stud, and a hat channel is then mounted into the clip to attach the drywall to. Isolation with this unit is typically around 6 to 8dB greater reduction than using standard resilient channel. Once again, there are several different manufacturers of this type of product.

Figure 4.14
Resilient sound isolation clips (RISC-1).

DUAL FRAME ASSEMBLIES

Dual wood framed wall assemblies come in a few different types. One of these is a staggered stud configuration, with single top and bottom plates (typically 2x6 or 2x8), and with the studs being staggered from one another on opposite sides of the wall. With framing 16" oc, that would place the studs on 8"centers and 12" centers for 24" framing. Figure 4.15 is a view of a typical staggered stud system.

Advantages include greater isolation than the use of single frame walls and decoupling of studs from one reduces the need for RC or RISC systems.

The disadvantage is that the common top and bottom plates become the weak points of this system, effectively acting as a bridge from one side to the other. This direct passage weakens an otherwise good system.

True double wall assemblies use separate top and bottom plates, as well as separate studs. This effectively completely decouples each wall from one another. Figure 4.16 is an example of double frame wall assemblies.

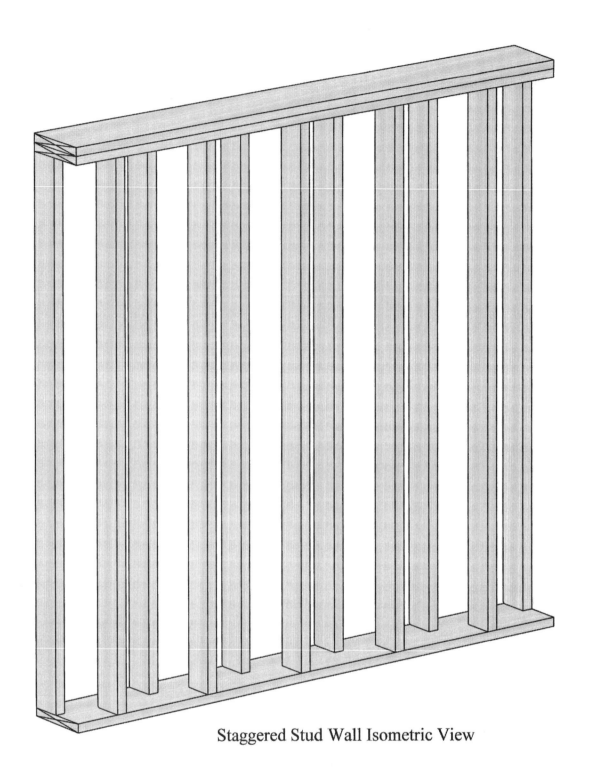

Staggered Stud Wall Isometric View

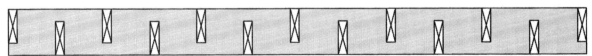

Staggered Stud Wall Plan View

Figure 4.15   Staggered stud framing.

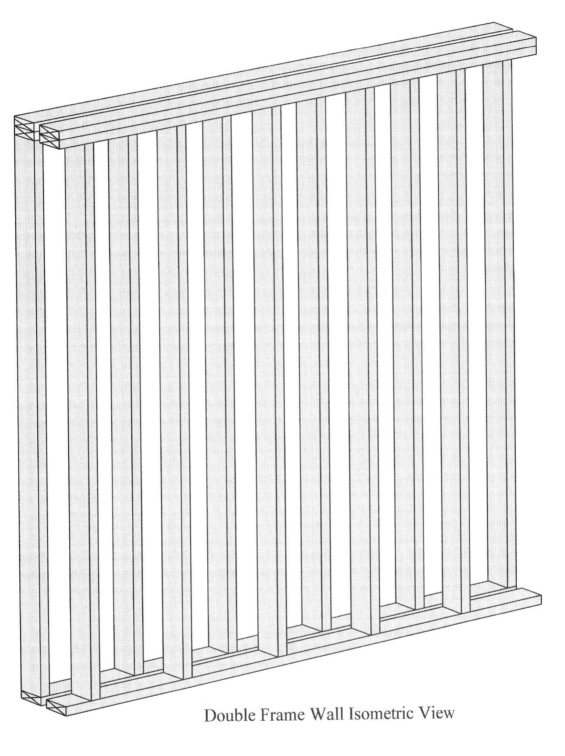

Double Frame Wall Isometric View

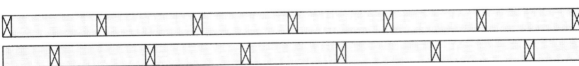

Double Frame Wall Plan View

Figure 4.16   Double wall framing details.

One point I want to be sure you get is that there is no advantage to using isolating clips or resilient channel with a true double wall assembly. Don't waste your money by thinking that more is better in this case. The only thing that should increase with a double wall system is mass (see Chapter 2).

The advantage to this is that it's not much more money than a staggered stud wall assembly, and it can achieve much greater isolation than any of the clip systems. The disadvantage is that it takes up more real estate (by this I mean room space) than the RISC, RC systems, or a simple staggered stud system with common top and bottom plates.

However, when isolation requirements are high, and you weigh the isolation benefit vs. the cost per square foot of construction, then the added isolation can be such a dramatic increase that the added cost is well worth the investment. You will reach a limit with the other systems (based on common connection points between the adjacent spaces), such that the flanking action of the frames will become the weak point. This is one of the great strengths of a double frame assembly.

Now, let me clarify that last statement. In all assemblies—unless care is taken to address flanking paths—there will come a point where the passage of flanking noise will take place over the value of the sum of the separate assemblies. For example, it would do you no good to build wall and ceiling assemblies with 70dB isolating values if you're on the second floor of a building and are sitting on a deck assembly, which is structurally connected to other parts of the building.

The sound that travels through the building structure will not decrease just because you continue to add more mass to the walls. If you can't create a condition where all of the elements of the assembly are balanced, then you will soon reach the point where you are throwing money at a problem without moving any closer to solving that problem.

STEEL FRAMING

Steel framing has some advantages over wood framing. It doesn't shrink, twist, or burn. It's a very stable material with uniform dimensions. Perfect fits are not as critical with steel framing as with wood. Fastening is as simple as screwing in a couple of self-tapping framing screws.

When we refer to heavy gauge steel framing, it's any material with a gauge greater than 25; 25 gauge or lighter framing is considered to be lightweight steel framing.

Light gauge steel framing has an advantage over wood framing or heavy gauge steel framing because a wall constructed with it has a greater STC rating than a similar wood or heavy gauge frame. So a simple wall framed with light gauge framing and drywall applied directly to both sides will achieve the same results as a wood frame wall with resilient channel installed.

The disadvantage of light gauge framing is that it will not carry loads that wood framing will carry with ease. Heavy gauge metal framing will carry the required loads, but it is generally more expensive than similar walls manufactured with wood.

Ceiling Construction

"One man's ceiling is another man's floor." Paul Simon, 1973.

Isn't it always the way? You want to make music, and some inconsiderate human being wants to quietly read a book, sleep, settle a baby down, etc. (fill in the blank based on your situation at home).

Constructing an isolated system is only as good as the weakest link in the assembly—with the greatest challenges being spaces directly above or below you.

Let's take a look at those challenges and methods of maintaining isolation.

WORKING WITH EXISTING CEILINGS/FLOORS

What steps can be taken to obtain isolation when building below other living spaces? First and foremost, keep your eyes on the basics—mass, mass, and more mass.

A typical deck in a modern home is generally 3/4" T&G (Tongue and Groove) plywood installed over floor joists or Truss Joist, (TJI's®[6]) with possibly pad and carpet or hardwood floors installed directly over this. Kitchens and bathrooms will generally have an additional layer of 3/8" plywood installed over the 3/4" deck, prior to the installation of resilient flooring or tile.

Figure 4.17 shows you some typical floor assemblies. Included are the approximate dead loads associated with these floors. Remember that the starting point for determining what may (or may not) be added to any structure begins with the existing structural capacity and weight.

One of the problems with just adding mass to the bottom of the existing joists is the transfer of sound directly through the joists themselves. Thus, the ceiling within your space has to be structurally decoupled from the floor above in some manner.

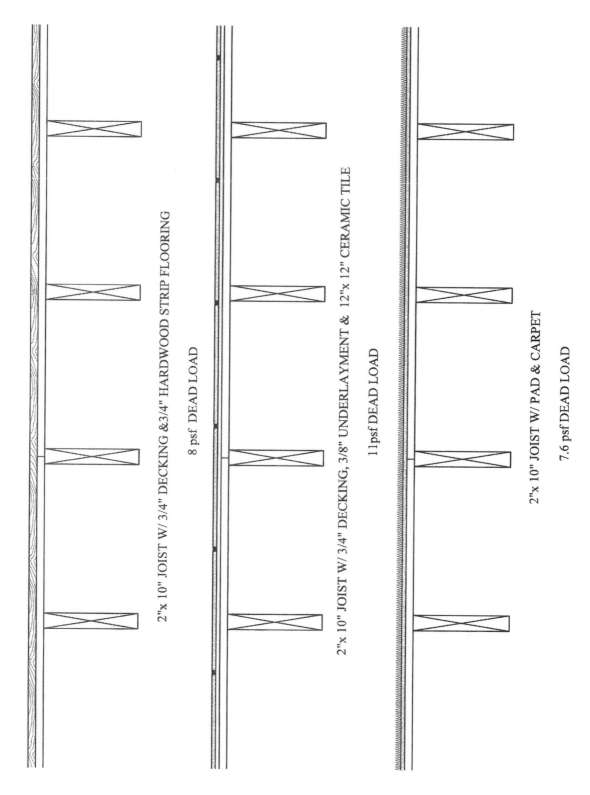

Figure 4.17   Varying deck assemblies.

In addition to this, additional mass should be installed (if structurally possible) on the floor above. Remember that mass on both leaves of an isolation assembly is important. This floor/ceiling assembly is only different from your walls (acoustically speaking) in the sense that people walk on it, so the footfall noise (impact noise) adds another dimension to the challenges associated with isolation.

Once again, everything begins with a structural analysis of the existing assembly to determine what it is capable of carrying. Typical home design is mandated for a 10 psf dead load and 40 psf live load in kitchens, living rooms, family rooms, dining rooms, and game rooms. Bedrooms are typically designed for 10 psf dead loads and 30 psf live loads. The dead load is the weight of the floor joist, any decking above, and loads imparted by walls resting on the deck, along with the weight of floor coverings. The live loads are based on furniture within the space and the loads imparted by people within the room.

Although you may think that 40 psf is a lot of capacity, when you look into an empty room and take into account your furniture, your spouse, and possibly a few children, it can suddenly become a critical load when you have a family reunion and 35 or 40 people fill up that room. (By the way, a family reunion on my mother's side of the family may have as many as 350 direct family members show up, so big loadings are a real possibility). The reason that I make this appear *very* important is because it really is.

Overloading a deck can cause long-term stress on it—with the result being a sudden and catastrophic structural failure. I cannot stress the importance of this enough.

If you are designing a new home, it's easy enough to determine what you need and make provisions for this in your design. Perhaps the placement of your studio above the garage—with an isolating mudroom connecting the two—would make sense. Or you could make sure you had a foundation that was 9 or 10 feet in height to allow enough room for a decent ceiling height in a basement studio, while maintaining completely isolated construction of the two spaces.

In this case, you would also want to add mass to the floor above and possibly even a lightweight concrete self-leveling slab (also known as Gyp-Crete), which helps tremendously with isolating traffic noise. We use this all the time in hotel construction with wood framed deck assemblies, gaining additional isolation, as well as creating a fire barrier between levels. See Figure 4.18 for a typical view of a wood deck with gyp-crete being applied.

We'll look more deeply at some isolating decks for new construction in the next chapter. However, in existing construction, we begin with establishing what we can safely carry in additional dead loads before proceeding.

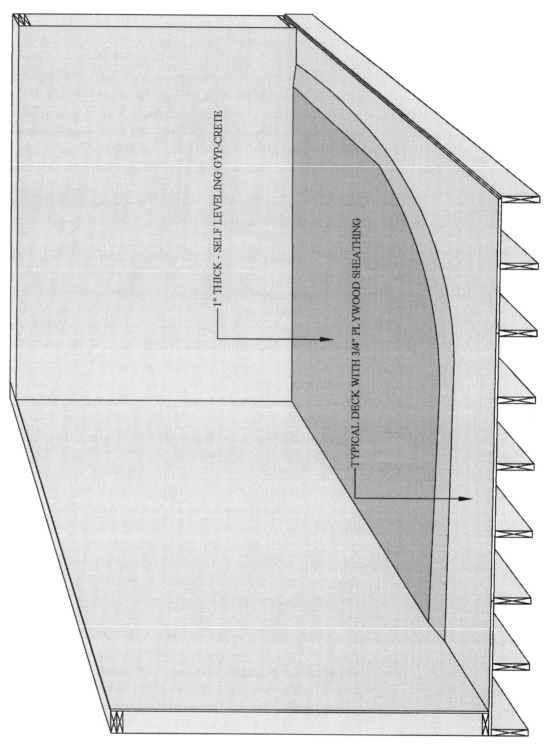

Figure 4.18   Gyp-Crete application over wood deck.

Now, assuming that your engineer sees no problems with adding load to the structure, you can begin by installing gypsum board directly against the bottom of your existing deck assembly. Fit the board so that it is about 1/4" from your existing floor joist, hold it in place temporarily with some 4d finish nails, and caulk all edges. Add as many additional layers as your joist can safely carry (see Figure 4.19).

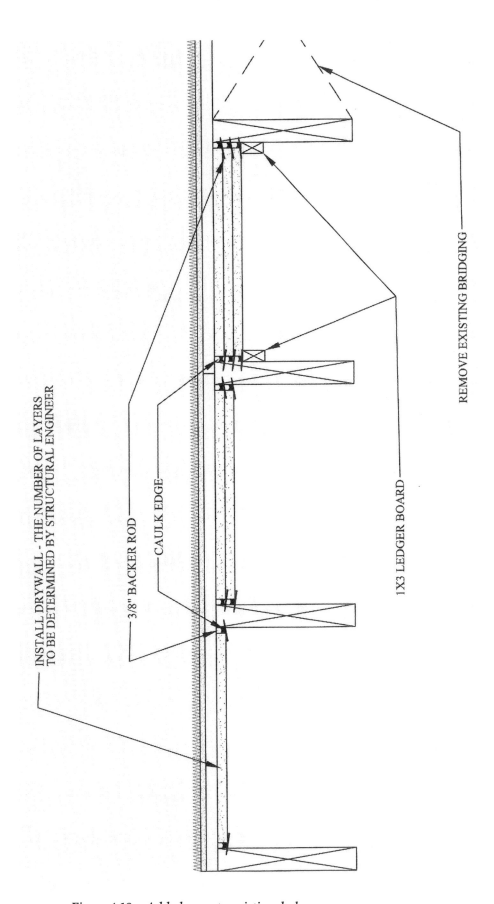

Figure 4.19   Added mass to existing deck.

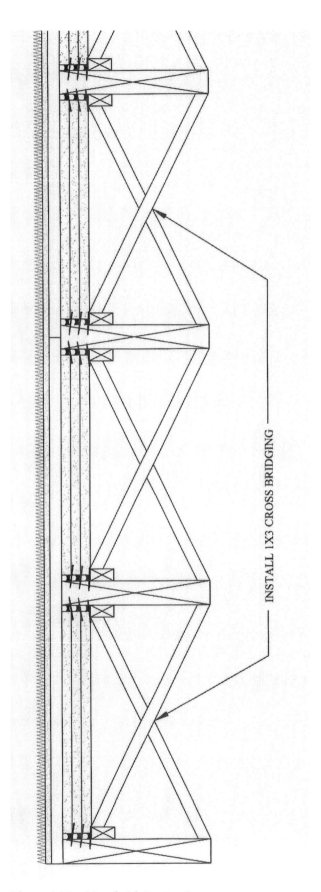

Figure 4.20   New bridging in place.

Generally, this will require the removal of some cross bracing members (known as *bridging*) in your deck assembly. Make certain to replace these, as they are critical to your floor design (see Figure 4.20).

After all of this is in place (or back in place with the case of the bridging), you will want to insulate below that to the bottom of the floor joist. I have seen a lot of recommendations for this material to be rockwool; however, standard fiberglass insulation will do just as well and for less cost.

Below this, we are now ready to install our new ceiling. Let's look at some options.

RESILIENT CHANNEL CEILINGS

Resilient channel works as well on ceilings as it does on walls, although I would recommend the use of the double-leg systems due to their capacity to carry a greater load than the single-leg system. Refer to the manufacturer's recommendations for the maximum spacing and load for their particular product.

RISC-1 clips and hat sections can also be used on ceilings with the same results you get on walls. Advantages to using this system are that the drywall ceiling can run directly to the perimeter of the existing wall assembly. This solves issues with weak isolation points at that location, as well as creating a good seal for fireblocking. The disadvantage is a lower isolation than totally isolated structural assemblies. Figure 4.21 is a typical installation of single-leg resilient channel on a ceiling.

Figure 4.22 is a double-leg resilient channel and Figure 4.23 shows the conditions with RISC-1 clip assemblies.

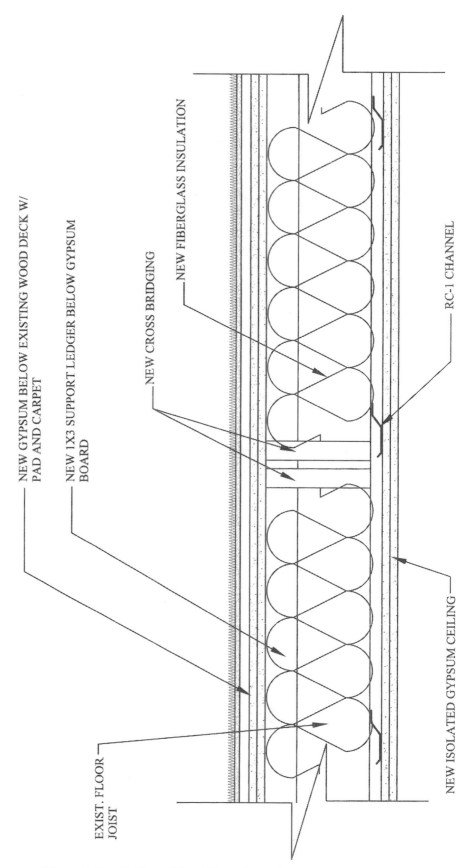

Figure 4.21   Ceiling with resilient channel.

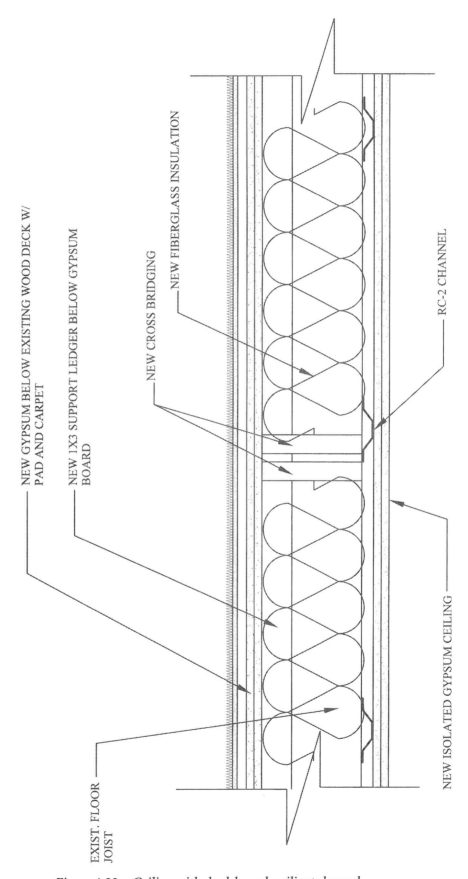

NEW GYPSUM BELOW EXISTING WOOD DECK W/ PAD AND CARPET

NEW 1X3 SUPPORT LEDGER BELOW GYPSUM BOARD

NEW CROSS BRIDGING

NEW FIBERGLASS INSULATION

RC-2 CHANNEL

NEW ISOLATED GYPSUM CEILING

EXIST. FLOOR JOIST

Figure 4.22   Ceiling with dual-legged resilient channel.

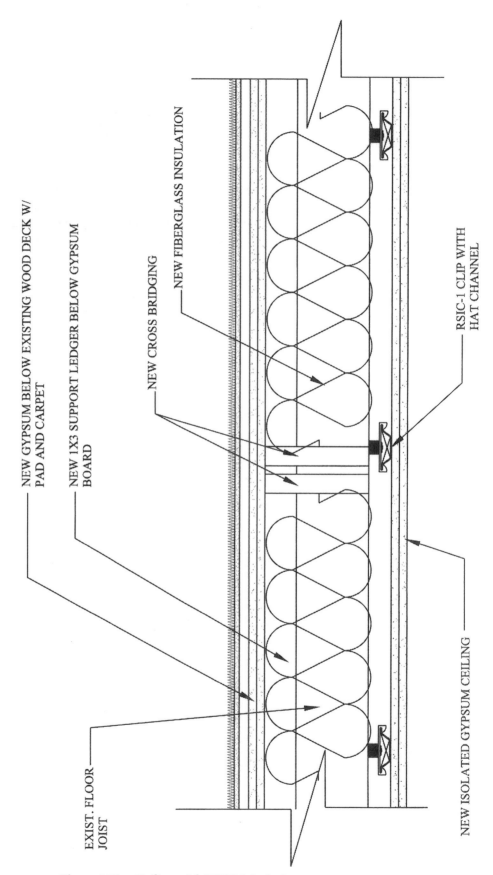

NEW GYPSUM BELOW EXISTING WOOD DECK W/ PAD AND CARPET

NEW 1X3 SUPPORT LEDGER BELOW GYPSUM BOARD

NEW FIBERGLASS INSULATION

NEW CROSS BRIDGING

RSIC-1 CLIP WITH HAT CHANNEL

EXIST. FLOOR JOIST

NEW ISOLATED GYPSUM CEILING

Figure 4.23   Ceiling with RISC-1 isolation.

SUSPENDED CEILINGS

Standard suspended ceilings, utilizing T-tracks with L-channels at the ceiling edges and laying in tiles, are not of any use for the purpose of serious isolation and should not be considered.

SEMI-INDEPENDENT FRAME CEILINGS

A semi-independent frame ceiling would be supported by your interior walls at the edges—with interior supports added to transfer some of the ceiling load back to the existing structure above. This is generally the case where you could not install a member large enough to support the entire load with a joist spanning the width of your room. This can be accomplished, with you still maintaining a good degree of isolation, through the use of isolation hangers carried by the structure above.

Once again, as with the floated slab construction, it is very important that you take into consideration the weight being carried by the individual hangers in order to make certain you load them up enough to engage the spring action of the isolator. Too much or too little load, and they will transfer sound energy through to the structure above. Again, the manufacturer will assist you in the calculations required for this system.

Figure 4.24 is a picture of a Mason Industries hanger made for this purpose. It's their WHR ceiling hanger.

Figure 4.24
WHR isolation hanger.

Figure 4.25 is a section through a deck (with the joist running lengthwise) that shows this hanger in use on a semi-independent ceiling assembly.

Figure 4.25a is another view of this with the section running through the new ceiling joist.

A downside to using this approach is (again) the load that it imposes on the existing structure, which will reduce the amount of mass you can add to the bottom of the deck above.

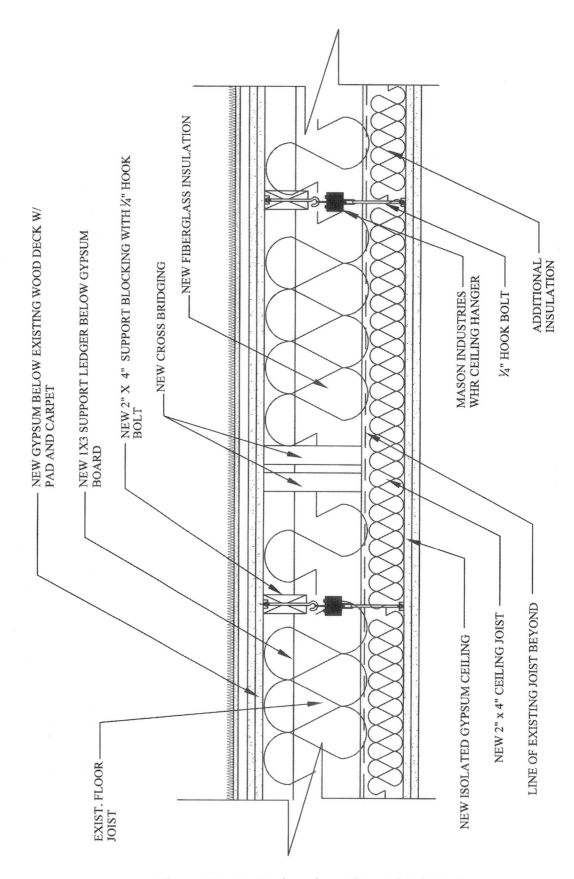

NEW GYPSUM BELOW EXISTING WOOD DECK W/ PAD AND CARPET

NEW 1X3 SUPPORT LEDGER BELOW GYPSUM BOARD

NEW 2" X 4" SUPPORT BLOCKING WITH ¼" HOOK BOLT

NEW CROSS BRIDGING

NEW FIBERGLASS INSULATION

MASON INDUSTRIES WHR CEILING HANGER

¼" HOOK BOLT

ADDITIONAL INSULATION

EXIST. FLOOR JOIST

NEW ISOLATED GYPSUM CEILING

NEW 2" x 4" CEILING JOIST

LINE OF EXISTING JOIST BEYOND

Figure 4.25   Semi-independent ceiling with isolation hangers.

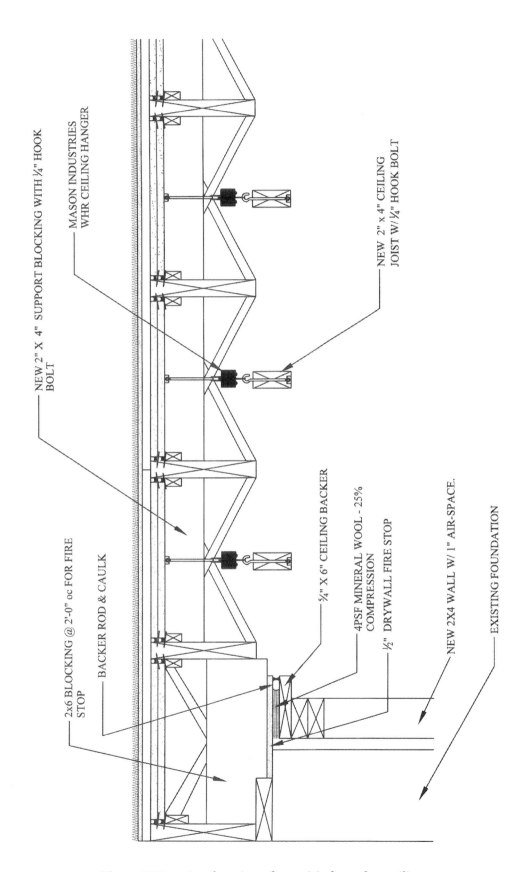

Figure 4.25a   Another view of a semi-independent ceiling.

INDEPENDENTLY FRAMED CEILINGS

Independently framed ceiling assemblies, carried by your new interior studio walls, are the best isolation you can achieve. One of the big advantages of this system is the fact that it imposes no weight to the existing structure, so you could add that much more mass to that structure to help with isolation. Figure 4.26 is an independently framed ceiling below an existing structure. Note how the new ceiling joist is offset above the bottom of the existing floor joist. This is the reason I suggest you use cross bridging rather than a solid block bridging for the existing assembly. Although solid bridging (a block made from the same dimensional material as the existing floor joist) creates a deck that is more solid than the cross bridging, it will not allow the new joist to enter the pocket of the existing joist.

In the case of Figure 4.26 (with 2x10 existing joist and new 2x6 ceiling joists), the difference would be losing 3 5/8" of framed ceiling height versus 6" with solid bridging. In tight spaces, such as existing basements, that extra few inches can make a world of difference in a room.

Take a moment and look at the firestop detail in Figure 4.26. It's important that you take care during construction to create assemblies that will not create chimney effects in the case of fire. The 1/2" drywall creates an effective firestop, yet maintains (as detailed) isolation between the two structures. Without this type of care taken during the construction process, a fire within the wall cavity could completely envelope the room in fire before you ever knew it was there. The creation of fire compartments within wall and ceiling cavities will provide a safe environment for you in case of an emergency.

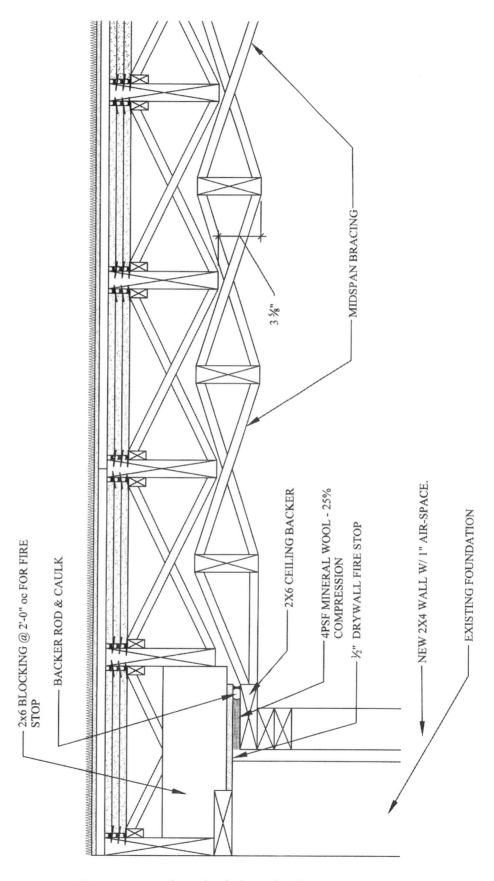

Figure 4.26   Independently framed ceiling.

Additional Isolation Products

There are a series of isolation products manufactured by Mason Industries. We'll take a look at how to use them properly in Chapter 10.

Figure 4.27 shows NPS Neoprene Partition Supports. Just as you can float slabs and ceilings, you can also float walls. These partition supports provide isolation from the existing slab to minimize slab transmissions into the wall structure.

Figure 4.27
Partition supports.

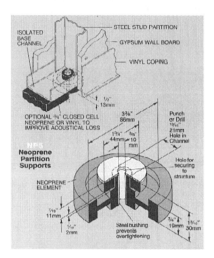

Figure 4.28 shows DNSB wall braces. Sway braces prevent buckling or overturning of tall or extremely long walls.

Figure 4.28
Wall braces.

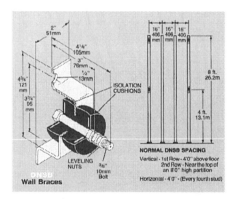

Figure 4.29 shows WIC and WCL sway braces. These products are ideal for lateral wall support where needed, while still maintaining isolation from the existing structure.

Figure 4.29
Sway braces.

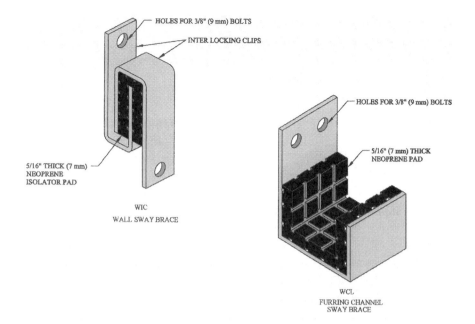

When bent, shear forces pull and stretch on the damping material.

Damping Systems

In a constrained layer damping system (CLD), a damping material is sandwiched between two other (usually stiff/rigid) materials. Damping occurs when the viscoelastic center of the "sandwich" is sheared (see Figure 4.30).

Figure 4.30
Constrained layer damping and how it works.

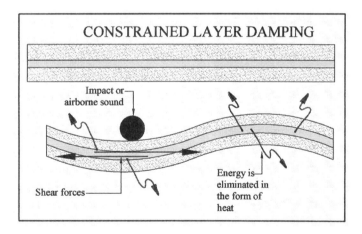

When bent, shear forces pull and stretch on the damping material. Energy is lost when the damping material is sheared. The vibration energy is not isolated, it's destroyed, and converted to heat at a rate defined by the efficiency of the damping material in any given system.

This is totally different than using an adhesive to glue multiple pieces of material together. When two pieces of drywall (for example) are joined together through the use of conventional construction adhesives, they bond, forming (essentially) one thicker piece of material. The effective isolation created from this type of assembly is less (as a whole) than the sum of the individual sheet themselves.

Thus, by gluing sheets together (using standard adhesives), you decrease isolation.

But with damping systems, the bonding actions that take place with conventional adhesives never occur, and the isolation is (potentially) greater than the sum of the two sheets themselves.

There are a large number of damping systems on the market: sheet loaded vinyl, polymeric materials incorporating mineral fillers, etc. But the only one that has caught my attention (providing greater isolation at low frequencies than standard drywall, while maintaining a cost performance that's reasonable) is a product called Green Glue, which is manufactured by Audio Alloy.

Is Green Glue more effective than just adding additional sheets of drywall? Well, if you remember mass law—each doubling of mass adds theoretically 6dB of additional isolation. But mass law stops at the drywall itself (in this case), so when it comes to a complete wall assembly, reality is closer to 4–5dB. So if you have two sheets on each side of a wall, the next step is four sheets each side for an averaged increase of a maximum of 5dB.

Figure 4.31 is a comparison of four wall assemblies, three of which were tested at Orfield Labs[7] for Audio Alloy. The first is a simple single stud wall with one layer of drywall each side. The second is a single stud wall with two layers of 5/8" drywall each side. The third is a single stud wall with two layers of drywall each side, with Green Glue sandwiched between the drywall on both sides. The fourth wall is an estimated performance for a single stud wall with four layers of drywall each side. Finally, at the bottom of the sheet, you see a chart line that shows you what mass law will gain you for each doubling of mass with this wall assembly, just for comparison's sake.

Figure 4.31
Isolation values for various wall types compared to a green glue assembly.

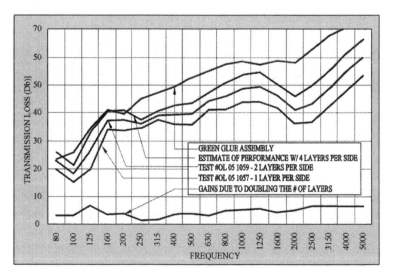

Note the increase in performance for the wall with only two layers of drywall on each face by adding Green Glue to the assembly. Note as well the superior performance of that wall to the wall with four layers of drywall and no green glue. Although they are close in the 125 to 200 Hz range, the green glue wall is far superior over 200 Hz, as well as around 100 Hz.

From a cost point of view, the Green Glue (with two layers of drywall) is fairly close to the cost of the wall with four layers of drywall each side, but the wall performance is so much more superior as to make it actually cheaper from the perspective of isolation value per square foot.

This is a product well worth considering if weight is a consideration in your structural analysis. It's a very effective means of increasing the ceiling floor assembly without the added weight that you have with strictly a mass approach to your construction.

Endnotes

[1] Sika-Dur Hi Mod is a registered trademark of Sika Corporation.

[2] Reprinted with permission of Mason Industries.

[3] Reprinted with permission of Mason Industries.

[4] Avoiding Flanking Noise Transmission: V. Young-Benidickson, "RAIC Update" 16(2), 1992, p. 7-8

[5] IR761 Gypsum Board Walls: Transmission Loss Data, R. E. Halliwell, T.R.T. Nightingale, A.C.C. Warnock, J.A. Birta, Internal Report IRC-IR-761, March 1988

[6] TJI is a registered trademark of Trus Joist, a Weyerhaeuser Business.

[7] Orfield Labs, LLC, 2709 E. 25th Street, Minneapolis, MN 55406, Contact: Mr. Steven J. Orfield, Phone: 612-721-2455.

CHAPTER 5

Window and Door Construction

So you understand about Mass Law, about isolation construction techniques, and about how important it is to seal up each and every square inch of space in your walls floor and ceilings. You know that where air goes—sound goes. Next, you're going to cut big gaping holes in these assemblies to put in huge windows and doors.

Yup, it's a fact of life—you need to be able to enter and leave the room. You also need to be able to see the people whom you're recording. On the subject of seeing the people you're recording, if this is a combination room, then you obviously won't need a window. (This is the case in my studio.) You also have the option, in a multi-room studio, of providing video feeds to other rooms versus windows. My preference, however, would be a window in this case. There is something about being able to see (face to face) the people you're recording that doesn't translate to a video screen.

In this chapter, we're going to look at exactly how we go about putting these assemblies in while still maintaining our isolation. We'll look at what we need to do to keep air from moving through the use of special gasketing assemblies. We'll figure out how to improve the quality of standard doors to get that extra isolation we need. We aren't going to do a step-by-step construction of these assemblies in this chapter. Rather, we are going to look at this from the perspective of the assembly as a whole, just to understand how it works as a unit, and which parts and pieces we will need when we finally do build it.

Glass

Because not only the windows, but often the doors will have glass in them, let's begin by taking a look at different types of glass and the advantages they have (or don't) in sound isolation.

FLOAT GLASS

Float glass (annealed glass) is the typical glass you are used to seeing in your windows at home. Most glass today is produced by the float process. The raw materials (primarily silica sand, soda ash, and limestone) are weighed, mixed, and conveyed to a melting furnace. Molten glass flows continuously from the furnace onto a bath of molten tin, where a continuous "ribbon" is formed. The glass floats on the tin and is pulled and stretched to the desired thickness and gradually cooled until it starts to solidify. The glass ribbon is then lifted out of the tin bath onto rollers and conveyed through an annealing lehr.

A lehr is a long oven that glass moves through on a conveyor belt. This allows for gradual cooling, which slowly relieves the stresses within the glass and allows the glass to properly anneal. The glass leaving the furnace passes between two metallic rolls that gives it the desired thickness. The glass is then slowly cooled until the glass exits the lehr, slightly above room temperature. At this point, the glass is flat and has virtually parallel surfaces. The glass is then cut, sized, and packaged. The standard specification for flat float glass is ASTM C1036.

Float glass has an advantage over tempered glass only due to its ability to be cut on-site. It's readily available from any of your local glass shops in thicknesses up to 1". No, I am not referring in this case to an insulated unit—that is the thickness of a single piece of glass. Float glass is the least effective glazing when considering acoustic isolation.

HEAT STRENGTHENED OR TEMPERED GLASS

Tempered glass is produced by taking an additional step in the manufacturing process of floating glass. The basic principle employed in the heat treating process is to create an initial condition of surface and edge compression. This condition is achieved by first heating the glass and then cooling the surfaces rapidly, which leaves the center glass thickness relatively hot compared to the surfaces. As the center thickness then cools, it forces the surfaces and edges into compression. Wind pressure, impact, thermal stresses, or other applied loads must first overcome this compression before there is any possibility of fracture. Understand though, a piece of tempered glass can be completely destroyed by a single nick on the edge that would never affect a standard piece of float glass. I had an insulated tempered glass unit literally explode in my face once while installing a piece of trim around a custom window opening. A 4d finish nail just barely nicked the edge of the glass, which was enough damage to force it to break into pieces.

Tempered glass is what you normally see installed in doors, door side-lights, sliding glass doors, etc. This glass is required as a safety means for glazing installed within 18" of a floor (this is a starting point—it gets more involved and has to do with pane size, mullion locations, etc.), for glass used in doorway passages, and for any glazing immediately adjacent to those passages. This glass is considered to be "safe," both due to its strength and its ability to break with a unique fracture pattern. Its strength, which effectively resists wind pressure and impact, provides safety in most applications. Also, when fully tempered glass does break, the glass fractures into small, relatively harmless fragments. This phenomenon (referred to as "dicing") reduces the chance of injury. Fully tempered glass is considered a safety glazing material if it is manufactured in accordance with ANSI Z97.1

Tempered glass is superior to float glass when acoustic isolation is a consideration; however, a disadvantage is that it cannot be cut once the tempering process is complete.

LAMINATE GLASS

A French chemist, Edouard Benedictus, invented laminated glass in 1909 and named it "Triplex." The process bonds two sheets of glass using a sheet of plastic, thereby producing a safety glass. Laminated glass is something you would normally see used for automobile windshields, but it is readily available in flat plate form as well. From a safety point of view, this glass is superior to either standard annealed or tempered for this purpose. Modern laminated glass panels are typically manufactured using a PVB interlayer. The manufacturing process for this glazing should adhere to ASTM C1172.

From an acoustical point of view, the big advantage of laminate glass is that the plastic inner layer (or laminate) provides a significant amount of internal structural damping for the glass. This damping effect has a major impact on the sound transmission properties of glass at high frequencies, especially near its critical frequency.

As mentioned earlier, the critical frequency is the acoustic frequency at which the wavelength of bending waves in a surface equals the wavelength of sound in air. At frequencies in the vicinity of the critical frequency, sound waves will pass through the glass much more readily than at other frequencies. As discussed in Chapter 3, this effect (reduced sound isolation in the region of the critical frequency) is called the *coincidence effect*.

Critical frequencies of glass are dependent on the glass thickness. Thicker glass will have a lower critical frequency than thinner glass. For example, 1/8" thick float glass has a critical frequency of 4800 Hz, while 1/4" thick float has a critical frequency of 2400 Hz, and 1/2" thick float has a critical frequency of 1200 Hz. Note that each doubling of thickness cuts the critical frequency in half.

Lab tests have proven that the isolation value of laminated glass in the coincidence region is greater than standard float or tempered glass. Thus, laminated glass provides better sound control than regular glass of the same total thickness. Just keep in mind that the benefit is really in the critical frequency range of the coincidence effect.

PLEXIGLASS

Plexiglass is a plastic sheet manufactured for a wide variety of uses. However, none of those uses includes sound isolation. This material just does not have the qualities you need. Remember that you need mass equal to the mass of the wall sheathing, stiffness to control the lowest frequencies, and a product that is going to hold up well over the lifetime of your studio (hopefully a long time). Plexiglass tends to scratch easily, and it can quickly become tiring to look through once this begins to happen.

So use this product for where it's designed—and use glass in your windows and doors.

Window Frame Construction and Isolating Techniques

The window is the easier of the two openings to deal with (which is why I began with it). If you have "room within a room" construction, you just determine what the mass is on your wall assembly and then match it with the window. Simple, isn't it?

Well, maybe not quite that simple. There are some construction techniques that you will have to use

WINDOW FRAMES AND TRIMS

In wall construction, it has been proven (through lab testing) that a heavy wooden window frame that runs continuously through the opening does not essentially weaken the TL value of a wall. Light-gauge steel frames (such as the type you would normally see in commercial applications for doors and windows) are a different story, however. So make it a point to stick with wood when building your window frames.

Some of the features of these assemblies will be identical, regardless of the wall type. I will make it a point to discuss only the differences in the assemblies, and I will try not to bore you by being redundant.

Figure 5.1 indicates a 5/4 stock window frame (1 1/4" nominal sized wood) in a 2x6 wood framed single wall assembly. It utilizes outside window stops made from standard 3/4" 1/4 round trim stock, a center stop of 1"x 6" pine (ripped to fit) with 1/2" and 3/4" glass. The exterior trims are just simple 1"x 4" pine.

NOTES:

1) WINDOW FRAME DETAILS ARE SIMILAR ON ALL 4 SIDES OF WINDOW.

2) TAKE CARE AT WINDOW CORNERS TO MAINTAIN WINDOW SEAL.

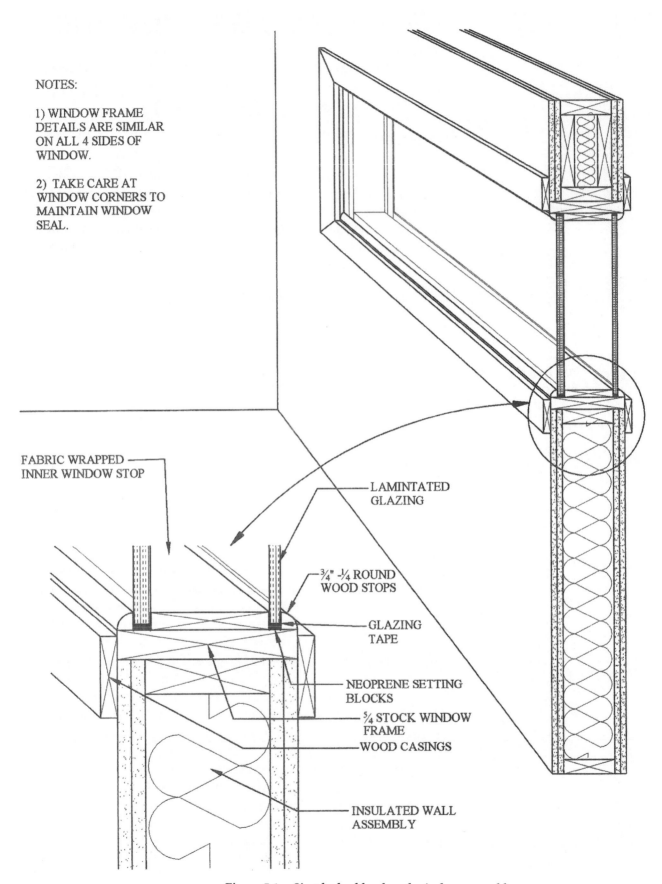

FABRIC WRAPPED INNER WINDOW STOP

LAMINTATED GLAZING

¾" -¼ ROUND WOOD STOPS

GLAZING TAPE

NEOPRENE SETTING BLOCKS

⁵⁄₄ STOCK WINDOW FRAME

WOOD CASINGS

INSULATED WALL ASSEMBLY

Figure 5.1   Simple double-glazed window assembly.

I like to take the inner stop and cover it with black felt, which adds a nice touch. Alternately, you could use a different fabric or finish the wood naturally. It doesn't make a difference from an acoustical point of view—it just makes a professional looking finished product.

Note the use of neoprene "setting blocks" to set the window on when installing it. These blocks help to maintain the window line in the opening, as well as allow caulking below the window to help create an airtight seal. Another piece of the seal assembly for this window is the use of glazing tape for both the inside edge of the window trim as well as the exterior. Glazing tapes are standard products that can be purchased from any local glass company. I like to use the Extru-Seal® manufactured by Precora Corporation for my windows. It's available in 1/16" and 1/8" thicknesses and 3/8" to 1/2" widths. Black and gray are the only colors, but I have never used anything other than black. Butyl caulks are perfect for the window perimeter, and they can be purchased at any local lumber center.

In staggered 2x6 stud construction, there is really no easy way with this wall type to isolate the frame from the separate stud assemblies, but when you take into account the coupling of the two wall faces with the top and bottom plate assemblies, you don't really lose a lot of isolation by continuing that "weak point" through the window assembly. However, if you build a staggered stud wall using 2x8 top and bottom plates and 2x4 studs, you can create an isolated frame by following the details in Figure 5.2. This window assembly is typical for an isolated wall, but it also can be used for a staggered stud wall. Care must be taken to ensure that the two frame faces never connect with one another. This can be accomplished by simply ripping the window framing plates to a width that ensures isolation (if need be).

Figure 5.2 is a typical window assembly with separate wall frames. Note how the frame for each window is totally isolated from one another through the use of a rubber seal surrounding the opening between the window frames (which I use to keep dust from settling into the window opening over time and also to increase the effect of the air spring within the window panels themselves). The areas between the separate inner window stops are then tightly fitted with rigid fiberglass insulation, and the finished layer is fabric wrapped. This gives a nice finish, and neither the rubber wrap nor the fiberglass can transmit sound from one wall face to the other. Another nice feature about this detail is that the seal gives you a good place to set some bags of desiccant to avoid the possibility of any moisture problems within the window cavity. Although this doesn't happen often, I have had people contact me to ask my assistance in this regard, so it can occur.

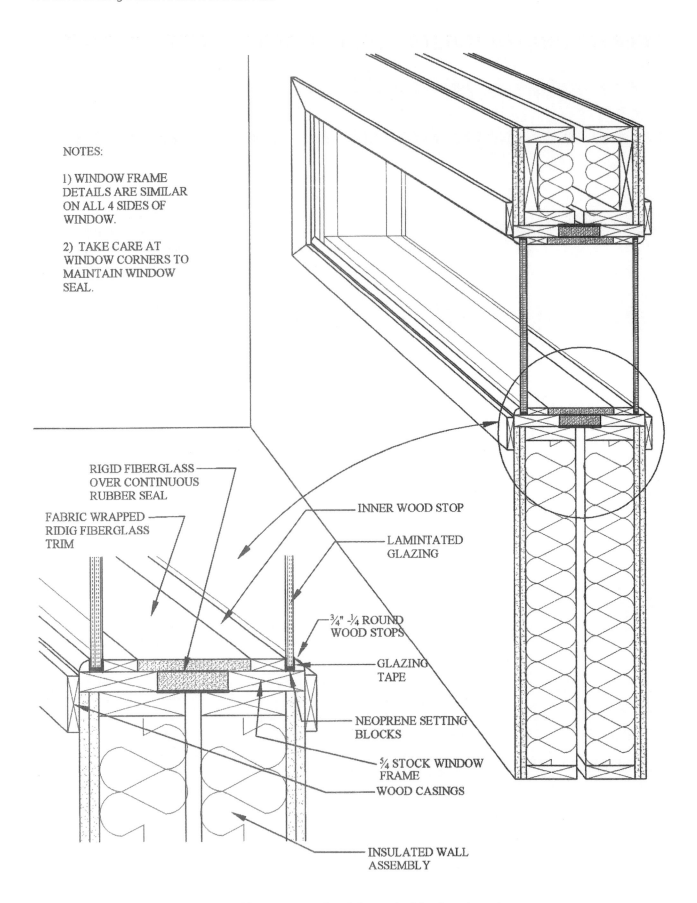

NOTES:

1) WINDOW FRAME
DETAILS ARE SIMILAR
ON ALL 4 SIDES OF
WINDOW.

2) TAKE CARE AT
WINDOW CORNERS TO
MAINTAIN WINDOW
SEAL.

RIGID FIBERGLASS
OVER CONTINUOUS
RUBBER SEAL

FABRIC WRAPPED
RIDIG FIBERGLASS
TRIM

INNER WOOD STOP

LAMINTATED
GLAZING

¾" ¼ ROUND
WOOD STOPS

GLAZING
TAPE

NEOPRENE SETTING
BLOCKS

⁵⁄₄ STOCK WINDOW
FRAME

WOOD CASINGS

INSULATED WALL
ASSEMBLY

Figure 5.2   Isolated frame double-glazed window

GLASS THICKNESS

By now you've noticed that I did not indicate any glass thickness in the previous drawings. You should be wondering (at this point) "Exactly how do we go about determining what glass thickness to use in our window openings?"

This is really one of the simpler things to do—just figure out what the weight of your mass on one side of the wall is, match this as a minimum for your thinnest piece of glass, and make sure you have at least 1/4" greater in thickness for the glass on the other side of the wall.

Remember the basics—it's all about mass. That doesn't change just because the material changes. For example, if you have two layers of 5/8" drywall on each side of your wall, then the mass = 2×2.625 psf (per layer) or 5.25 psf of mass (on each side of the wall) for the drywall. Standard plate glass (annealed) weighs 1.64 psf for glass 1/8" thick. Thus, a 3/8" piece of annealed weighs 4.92 psf (a little light), so you need a piece of 1/2" for one side and 3/4" for the other. Thus, the glass weights will be 6.56 psf and 9.84 psf, respectively. Don't worry about the fact that the glass weighs more than the wall—remember the added benefit you get from thicker glass with the lower coincidence effect. That, plus the fact that the coincidence level for each piece of glazing is different, will help you to increase isolation. Because of this, the wall assembly surrounding the window will be your weakest point, and the effective isolation will be as if you had never penetrated the wall at all.

Finally, I want to touch base with you on the issue of splayed glass (which is when the two pieces of glass are farther apart at the top then they are at the bottom) versus parallel panes of glazing.

Maximum volume equals maximum isolation. So placing the glass more closely together at the bottom is decreasing the isolation value of the window. But the splaying of the glass also helps you in a few respects— the first of which is that it stops you from seeing reflections in the glass (by reflections I mean images, not sound). It also helps to stop glare from lighting—both of which make it much less tiring to look through. An additional benefit (from my perspective) is that it helps to stop early reflections off the glass (by reflections, I'm referring to sound coming from the speakers) from causing a problem. Instead of having sounds reflect from the glass into your face, they will reflect down towards the floor or into the back of your console.

In my mind, the loss in isolation from the air spring is made up for in mass. We will always have greater mass than the wall surfaces if we do this right, so what little difference there may be we just live with. In Chapter 1, we looked at the fact that in the real world sometimes there are things that we just live with. This is one of those things.

However, if you want to gain the maximum isolation benefit (at this point the walls will be the weak point and control your total isolation), then feel free to install the glass parallel. This is the sort of thing that is really a matter of personal choice, and it won't affect the outcome to any great degree, so I won't push you in any one direction. It's only important to me that you understand enough about the subject to be able to make an informed decision.

Figure 5.3 details a typical splayed window unit. Note that I have now switched from a quarter round window trim to square edge stops. This glass weights quite a bit, and the greater the window splay, the more weight is carried by the topmost window stop. Don't take chances with small stock if you're heading this route, make sure that you don't have any surprises coming down the road—use the larger stock.

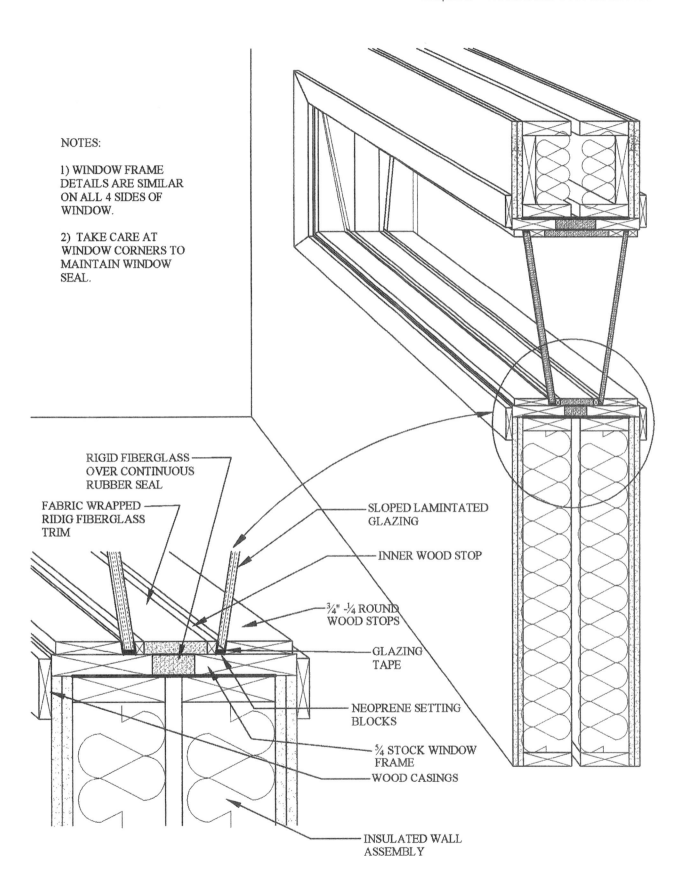

NOTES:

1) WINDOW FRAME DETAILS ARE SIMILAR ON ALL 4 SIDES OF WINDOW.

2) TAKE CARE AT WINDOW CORNERS TO MAINTAIN WINDOW SEAL.

RIGID FIBERGLASS OVER CONTINUOUS RUBBER SEAL

FABRIC WRAPPED RIDIG FIBERGLASS TRIM

SLOPED LAMINTATED GLAZING

INNER WOOD STOP

¾" -¼ ROUND WOOD STOPS

GLAZING TAPE

NEOPRENE SETTING BLOCKS

⁵⁄₄ STOCK WINDOW FRAME

WOOD CASINGS

INSULATED WALL ASSEMBLY

Figure 5.3   Isolated frame double glazed splayed window

MANUFACTURED WINDOW UNITS

Just to cover the all the bases, you can purchase manufactured acoustic window units. Over the years, I've worked successfully with products manufactured by the Overly Door Company. Their window line provides special steel frames with dual-glazed systems, offering acoustic ratings up to STC 55. This rating was achieved with a clear glazing area of 21sf, using 3/4" and 1/2" laminated glass. The cost for these units is pricey when compared to DIY windows, but if you do not feel up to constructing a window and would rather purchase one, then Overly would be a manufacturer you could not go wrong with. An example of their products can be seen in Figures 5.4 and 5.5. These pictures are from the Quincy Public Access TV Studio located at the Thomas Crane Public Library in Quincy, MA.

Figure 5.4
Overly Door Co. window.

Figure 5.5
Overly Door Co. window.

Doors

With door construction, the basics stay the same (at least with the door itself) and that means mass, mass, and more mass. Funny how that theme follows us though this book, isn't it? But, when it comes to the remainder of the door assembly, it's all about stopping the movement of air.

Unlike a window (where you punch a hole through a wall and then seal it up tight again), a door is built with the intent that you are going to continually violate the seal of the wall. So, sometimes you want the wall air tight, and sometimes you don't. Here everything becomes an issue of seals. Multiple seals, a layering of seals, seals upon seals upon seals, etc.

Do you remember back in Chapter 3 when we looked at that small crack at the bottom of the wall and what that equated to when compared with a hole through the wall? Well, the door is very much like that wall—only with a very big crack at the door bottom and a smaller crack on the remaining three sides. The pain is this—in order for the door to operate properly, you need the door to be fitted to create all those relatively big cracks. Thus, we are forced into those seals mentioned above.

By the time you finish a door, you will be dreaming about seals, because this is going to be make it or break it time for your room. Do this right, and you have it made, but screw this one up, and no matter how good the remainder of your construction is, you just lost it.

Now, in all fairness, the one nice thing about this is that the door is available to take apart without removing all of the assembly (unlike a wall, floor, or ceiling once they're completed), so you can work, then rework, and then rework again if required, but in the end, if it isn't right, neither is your room. So this is a place where you may want to bring some professional help in if you don't feel up to the task.

Another reason to consider this (if you are not a carpenter or a real handy DIY'er) is that the materials for a proper door assembly can get pretty expensive real fast. And if they are accidentally cut short—or otherwise get ruined to the point where they don't work—then replacing them can sure eat into your project budget. Better to keep your extra money for room gear if you aren't up to this one.

OK, now that I've warned you—on to the task at hand.

DOOR FRAME CONSTRUCTION

There are a few different ways of attacking door openings through walls. One being what I call a "super door," which is a modified solid core door. The second one is through the use of two standard solid core doors in the same opening. My preference is the super door. Let's take a look at both.

I'll let you know right now that this is one place I don't worry about maintaining the separation of wall assemblies with the frames, even when using totally separated assemblies. When it comes to carrying a door that might weight well over 300 pounds (if you build them like I do), or even standard solid core doors, you do not want your door frame attached to a stud that can move over the years. As I noted above, tests have proven that a through jamb does not effectively lessen the total isolation value of a wall assembly to any great degree. So don't worry about any miniscule amount of isolation you may lose. Just build the frame straight through the cavity.

I would also recommend against using the standard 5/8" jambs that are typically used with pre-hung doors, because the jambs will not hold up against the weight of the "super door" assembly. Often, neither will a standard hinge. Use 5/4 stock lumber for your frames; 3/4" pine is fine for door stops. Then use a variety of special seals to make this baby airtight.

Figure 5.6 is a plan view of a typical door assembly. I begin with a standard solid core door, and in this case, any manufacturer's door is as good as any other door. As long as it's solid core, don't bother worrying about what the core material is made of.

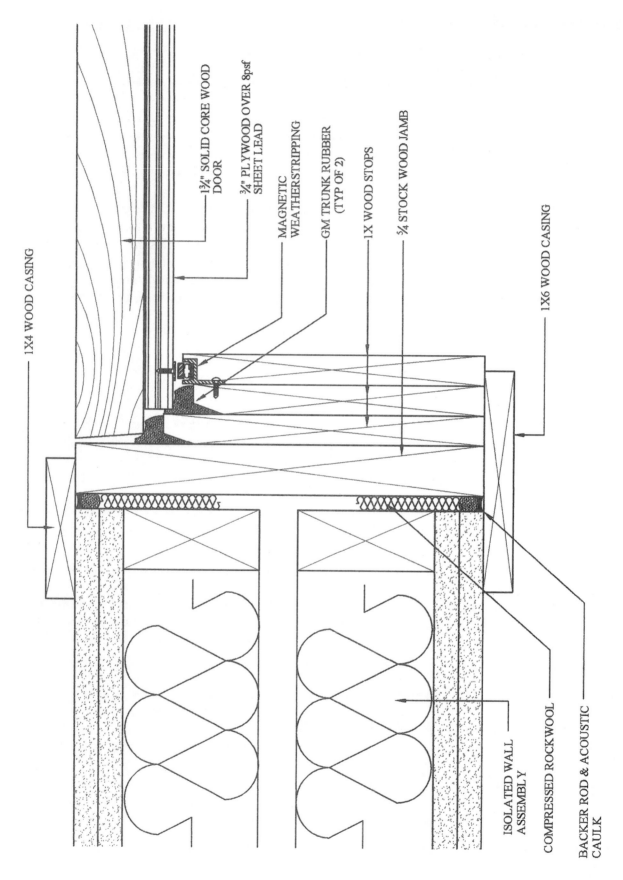

1X4 WOOD CASING

1¾" SOLID CORE WOOD DOOR

¾" PLYWOOD OVER 8psf SHEET LEAD

MAGNETIC WEATHERSTRIPPING

GM TRUNK RUBBER (TYP OF 2)

1X WOOD STOPS

⁵⁄₄ STOCK WOOD JAMB

1X6 WOOD CASING

ISOLATED WALL ASSEMBLY

COMPRESSED ROCKWOOL

BACKER ROD & ACOUSTIC CAULK

Figure 5.6   Typical door assembly.

The door itself is improved by adding mass to the inner face. My preferred method is the use of 8 psf sheet lead, which can be purchased at any local masonry supply store in varying widths. This is sandwiched between the door and a piece of 3/4" plywood. The plywood and lead are held back of the door edge 1" (on the two sides and the top) to allow for weather-stripping the door. The door is then hung with heavy duty hinges, weather-stripping is installed, a bottom drop seal (with threshold) is put into place, and then, finally, door latches complete the project.

The final part of this assembly is a door closure. Order a good quality commercial closure for your door. You want this for two reasons, the first of which is safety. Yes, safety. A door with this much mass could break bones, or even remove body parts, if they happened to be between the door and the jamb when it closed. Although you might never have this happen to you (as an adult), the possibility of this happening with a child is greater than you might think. A good commercial door closure has the strength to handle a door of this weight, and it has two distinct closing settings. The first setting is with the door in a wide open position, and it controls the closing speed of the door to within (roughly) 8" to 10" of the jamb. Then the latch speed takes over, which can be adjusted to complete the closing at a very slow, gentle rate. Not only does this give you some safety (as mentioned above), but it will also help your door assembly to live longer. By this I mean that the slamming of a door like this will cause screws attaching it at the hinges to loosen up, which should be avoided.

By now you understand that this is going to be an expensive piece of your studio cost. None of these items is inexpensive. But this is one place you do not want to skimp on expenditures. Remember that your entire assemblies are as good as your weakest link.

An alternative to constructing a door like this is to use two doors on opposite sides of your isolated walls, in which case you would construct in accordance with Figure 5.7. Note that although you save the cost of the sheet lead and cabinet grade plywood, in this case, you will have to purchase two times as much gasketing, drops seals, thresholds, and closures. But this is still an option should you choose to use this technique.

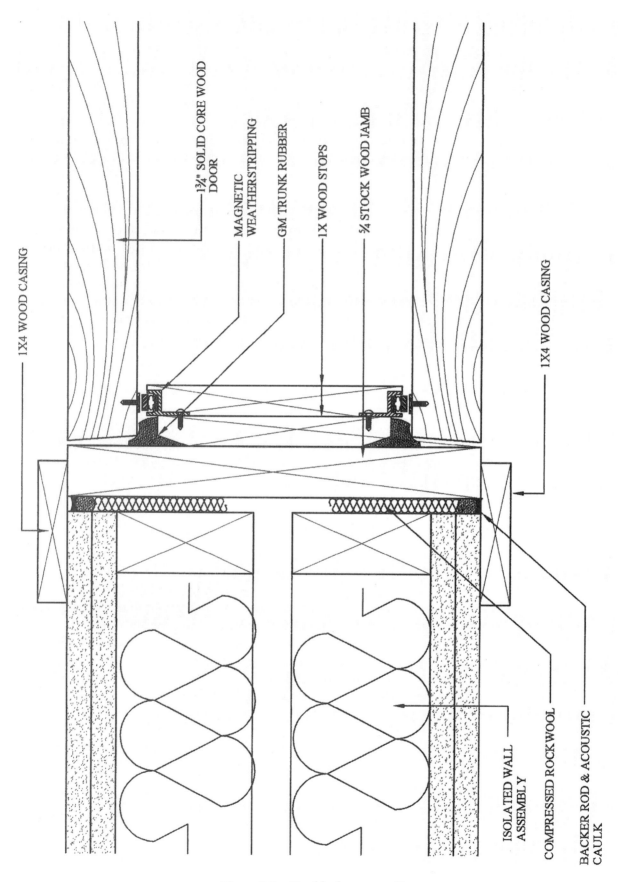

Figure 5.7   Double door assembly.

WINDOWS IN DOORS

Installing windows in doors is similar to the installation in walls—you want an air space and airtight construction. However, you become limited in air space and window thickness, depending on the thickness of the door assembly.

If you use a double door assembly, then you would use the same glass thickness that is used on the walls. For example, one door would have 1/2" glass, and the other would be 3/4". Remember that you cannot use float glass in this application.

In a single super door, you can use two separate pieces of glass. The door itself is 1 3/4" thick, and the additional lead (1/8") and 3/4" plywood make a final thickness of 2 5/8". A typical 3068 super door will weight around 304 pounds, thus about 15.2 psf. So a piece of glass 3/4" thick, coupled with a piece 3/8" thick would give comparable mass to the door and would allow for a 1 1/2" air gap between panes using flush window stops.

DOOR HARDWARE

In order to create airtight assemblies, special hardware is required. I use a soft gasket, manufactured by General Motors for the trunk rubber seal on some of their automobiles, as a part of my assemblies. Type "K" is the rubber gasket that works best. Figure 5.8 is a close-up view of that seal.

Figure 5.8
General Motors Type "K" trunk rubber—close view.

I also like seals manufactured by Zero International. They manufacture the following products that I would recommend for door gasketing. Figure 5.9 shows a typical magnetic weather-stripping.

Figure 5.9
Magnetic weather-stripping.

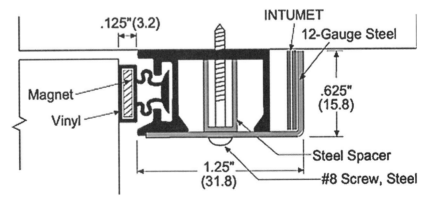

Figure 5.10 is an example of their drop seals for door bottoms.

Figure 5.10
Drop seal assembly.

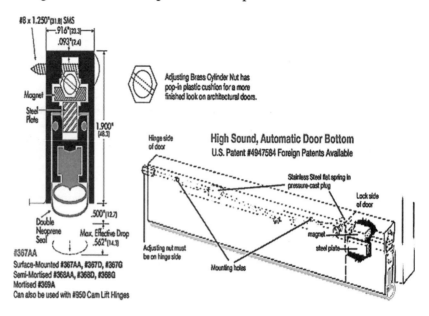

Figure 5.11 is a threshold that incorporates an additional rubber seal at the door bottom.

Figure 5.11
Sealing threshold.

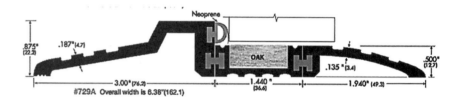

MANUFACTURED DOORS

As with windows, should you choose not to construct your own doors, you can purchase manufactured units specifically made for sound isolation. Again, I have had good luck in the past with Overly. They manufacture steel and wood acoustic door assemblies with special hardware, integral gasketing, and isolated steel frames. Their steel doors have isolation values up to STC 55, while the wood units are available with ratings to STC 49.

Only a few more chapters, and we'll begin to look at how this all comes together.

CHAPTER 6

Electrical Considerations

Let's begin this chapter (and the next for that matter) with my explaining that I do not intend to tell you how to wire electrical outlets or install HVAC Systems.

Over the next two chapters, I want to explain enough about the subjects to help you avoid some problems, allow you to make some decent judgments, and get you ready to deal with the subjects.

If you want to learn how to wire or how to install HVAC systems, there are already some excellent books on the market to help you along, so please buy one of them.

Line Voltage

You need to begin with understanding your electrical service and panel, along with the parts and pieces of your room and gear.

Typical home electrical service will be single phase 230V AC. This consists of a three-line service from the power company into your electrical panel—two "hot" legs of 110V and one neutral (return) leg (see Figure 6.1).

A Comment on Power Company Service

Most schematics for this would indicated the neutral feed flowing in the direction of the service; however, I indicate this as flowing out of the service back to the power company, for that is really its purpose. The neutral returns residual electricity back to the power company's ground.

Figure 6.1
Home electrical service details.

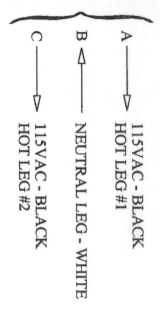

SOURCE FROM POWER
COMPANY TRANSFORMER

C — 115VAC - BLACK HOT LEG #2

B — NEUTRAL LEG - WHITE

A — 115VAC - BLACK HOT LEG #1

TO SERVICE PANEL

Most of your use will require a single pole circuit, which utilizes one of the hot legs, the return, and a ground. On your main panel, the ground bar and neutral bar will be "bonded" which means they are joined together.

One thing that's important for you to understand is that your panel is not built for power leg #1 to feed the left side of the panel, with leg #2 feeding the right side. Rather, power in a panel usually feeds from top to bottom and rotating. So leg #1 are the odd numbered breakers top to bottom, and leg #2 are the even breakers top to bottom.

Figure 6.2 indicates a typical panel with the main breaker, the neutral buss bar, the ground buss bar, and the sub-breaker configuration. Pay attention to the sub-breaker configuration because this will be important to you when wiring your studio.

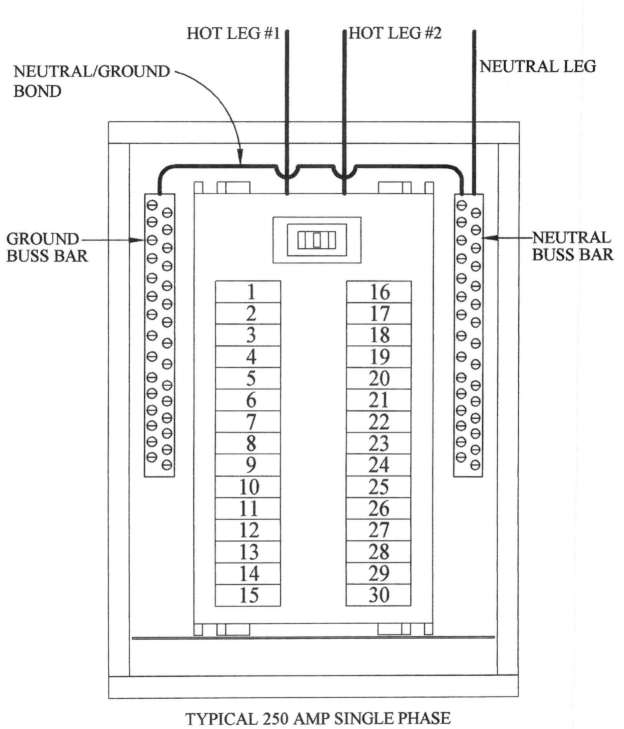

Figure 6.2   Typical electrical panel.

One of your goals with studio wiring is to put all of your gear on one leg of the panel, and all other loads such as lighting, HVAC equipment, refrigerators, etc., on the second leg. This will help you avoid things like 60 Hz motor transmissions from showing up as noise in your recordings.

Although this sounds easy, it may not be the case. This is due to the fact that your panel also needs to have what is called a "balanced load." Picture a hot summer day, all the AC units running, refrigerator running, a load of clothes in the wash, another one in the dryer, hot water heater on, most of the house lights on, someone running a TV, someone else at a computer, and you in your studio with a band. If the total load for your electrical service (at that time) were 170 amps, you would want roughly 85 amps on one leg and the other 85 amps on the second leg. That's a balanced load.

Why? Picture a 200 amp 120/240V residential service with the entire house wired to one phase. Imagine 210 amps of 120V line-to-neutral loads being connected to this phase. This setup will only allow half of the possible amperage load before the main breaker trips. This is because the load on that pole of the breaker exceeds 200 amps. Now, if you take that same load and spread it out over two phases (110 amps per phase), then the main breaker will be fine because the 110 amps is well below each pole's capacity.

Another reason this is desirable is due to the fact that the more balanced the load is on a service, the less current will be carried through the neutral. In a perfectly balanced panel, the current present in the neutral would be 0 amps. This is a safety feature for both the workers for the local electrical company, as well as you (or anyone else) who might work on your wiring in the future. It's a real pain (potentially a life-threatening pain, in fact) to go to work on a circuit that you've turned off the current to and have current present in the neutral on that circuit that decides you're a good source to ground.

Low Voltage

Low voltage wiring should be kept as separate as possible from line voltage sources. In an ideal world, the low voltage wiring runs low in the room, and line voltage wiring runs high (or vice versa). If you have to cross low and line voltage wiring, then cross them at a 90° angle. Do not run them parallel to one another.

Taking care when running these lines will help to minimize noise in your final product.

Electrical Noise

Here's something I hear on a regular basis. "I wired my studio up and everything seems to be wired right, but I have this buzzing sound in my monitors. What did I do wrong?"

Well, even if you did everything right, you can still have noise crop up in your systems. Electrical noise is caused by the transmission of RFI (Radio Frequency Interference). RFI transmissions can be transmitted through the air or through your electrical wiring system.

Right off the bat, you can have ground loops in your existing wiring system that never show up until you begin to wire in studio quality gear. So what exactly is a ground loop? It's current that flows in conductors connecting two points (through varying paths) that should have the same potential (i.e., ground), but are actually at different potentials.

Not quite clear yet? For example, when two or more devices are connected to a common ground through different paths, ground path noise, or a ground loop, can occur. Thus, a system grounded at two different points, with a potential difference between the two grounds, can cause unwanted noise voltage in the circuit paths. Current flows through these "multiple paths" and develops voltages, which can cause damage and noise (50 Hz/60 Hz hum) in audio or video equipment.

Here's an example of a ground loop and its cause. A world-class studio we constructed had hum and buzz problems with single loop guitar coils. The buzz would change as the guitar was moved—from almost totally silent to loud—*real loud*. A test with an oscilloscope indicated a strong 60 Hz signal on the ground of a circuit with nothing running on it.

It took almost a month to finally trace the problem. When the building was constructed, the water service to the building was provided from the adjacent building on the property. It was more than enough service to provide our needs for the few bathrooms we had in the new building. However, it was bonded in the original building to the earth ground, and then again to the earth ground for our new electrical service. That created the path to two grounds from one source.

To solve the problem, we installed a non-metallic connector on the water service between the two buildings, thus breaking the second path to ground.

Simple problem—simple solution—four weeks to figure it out.

Ground loops can be eliminated in one of two ways:

▶ Remove one of the ground paths, thus converting the system to a single point ground, in a similar manner to our problem with the water service.

▶ Isolate one of the ground paths with an isolation transformer, common mode choke, optical coupler, balanced circuitry, or frequency selective grounding.

In my opinion, the easiest (and usually a fairly cost effective) method for doing this would be to use an isolation transformer. An isolation transformer is a device that allows all the desired signals to pass freely, while interrupting ground continuity, hence breaking ground loops.

There can be other sources of noise in your gear that have nothing to do with ground loops and can occur even if you install an isolated ground transformer. Creating a quiet electrical system requires careful planning of your service to the studio.

Let's look at some things we can plan that will help to ensure clean power in our studio.

Isolated Ground Receptacles and Star Grounding

Something you might want to consider when planning the wiring for your studio is the use of hospital grade, isolated ground receptacles and a star grounding system. This is the most commonly used system for technical grounding. Hospitals use this approach to power distribution as a matter of course. It helps them to ensure that their critical equipment will not fail due to dirty electrical circuits. It has a minimum of technical compromises, meets the requirements of equipment grounding, and provides a system that is relatively practical to install, troubleshoot, and maintain.

Figure 6.3 illustrates the basic geometry for a star ground system. Note that the isolated ground wires have been run back to a separate ground panel. The ground buss within that panel is then tied to the earth ground for the building service.

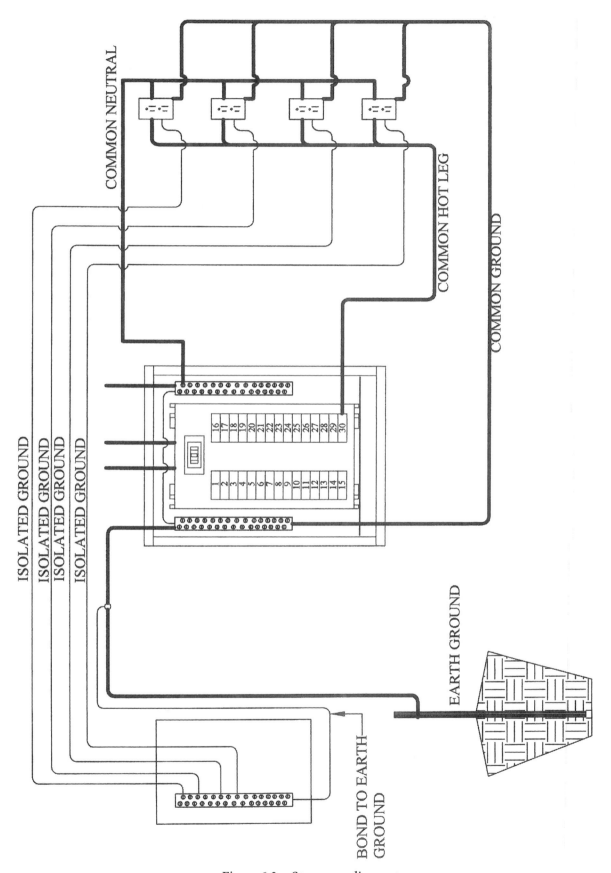

Figure 6.3   Star grounding system.

The usual three wires for the receptacles are run normally. Black wire (hot leg) to brass screw, neutral (white wire) to silver, bare ground to box, but then a separate jacketed ground is run back to the ground buss. Typically, this would be run within a conduit (it is required to be protected by the National Electrical Code or NEC) and should be run in close proximity to the cable used for the receptacle service. Standard junction boxes can be used for this purpose to allow for multiple conductors to be run within one conduit rather than individual ones. The wires can run back to the original ground buss in the main panel, or a separate ground panel with its own ground buss can be used adjacent to the main panel. It's important that this then be tied back to the ground wire running to earth ground on the main panel.

Lighting

Avoid the use of fluorescent lighting. Although the lighting itself is great and is relatively inexpensive, the ballasts (and yes, this includes electronic ballasts) are very noisy.

If at all possible, avoid the use of dimmer systems. You can plan your lighting to achieve almost the same effect by using a greater number of lights with smaller wattage bulbs, and you can control intensity through the use of individual switches controlling the lighting symmetrically in pairs.

If you really need (or just want) a dimmer system, stick with good quality professional systems, not the single slide bar controls that you use for your living room, and understand that you might have to add remotely mounted systems specially designed to get rid of any problems that may crop up down the road.

I have used lighting systems manufactured by Lutron Electronics, Inc. successfully in the past; however, care must still be taken. The following information comes from Lutron.

What Is Radio Frequency Interference (RFI)?

RFI is a buzzing noise, which may occur in some audio and radio equipment when solid-state dimmers are used nearby. Although every Lutron dimmer contains a filter to suppress RFI, additional filtering may be required in some applications. Typical examples of RFI-sensitive equipment are AM radios, stereo sound systems, broadcasting equipment, intercom systems, public address systems, and wireless telephones.

RFI can be transmitted in two ways: radiated and conducted.

Note: These suggestions will help minimize RFI; however, they do not guarantee that RFI will be completely eliminated.

RADIATED RFI

Any sensitive equipment that is in close proximity to dimming equipment can pick up the RFI and generate noise into its system.

The following are three possible ways to minimize radiated RFI:

▶ Physically separate the RFI-sensitive equipment from the dimmer and its wiring.

▶ Run dimmer wiring in its own metal conduit.

▶ Use a lamp debuzzing coil (available from Lutron) to filter the RFI.

CONDUCTED RFI

In some cases, RFI is conducted through the building wiring and directly into the AC power supply of the sensitive equipment.

To minimize conducted RFI, follow these guidelines:

▶ Feed sensitive equipment from a circuit without a dimmer on it.

▶ Add a power-line filter to the sensitive equipment.

▶ Add shielded wire for all microphones and input cables. Also, use low-impedance balanced microphone cables, which are less susceptible to interference than high-impedance types.

▶ Make sure that all the equipment is grounded. Connect all shields to the ground at one point. Ground lighting fixture metal housings properly.

▶ Use a lamp debuzzing coil (available from Lutron) to filter the RFI.

Lamp debuzzing coils (LDCs) are the most effective way to reduce RFI. One LDC is required for each dimmer. Select the LDC according to the connected lighting load. The LDCs may be wired in series on either the line side or the load side of the dimmer. For maximum RFI suppression, keep the wiring between the LDC and the dimmer as short as possible.

Since the LDC itself makes an audible buzz, mount it in a location where the noise will not be objectionable (e.g., an electrical closet, a basement, or above a drop ceiling). LDCs are designed to easily mount onto a standard 4"x4" junction box. They are UL listed and thermally protected. [1]

The How's and Why's of Lighting Noise

Why does it work this way? Why do lights make noise when dimmed?

Solid-state dimmers are electronic switches that rapidly turn the current feeding a lighting circuit on and off, 120 times per second, to produce the dimming effect. This rapid switching can cause incandescent lamp filaments to vibrate, resulting in a buzzing noise. Lamp buzz is generally noisiest at mid-range (50%) dimming level. Some lamps are noisier than others when dimmed, depending on the physical characteristics of the lamp filament. Lamps of higher wattage (100W and above) tend to produce a louder buzz. Therefore, use a lower wattage lamp whenever possible to reduce lamp buzz.

How does a lamp debuzzing coil (LDC) work? When an LDC is wired in series with the dimmer, it slows down the inrush of current during the rapid switching cycle of the dimmer. As the current inrush is slowed down, the lamp filament vibration and lamp buzz are reduced. This helps to quiet not only the lamp itself, but also the amount of RFI transmitted through the wiring system.

Diagnosing and Troubleshooting Problems

To accurately determine the correct solution to a problem, you first have to find and isolate it. For example, if you simply start flailing away, swapping gear and cables and everything all at once, you may never know what actually caused (or fixed) the problem. In addition, you may end up making more and more work since you are expending energy in areas that don't have any effect on the problem at hand.

Start simple. Troubleshooting ground loops involves taking things in order and checking a few basic, common elements to see if the problem is simple or complex. For example, if adjusting the volume on your processor/receiver does not alter the hum level, then the problem must be occurring *after* that point. If it occurred prior, then the processor/receiver would typically alter the overall level of noise. Make sense?

Work in the following methodical manner. Begin by taking one piece of the chain out of the loop at a time. If the noise suddenly disappears when you disconnect a compressor (for example), then the problem lies there, either within the compressor itself or within its power supply.

Another example would be to check your mic or equipment cords. Quite often a bad cord will cause a hum. Begin (again) by checking one cord at a time. Pulling out a bunch of cords all at once might well solve your problem, but it won't let you know which of those cords was the real problem.

Some Common Problems

First, check to see if you have a power cord or an outlet in the wall that is worn out and will not grip. If the hot/neutral/ground prongs on the plug are making intermittent or light contact with the tang on the inside of the outlet, it can cause a hum through the system. The best solution for this is to replace the cord with a new one or the outlet with an industrial version. Industrial outlets have better gripping and will hold power cables more securely.

Second, check the polarity of the outlet because it may be wired backwards. You can get a polarity checker for about $5. This is one of the first things you may want to check after you finish wiring your studio. Check this even if you have a professional electrician do the wiring for you. You would be amazed the number of times I find problems with polarity in an outlet on projects wired by licensed electricians. Remember—they're human—they make mistakes.

Third, light dimmers, fluorescent lamps, and other appliances that share the same circuit or common ground with your equipment can cause hums.

Fixing the Problem

If your problem relates to any of the three items above, then change the cords, fix the polarity, or put those lights on a different leg of the service.

Understand though that troubleshooting all of the possible sources for hums and buzzes could easily cost thousands of dollars of a professional's time.

"OK, so I've done everything right, still have noise, and found out that the problem stems from the power company itself. They've told me that the power is clean enough for residential use, and there is nothing they can (or will) do to fix it. Where do I go from here?"

If this is the case, then you will have to consider the use of an isolation transformer for your gear.

Tripp Lite is a manufacturer of small isolation transformers. Costs for their units range from around $135 for a two-outlet, 250 watt transformer (see Figure 6.4) to about $343.00 for a four-outlet 1,000 watt hospital grade transformer (see Figure 6.5).

Figure 6.4
250 watt isolated transformer.

Figure 6.5
1,000 watt isolated transformer
(hospital grade).

Tripp Lite uses a design incorporating a Faraday Shield for effective isolation. The Faraday Cage was invented by Michael Faraday (1791–1867). In 1836, Faraday built a room, coated it with metal foil, and allowed high-voltage discharges from an electrostatic generator to strike the outside of the room. He then used an electroscope to show that there was no excess electric charge on the inside of the room's walls and volume.

The same principle is used for shielding of electrostatic RFI from any of the higher quality isolation transformers on the market. Use of these units is simple. You purchase a unit, plug it into your power supply, and then plug your gear into the available outlets. Hopefully, it won't come to this, but these units are always available solutions should the need arise.

Endnotes
[1] Reprinted with permission of Lutron Electronics, Inc.

CHAPTER 7

HVAC Design Concepts

This is probably one of the most overlooked items when it comes to home studios. I am constantly bombarded by people coming to ask how they can fix their room. The work's all done, it's airtight, beautiful, sounds great, and they suddenly realize that they need fresh air—air conditioning, heat, the usual amenities.

I shake my head in wonder as I think about how many people miss this so very basic requirement. Re-work is always a lot more expensive than doing it right the first time. So save your money, keep your sanity, and plan for this now.

Again, remember, this chapter isn't going to teach you how to install these systems. It won't tell you how to sweat a copper joint or how to braze compression lines for coolants. It will give you the knowledge of the design concepts with enough depth to intelligently discuss your needs with professionals. Beyond this, you need professionals for the final design and installation on HVAC systems. There are too many different factors that come into play with HVAC systems to cover them all in this book. Heck, you could fill an entire book by itself just going over the basics in design, but if you did that, you wouldn't ever get to the part about building your studio.

Getting Started

First and foremost, understand that you have a superinsulated structure to deal with. All of this work that you're going to do to keep sound in (and out) also helps tremendously to reduce thermal transmissions through the structure. Thus, the design *cannot* be based on the same criteria as your home.

Next, if you have separate control and sound rooms, then you have two very different requirements for these. The control room (for example) will typically be smaller in volume than your sound room, but will generally have more gear producing heat that needs to be dealt with. The sound room (on the other hand) will usually have greater heat and moisture from the human body than the control room, and this too needs to be dealt with.

So it isn't as simple as it might appear. Let's begin with your control room.

Room Design Criteria

The beginning of this is an assessment (on your part) as to the equipment you have (and will have) within this space. Yep, you have to reasonably anticipate what's coming in the future. The reason for this is that all of this equipment gives off heat when it's working, and you need to deal with it. Once you have this figured out, make up a list and include, as a part of that list, what the total wattage is for each and every piece of gear.

If you are going to install an isolation transformer in a location that will transfer heat into the room, you should include this in your calculations. Again, provide the total wattage for the unit. The same would go for a computer, UPS, etc.

Lighting adds quite a bit of load to room cooling requirements, so a simple calculation based on the area of the room should be enough to cover this, unless you have some plans for very heavy lighting loads.

Next, you have to decide just how many people are going to be inside that room besides yourself. Once again, wattage is the data required for design. Yes, the heat that people give off can be calculated as wattage—you'll learn how it's done.

Finally, fresh air is taken into account.

All of this information is critical to proper HVAC design.

BTU OUTPUT
Let's take a look at how this info is utilized.

One Btu (British thermal unit) is the amount of heat required to increase the temperature of one pound (one pint) of water by one degree F. This is roughly equal to the heat produced by one standard wooden match.

Thus, to bring one pound of water from freezing (32°F) to the state of boiling (212°F) requires 180 Btu (i.e., 212°- 32° = 180° = 180 Btu).

To convert wattage into Btu output, you multiply watts by 3.4129. To convert Btu's to watts, simply multiply by 0.2930711.

The People Factor

Calculating what people contribute to a room gets a little more involved.

To accurately calculate the Btu output of a person, you first have to determine their BSA (Body Surface Area). To determine this, you could use one of several mathematical models available. I prefer the Mosteller[1] formula, but other popular methods exist. My reason for preferring this formula over the others only has to do with the ease of use this one presents. The calculations can be performed with a simple handheld calculator.

The Mosteller formula is:

$$BSA\ (m^2) = ([Height(cm)\ x\ Weight(kg)]/3600)^*\ .5$$

A person 5'-10" tall (177.8cm) weighing 180.78 pounds (82kg) would have a BSA of 2.02594m^2

$$BSA\ (m^2) = ([177.8cm \times 180.78kg\ ]/3600)^*\ .5 = 2.02594m^2$$

To convert meters^2 to feet^2, simply multiply it times 10.7639104. So your friend above has a BSA of 21.807 feet^2, and let's call him Mr. "A."

OK, now that you've dragged yourself through all of that—where do you go from here?

Well, if you look at Figure 7.1 you'll see a set of values for the metabolic rate of people doing various tasks. The values are indicated as "met units." One met unit equals the output of one square meter of skin.

Activity	Metabolic Rate (met units)
Reclining	0.8
Seated, quietly	1.0
Sedentary activity (office, dwelling, lab, school)	1.2
Standing, relaxed	1.2
Light activity, standing (shopping, lab, light industry)	1.6
Medium activity, standing (shop assistant, domestic work, machine work)	2.0
High activity (heavy machine work, garage work)	3.0

One met = 58.2 W/m2 = 18.4 Btu/h ft2

Figure 7.1 Metabolic rate chart.

This value (for 1 met unit) is 58.2 watts per meter squared or 18.46 Btu per hour per square foot (58.2 watts * 3.4129)/10.76 = 18.45Btu/h f^2) In an office setting, you would multiply this times 1.2 for a total of 69.84 watts (22.14Btu/h f^2).

So, using the example above, Mr. "A" will produce (in a typical office setting) 482.81Btu/h or 141.48watts/h (22.14Btu/h × 21.807 feet²). You're going to use the data from Mr. "A" to represent the "typical adult" throughout these exercises.

Room Calculations

Let's create a 16'x20' control room and fill it with the following equipment:

▶ 1- 24 Channel Mixing Board with 250w power supply

▶ 1- Stereo Vacuum Tube Power Amplifier—500w

▶ 2- Dual Channel Tube Mic-Preamps—35w ea.

▶ 4 - 4 Channel Stereo Compressor Limiters—35w ea.

▶ 1 – Stereo Tube Limiter & Mic-Preamp—75w

▶ 1- Stereo EQ—72w

▶ 6 – Effect Units—16w ea.

▶ 1- 6 Channel Headphone System—210w

▶ 1- 24 Channel Digital Recorder—50w

▶ 1- 2 Track 1/4"x7" Stereo Reel to Reel —30w

That's 1,493 watts of gear in a 320 sf room that will hold a maximum of five people during mix-down. You decided you want clean power, so you're using a 500 watt isolation transformer that will sit besides your desk.

If you're building a studio with any serious sound isolating capabilities, then you don't have to bother taking passive solar gain into consideration, nor is thermal loss of any real consequence. There is, however, one other item to deal with—fresh air, which we will examine in a little bit.

Table 7.1.a is a simple worksheet to calculate the heat-load within the room. If you put this all together and use the formulas in the table, you'll see that the total Btu's per hour of generated heat are 9,770.8.

Heatload Calculation Chart "a"

ITEM	REQUIRED INPUT	CALCULATION	HEAT OUTPUT
Gear	Full Power Load in Watts	Total Wattage Load	1493.0 WATTS
Lighting	Room Area in Square Feet	Floor Area x 2.0	640.0 WATTS
Power Distribution	Power System Rating in Watts	(0.02 x The Power System Rating) + (0.02 x Gear Above)	22.8 WATTS
People	Maximum Occupancy Load	160.94 x each person	804.7 WATTS
Total		Total From Above	3410.5 WATTS
Conversion		Multiply Wattage Total x 3.4129	11,639.7 Btu's / Hr.

Table 7.1.a

It takes 12,000 Btu's to create one ton of cooling, so your needs are .81 tons of cooling per hour for the control room.

Now let's add a tracking room to the equation. It's going to be 15'x21.5'.

Let's start again with a gear takeoff:

▶ Guitar Amp—300w

▶ Bass Amp—500w

▶ Keyboard Amp—250w

▶ PA System—500w (Although you won't use this for recording, if the room doubles as a practice room, you should add it to the equation.)

In a tracking room, everything stays pretty much the same (from a calculation point of view) with the exception of the latent load per person. Musicians can generate as much Btu output as anyone who's working fairly hard, so we will use a met rate of 3.0 for this space (353.56w per person). Also (in this case), you won't be using an isolation transformer for the space. Let's calculate using a four-piece band working in this room.

If you create another worksheet (Table 7.1.b), you'll see that the requirements in this room are different from the control room. Although the total load is only about 1/3 greater than the control room, the heat load due to people is fully double. The total load for this room is 1.03 tons.

Heatload Calculation Chart "b"

ITEM	REQUIRED INPUT	CALCULATION	HEAT OUTPUT
Gear	Full Power Load in Watts	Total Wattage Load	1550.0 WATTS
Lighting	Room Area in Square Feet	Floor Area x 2.0	645.0 WATTS
Power Distribution	Power System Rating in Watts	(0.02 x The Power System Rating) + (0.02 x Gear Above)	0.0 WATTS
People	Maximum Occupancy Load	321.89 x each person	1609.4 WATTS
Total		Total From Above	3804.4 WATTS
Conversion		Multiply Wattage Total x 3.4129	12,984.1 Btu's / Hr.

Table 7.1.b

Remember that you still have to deal with fresh air and what it adds to the equation.

Sensible Loads and Latent Loads

When you deal with cooling requirements, there are two very different loads you need to contend with. One of these you are familiar with, and the other you probably have never encountered.

Sensible loads are what you are used to seeing when you read a thermometer. You want it to be 70°F (21°C), and it's 85°F (29°C). So you need to cool down by 15°F (8°C) Simple right? Yes, it is—it's the actual, measurable, change in temperature.

Latent loads (on the other hand) are a bit more involved. When dealing with latent loads, what you are actually doing is determining the amount of moisture that needs to be dehumidified, with the understanding that this will not change the temperature in the least.

Latent heat is defined as "heat that when added or removed, causes a change in state, but no change in temperature."

Back to People

For the purpose of air-conditioning design, the total Btu output from people is broken down further into sensible and latent loads. However, this is not linear. It isn't a matter of 60/40% or any other fixed ratio. Just as the greater the activity, the greater the Btu output from your body—the greater percentage of that output is latent heat.

Take a minute and examine Table 7.1.c. It indicates how all of this goes together for a person. Note that on the right-hand side of the chart, the total output per person is broken down in Btu value as a percentage between sensible and latent output for the various activities we have been discussing.

Heatload Breakdown per Activity

ACTIVITY	MET RATE	Wattage Output (m²)	Conversion to S.F.	Wattage Output (f²)	Btu Output	Watts Out Mr "A"	Conversion to Btu Output	BTU Out Mr. "A"	Sensible Heat%	Latent Heat%	Sensible Btu/h	Latent Btu/h
reclining	0.8	46.56	10.7639104	4.33	14.76	94.28141	3.4129	322	60%	40%	192	130
seated quietly	1	58.2	10.7639104	5.41	18.45	117.8518	3.4129	402	66%	34%	267	135
sedentary activity	1.2	69.84	10.7639104	6.49	22.14	141.4221	3.4129	483	62%	38%	298	185
standing relaxed	1.2	69.84	10.7639104	6.49	22.14	141.4221	3.4129	483	62%	38%	298	185
light activity	1.6	93.12	10.7639104	8.65	29.53	188.5628	3.4129	644	52%	48%	334	310
meduim activity	2	139.68	10.7639104	12.98	44.29	282.8442	3.4129	965	31%	69%	295	670
high activity	3	174.6	10.7639104	16.22	55.36	353.5553	3.4129	1,207	30%	70%	357	850

Table 7.1.c

Fresh Air

A good rule of thumb for providing fresh air is 15cfm (cubic feet of air per minute) per person. So in keeping with our five people, 75cfm would be required for the control room and 60cfm for the sound room. This air is also going to have to be conditioned.

Accurately calculating the amount of humidity that fresh air adds to the "mix" here is no easy feat, but to help you understand the basics, I'll pass on some information from ASHRAE (The American Society of Heating, Refrigerating, and Air-Conditioning Engineers).

In 1997, ASHRAE developed what they referred to as the "Ventilation Load Index" (VLI), which is the total load generated (in one year) by fresh air, calculated at the rate of 1 cfm supplied to a building from the outside world. This index consists of two numbers, which separate the loads into dehumidification (latent) and cooling (sensible) loads for easy comparison. Thus it reads: latent ton-hours per cfm per year and sensible ton-hours per cfm per year.

Understanding the system is easy; for example, in Hartford, CT, the latent load is 3.0 ton hours cfm per year and the sensible load is 0.3 ton hours cfm per year. Based on your control room fresh air supply of 75cfm, that would translate to 225 tons (2,700,000 Btu's) of dehumidification required per year and 22.5 tons (270,000 Btu's) of cooling required per year.

Likewise, in Key West, Florida, it would be 21.6 + 3.5, indicating a need for 1,620 tons (19,440,000 Btu's) of dehumidification required per year and 262.5 tons (3,150,000 Btu's) of cooling required per year. One more example, and we'll move on. In Reno Nevada, it's 0.0 + 0.8, thus 0 tons (0.0 Btu's) of dehumidification required per year and only 60 tons (9,600 Btu's) of cooling required per year.

The reason you have to pay attention to this is due to the fact that what fresh air adds to the room (unlike gear, people, and lights) is not a constant. As you can see, it can be anywhere from no real concern (Reno) to a huge concern (Key West), or anywhere in between (Hartford).

If you want to check what the index is for your area, you can download the ASHRAE document at the Web site of the Energy Resources Center, University of Illinois at Chicago. Search for "Dehumidification and Cooling Loads From Ventilation Air."[2] Understand one thing—this is not a factor you plug into your design calculation. It is simply a tool you can use to determine the extent of concern you should have with the design side of your system. The designers of the system will have to base their calculations on peak design loads.

WHY SHOULD I CARE ABOUT HUMIDITY?

Once again—looking at those ever so average adult human beings—they produce about 2.8kg of vapor per day, which is roughly 98.77 oz. So our five people will produce about 14kg or almost 494 oz (3.86 US gallons) of vapor per day.

That's on top of whatever is brought in with the outside air, and all of this in a room that you want to maintain at a maximum of about 45% relative humidity.

In order to understand relative humidity, I want you to picture blowing up a balloon. You already know that you exhale vapor (among other things), so when you blow up that balloon, you will breathe a certain number of grains of vapor into it. The actual number is not important. After you blow the balloon up, look at it (in your mind's eye, of course—after all, you are just picturing this, aren't you?). It's nice and plump because you did a good job of blowing it up. Now tie and seal the end.

Take the balloon and place it in your freezer. Let it sit there for a few hours. When you finally go look at it, you'll find that it looks as if someone let some of the air out. They didn't, but it still looks like it. However, the moisture within the balloon remains constant. The actual grains of vapor within the balloon did not change, but the amount of vapor relative to the volume of the air did change. If the balloon (in the state it was in when you blew it up) was 1cf of volume with 400 grains of vapor, and in the cold state was 1/10cf of volume, it would still contain the same 400 grains of vapor.

So the amount of vapor relative to the volume increases, hence the term "relative humidity."

Picture now pulling 75cfm of fresh 95°F air with a relative humidity of 85% and placing it into your refrigerator of a room. The relative humidity is going to rise tremendously. You could literally end up with water running down your walls if it isn't properly dehumidified. When air is 50% saturated, it contains only one half the amount of water that it can contain at the same temperature and pressure. As the relative humidity approaches

100%, the air can take on less and less moisture, and at 100% relative humidity, that air cannot hold more water.

Relative humidity is determined by means of wet bulb and dry bulb thermometers. The dry bulb temperature is the temperature of air as determined by a standard thermometer. The wet bulb temperature is determined by tying a wet wick over the bulb dipped in a reservoir containing distilled water. Airflow around the wick causes the evaporation of moisture, thus lowering the temperature and producing a reading lower than that on the dry bulb thermometer.

By taking the differences between these two readings and referring to a psychrometric chart, you can determine the relative humidity in a space. A psychrometric chart is nothing more than a graphical representation of several interrelated air parameters brought together.

A sling psychrometer is a tool often used to do this. This is the most common type of hygrometer. Figure 7.2 is a sling psychrometer manufactured by Bacharach, Inc. It's designed to accurately determine the percent of relative humidity without the necessity of consulting complex tables. There is no need to wet the wick each time a reading is taken, and it contains a slide rule calculator, which correlates wet and dry bulb thermometer indications for direct reading of relative humidity. When not in use, the thermometer case telescopes into the handle for protection. You open it up and spin it around for a few minutes to get your readings; then adjust the slide rule to see the humidity level.

Figure 7.2
A typical sling psychrometer.

There are also easier ways to do this. Digital psychrometers and hygrometers are available with pricing running anywhere from around $100 to over $1,000. The $100 instruments are only usually accurate to ± 5%rh. The instruments with accuracy to ± 2%rh, cost around $300.

Being able to accurately measure the relative humidity in your space makes sense once you get things up and running. This way you will have the information you need to fine-tune your HVAC systems. Something else you have to be concerned with (when considering humidity levels) is the potential for mold growth.

Mold

Let's try to keep this short. Mold tends to become a problem when relative humidity is around or above 50% for any length in time.

There are more than 100,000 mold species in the world. Molds are microscopic organisms that produce enzymes to digest organic matter and spores in order to reproduce. These organisms are part of the fungi kingdom, a realm shared with mushrooms, yeast, and mildew. In nature, mold plays a key role in the decomposition of leaves, wood, and other plant debris. However, problems arise when mold starts digesting organic materials we don't want them to, such as our homes. Once mold spores settle in your home, they need moisture to begin growing and digesting whatever they are growing on. There are molds that can grow on wood, ceiling tiles, wallpaper, paints, carpet, sheet rock, and insulation. When excess moisture or water builds up in your home from say, a leaky roof, high humidity, or flooding, conditions are often ideal for mold growth. Long-standing moisture or high humidity conditions and mold growth go together. Realistically, there is no way to get rid of all mold and mold spores from your home; the way to control mold growth is to control moisture.

The goal is to keep the RH in your space between 40% and 45%. This is close to ideal for most instruments and will help to keep mold at bay.

UNDERSTANDING THE SYSTEM AS A WHOLE

How does this actually work?

This is where things get "sticky." When it comes to HVAC design (as mentioned earlier), you have sensible cooling loads and latent cooling loads. Sensible cooling relates directly to the ability of the unit to cool the air, while latent cooling relates to the ability of the unit to dehumidify the air. Gear and lighting loads do not add humidity to the air in a space, but people do, as can fresh outside air.

It's important for you to understand the sensible versus latent loads in your rooms and to purchase equipment that meets those needs, which is no small challenge. It might surprise you to know this, but the vast majority of mechanical contractors get this wrong—even on something as "simple" as a home. They tend to use calculation methods that are questionable at best, and then add "fudge factors" to cover themselves.

If their calculations come to 3 1/2 tons of cooling for your home, they'll tell you to get 4, explaining to you that this will make sure that on even the hottest days of summer you'll always have plenty of cooling. Although this is partly true, it's also very wrong. It's partly true because you will never have to worry about having enough cooling. It's very wrong because it isn't the right kind of cooling. What happens is that the unit is so oversized that it super-cools your home, utilizing very short run-times, which means that you don't get enough air moved across the coils to properly dehumidify your home. This also could cause additional wear and tear on your compressor motor and higher electrical bills for you.

Air conditioners are generally inefficient in the first stages of operation, while their efficiency increases the longer they run. If the on-time of an air conditioner is only five minutes, the efficiency (EER) is somewhere around 6.2. On the other hand, with a properly sized air conditioner, the same amount of cooling would take place in a little less than 10 minutes, and the efficiency would rise to 6.9. This additional run-time would save the customer about 10% of their energy costs.

The ability of an air conditioner to remove moisture (i.e., its latent capacity) is lowest at the beginning of an air conditioner cycle. In order to remove moisture from the air, the coil has to cool to the point of creating dew point, and then it has to have time to cycle the room through complete air changes. As the warm moist air passes over the coils, the moisture wets the coil and (when the unit runs long enough) flows off the coil into the drip pan. It is then removed, either through the use of gravity drains or with condensate pumps. When the compressor short cycles, the moisture on the coil does not complete condensing, and, when the unit stops, the moisture on the coil evaporates back into the indoor air.

Volume Versus Velocity

The volume of air you push into a room is measured as cubic feet per minute (cfm), whereas the velocity (the speed of air through the ducts) is measured as feet per minute (fpm). We'll use cfm and fpm for the remainder of this conversation.

One of the tricks to creating a quiet HVAC system is to maintain large amounts of volume with low speed. So, where a typical air handler system (by typical, I mean a normal home system or a system in an office) might have velocities in excess of 1,000 fpm (850 is preferable), in a studio system I like to see velocities below 300 fpm, and if at all possible, 100 fpm. This isn't that difficult to obtain and still maintain the same volume required for the room. You just increase both the duct size and the number of supply ducts to provide the volume required.

Picture that in a typical 4" round duct you can achieve 100 cfm with velocity of 1,167 fpm with static pressure of 3/4" in 100' of pipe. Now, if we lower the velocity to 300 fpm and keep everything else relative, a duct size of 13.5" diameter will handle the job. So that's one of the goals of the studio design: high volumes—low velocities.

System Options

There is a wide variety of systems available for cooling your recording studio. Now that you understand the basics of design and the amount of money you plan to devote to your system, you can look at the options you have to get the job done.

SPLIT/PACKAGED DIRECT-EXPANSION (DX) AIR CONDITIONERS

Figure 7.3 is a typical setup for a split AC system. With these units, an air-handler is installed inside the building, while the condenser/compressor for the unit sits outside. This helps to keep the sounds from the condensing unit's fan in the compressor from entering your space. It's important to locate the condenser so that it is free from shrubbery and other conditions, as that would reduce the free flow of air to the unit. This reduces the unit's efficiency.

Note the use of isolation hangers for the air-handler unit inside the building. This stops the transfer of vibration from the system into the structure above. Also, note that the duct work is connected to the system through a series of 90° bends in the duct work, which is also important in helping to reduce the transmission of air-handler noise (fan motor, etc.) into the room.

Fresh air is introduced into the system by a ducted connection (to outside air) immediately adjacent to the unit on the return side of the fan. A barometric release (which is also ducted to outside air) is connected into the system to maintain a small amount of positive pressure in the room, while allowing any pressure buildup beyond that to release. This is an important part of the system. Otherwise, the room will achieve the static pressure capacity of the fan and will no longer be able to bring fresh air into the space.

A supply duct running adjacent to the wall/ceiling assembly helps to maintain isolation from above while maximizing ceiling heights in the room.

As far as the duct material you choose to use, it can be lined galvanized duct, or a polymer lined fiberglass duct-board, but understand that the lining is an important part of achieving sound attenuation for the system as a whole. Don't forget, if the duct is galvanized, a canvas connector is required between the duct and air handler unit to stop the transmission of mechanical vibrations from the fan assembly through the body of the duct work. Fiberglass duct board will not transmit those sounds.

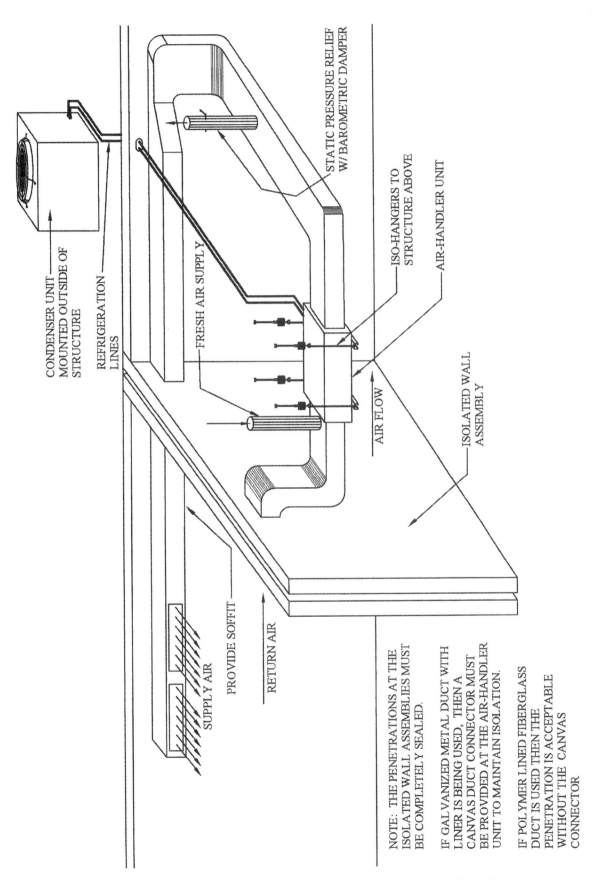

Figure 7.3   Isometric view of a split air-conditioning system.

THROUGH-THE-WALL SYSTEMS

In the tracking room, you can always use a window or through-the-wall unit—if you take care to construct a manner of closing it off when you record. A through-the-wall unit is an air conditioner that installs in a sleeve that goes through a framed opening in the wall. These are similar in nature to the units you see installed in windows, but a through-the-wall unit is a year-round installation, whereas the window unit is typically temporary.

If you picture it, the amount of time it takes you to record is only a few minutes, after which you can always open things back up and turn the unit back on.

This doesn't really lend itself well to a control room situation, however, due to the fact that you will sometimes spend hours on end while mixing down, with only seconds between stopping and starting between songs, or working the mix on the same songs.

Figure 7.4 is one manner of dealing with the penetration and still maintaining isolation.

DUCTLESS MINI-SPLIT SYSTEMS

Mini-split systems offer fairly high efficiency and reduced noise without a large hole in the wall or an open window. By separating the compressor and condenser coil from the fan and evaporator coil, the noisiest component is away from the room. The indoor unit will usually have remote control capabilities and a timer to cycle the system only when needed. The indoor unit is still called an air handler because it has the evaporator coil, blower, and controls inside. The outdoor unit is still called the condenser. They are connected together with refrigerant piping and control wiring, similar to a standard split system. Some of these units employ very quiet fans for the air-handler unit and would be quite compatible with the needs of either control or tracking rooms.

Some manufacturers use low voltage to control the system, while still others use line voltage. Caution must be taken when opening up the cabinet to shut power off when servicing. The most important service item is dirt. Screens or filters can usually be found behind the front grille of the air handler. Tabs allow them to slide out for cleaning. As with the condenser unit on split systems, keep vegetation and debris away from the outdoor unit to allow good air flow for maximum cooling efficiency. An occasional blast from a garden hose with the system shut down will help keep the condenser clean.

Relatively new to the American market, ductless split systems have been in use in Japan and other markets for a long time. Until recently, none were of U.S. manufacture, but increased demand has changed that.

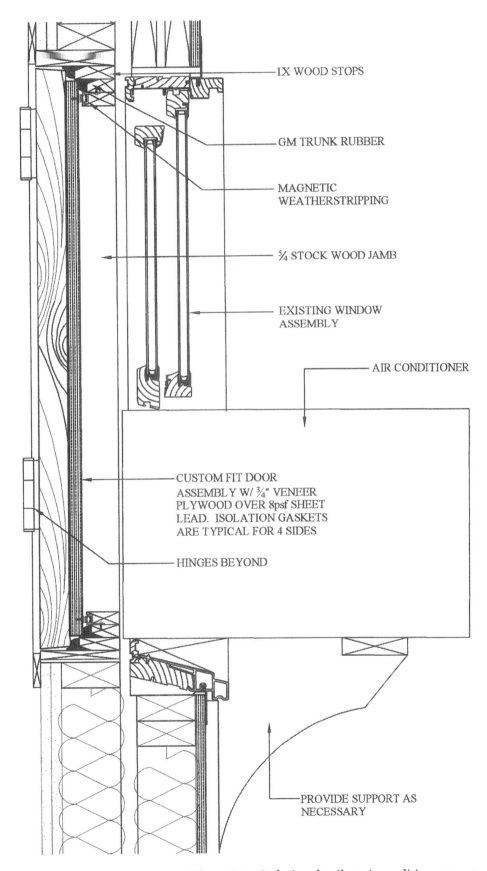

1X WOOD STOPS

GM TRUNK RUBBER

MAGNETIC
WEATHERSTRIPPING

⁵⁄₄ STOCK WOOD JAMB

EXISTING WINDOW
ASSEMBLY

AIR CONDITIONER

CUSTOM FIT DOOR
ASSEMBLY W/ ¾" VENEER
PLYWOOD OVER 8psf SHEET
LEAD. ISOLATION GASKETS
ARE TYPICAL FOR 4 SIDES

HINGES BEYOND

PROVIDE SUPPORT AS
NECESSARY

Figure 7.4   Isolation detail at air conditioner penetration.

PORTABLE AIR CONDITIONERS

Portable air conditioners are one of the newest types of air conditioners. Although they still have an exhaust tube that must be vented out somewhere, they are truly portable in the sense that they require no permanent installation.

Portable air conditioners virtually always have caster wheels for portability. They consist of one "box" that holds both the hot and cold side of the air conditioner in one, and they use their exhaust hose to expel heat. There are several ways to get rid of the water that the air conditioner condenses out of the air. Most units collect this water in an internal drain bucket, but some units exhaust the water through their drain hose. Some units have pumps that pump the condensate water out through a tube in their drain hose. Most models that collect condensate water in an internal bucket can also be adapted for direct drain-off.

Since portable air conditioners have both the hot and cold sides of the air-conditioning cycle contained in one box, they have to cool their condenser coil with air they intake from the room they are cooling, and then this air is expelled through their exhaust hose. For this reason, portable air conditioners usually create a negative air pressure in the room in which they are run. Air is continually seeping into this room from the rest of the house or building to replace the air that the portable air conditioner expels. Some portable air conditioners have solved this problem with a two-hose connection to the outside—one hose to intake air to use to cool the compressor, and one hose to expel this air. In fact, most industrial portable air conditioners use this type of setup. This setup will be required for your space unless you provide another (separate) method for the fresh air supply.

Some of these systems run quietly enough that operating them in your rooms won't cause you problems. I've heard a lot of home studio owners sing their praises. Your best bet is always to check them out for yourself to decide whether they'll work for you.

Advantages: No ductwork to install—very small penetration to the outside of the room.

Disadvantages: 13,000 Btu systems are the largest (at this time) that provide two-hose connections.

EVAPORATIVE COOLERS

It would be wrong not to cover the evaporative cooler in this book, even though only a very small part of the population can use these systems.

Nature's most efficient means of cooling is through the evaporation of water. Evaporative cooling works on the principle of heat absorption by moisture evaporation. The evaporative cooler draws exterior air into special pads soaked with water, where the air is cooled by evaporation and then circulated. Evaporative cooling is especially well suited to places where the air is hot and humidity is low—and, in effect, acts as not only a means of cooling the air, but also as a means of providing humidity.

Remember that in climates like Reno, Nevada (one of the examples cited previously), the fresh air will add 0% humidity to the room, and your levels will fall well below the 40% to 45% range that you want to maintain in your studio. These units help you achieve that goal. They are available in either portable or ducted arrangements.

One of the nice features of these systems is the fact that there is no compressor, so operating costs are much lower than with standard air-conditioning systems. A disadvantage of these systems is that they require negative pressure in the space to work efficiently. An additional exhaust fan will generally be required to provide that condition. This can be inter-locked with the unit for operating purposes.

EXCHANGE CHAMBERS
An exchange chamber is a small room adjacent to your studio, which uses a through-the-wall (or window type) air conditioner to pre-condition the air prior to it being exchanged with the air in your space. The air exchange is then handled through the use of exhaust ducts with inline fans to force the air movement you require.

This is a fairly inexpensive method of providing fresh/conditioned air to your space while maintaining isolation. It is (however) contingent on your having a wall above grade to install the unit, as well as being able to devote enough space needed to create the chamber itself. Figure 7.5 is one example of how to construct an exchange chamber.

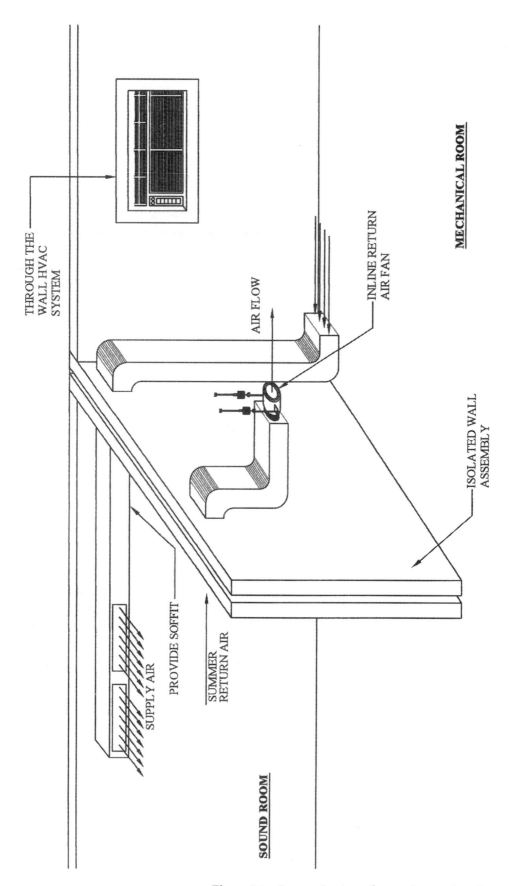

THROUGH THE
WALL HVAC
SYSTEM

AIR FLOW

INLINE RETURN
AIR FAN

MECHANICAL ROOM

ISOLATED WALL
ASSEMBLY

SUPPLY AIR

PROVIDE SOFFIT

SUMMER
RETURN AIR

SOUND ROOM

Figure 7.5   Isometric view of an exchange chamber.

Combination Cooling/Heating Systems

Until now, we've only been looking at the cooling side of the equation. If you're located in a climate where heating during winter months is a requirement, then it may well make sense for you to consider combination systems that can handle both your cooling and heating needs.

SPLIT SYSTEMS

Split system is a term that covers a couple of different type of air-conditioning setups. What it is basically telling you is that there is an interior air handling unit (basically a fan with a cooling coil) and a separate outside unit. Let's take a look at some of the options you have with these units.

Split Systems with DX Coils

The air handler unit for a typical split system can be ordered with either an electric or hydrostatic heating coil (in addition to the cooling coil) as a part of the unit. So the only additional parts required for this system would be a connection of additional power for an electric coil, or the connection to your boiler for a hot water loop. The existing ductwork is used for circulation purposes.

One thing you should add to your system, if using this for heat, is a low return for the heating season. This is coupled with damper controls to change the air flow between seasons. The reason for this is simple —heat rises. A high return in the cooling season makes perfect sense—peel away the hotter layer near the ceiling, and the cool air drops to the floor.

In the heating season, though, pulling hot air from the ceiling defeats one of the principles of room heat—and that is creating a thermal layer of warmer air until (finally) at 5' above the floor, you reach the temperature the thermostat is set to. In addition, as the air cools, it settles to the floor, and it is this cool air that returns to the coil to be reheated and recirculated through the room. This circulation helps to pull warmer air down towards the floor, making it that much more comfortable in the room. Figure 7.6 is the original system with the return duct modified for winter return.

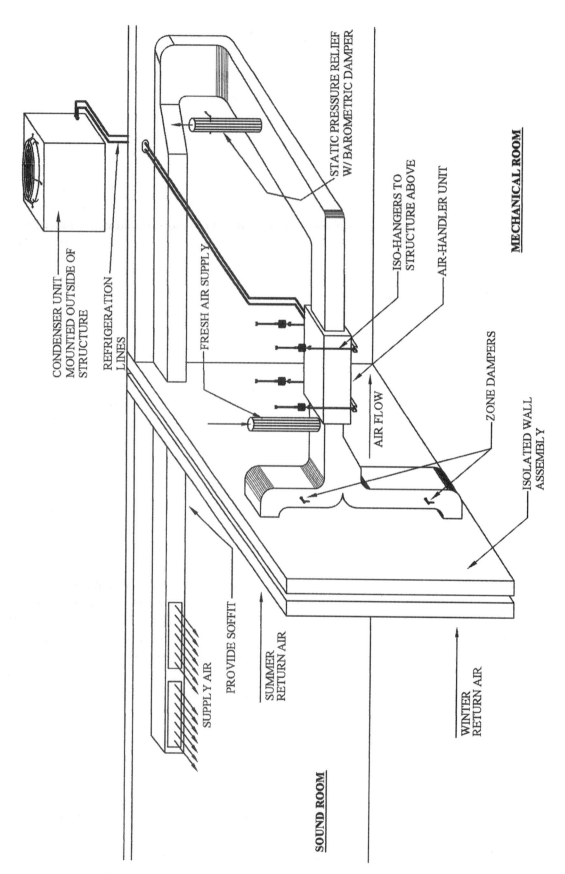

Figure 7.6   Isometric view of a split air-conditioning/heating system.

During the heating season, simply close the damper for the upper register and open the bottom damper. Reverse the process during the cooling season.

Split Systems with Heat Pumps

For climates with moderate heating and cooling needs, heat pumps offer an energy-efficient alternative to furnaces and air conditioners. Like your refrigerator, heat pumps use electricity to move heat from a cool space into a warm one, making the cool space cooler and the warm space warmer. During the heating season, heat pumps move heat from the cool outdoors into your warm house; during the cooling season, heat pumps move heat from your cool house into the warm outdoors. Because they move heat rather than generate heat, heat pumps can provide up to four times the amount of energy they consume.

The most common type of heat pump is the air-source heat pump, which transfers heat between your house and the outside air. If you heat with electricity, a heat pump can trim the amount of electricity you use for heating by as much as 30%–40%. High-efficiency heat pumps also dehumidify better than standard central air conditioners, resulting in less energy usage and more cooling comfort in summer months. However, the efficiency of most air-source heat pumps as a heat source drops dramatically at lower temperatures, generally making them unsuitable for cold climates, although there are systems that can overcome that problem.

For homes without ducts, air-source heat pumps are also available in a ductless version called a mini-split heat pump. In addition, a special type of air-source heat pump, called a reverse cycle chiller, generates hot and cold water rather than air, allowing it to be used with radiant floor heating systems in heating mode.

Higher efficiencies are achieved with geothermal (ground-source or water-source) heat pumps, which transfer heat between your house and the ground or a nearby water source. Although they cost more to install, geothermal heat pumps have low operating costs because they take advantage of relatively constant ground or water temperatures. However, the installation depends on the size of your lot, the subsoil, and the landscape. Ground-source or water-source heat pumps can be used in more extreme climatic conditions than air-source heat pumps, and customer satisfaction with the systems is very high.

THROUGH-THE-WALL SYSTEMS

Through-the-wall HVAC units come in a variety of systems. But they all have one thing in common, they are a complete, self-contained system, and one side of the system is exposed within the room, while the other end is exposed to outside air. A standard air conditioner, the window unit style, is an example of the easiest way to accomplish the installation of one of these units. You can also purchase sleeves that are designed to fit in framed openings in an outside wall for a permanent installation of the equipment.

There are a number of reasons these types of units are preferable to split systems. The first big one is cost. A through-the-wall system can be purchased for roughly 20% of the cost of a similar sized split system. The next is that they are designed to provide fresh air as a part of their operation, thus handling the need for fresh air within the space. Because of the fact that the fresh air is pulled directly through the cooling coil, dehumidification is handled without the need for additional ducting.

However, one downside is the big hole you just cut through the exterior of your building and the noise that it will let in and out. Another problem with these units is that the compressor is encompassed within the unit, and, even with quiet units, you can hear these when they turn on.

There are steps you can take to use these unless your actual recording times are long. You can install a soundproof enclosure with an interior "door" to close over the opening when you record. You can also tie the power supply into a simple kill switch at your recording desk.

Having looked at the ups and downs to the systems, take a look at the types of systems available to you.

Packaged Terminal Air Conditioner (PTAC)

A PTAC unit is a separate encased combination of heating and cooling that is normally mounted through the wall. It has refrigeration components and forced ventilation, and it utilizes reverse cycle refrigeration as its prime heating source. It normally has another heating supplement, generally an electric element heater for backup in the coldest winter days. This type of unit is usually larger than a typical through-the-wall air conditioner and is often seen in motel rooms and apartment buildings.

Electric Heat Air Conditioners

These units are available in either through-the-wall or window installations. They are the same as standard air conditioner units, with the addition of an electrical heating element for winter months.

EXCHANGE CHAMBERS

Any through-the-wall or window unit can be utilized within these chambers. As with any other ducted system, you want to draw the return air from floor level in the winter and near the ceiling in the summer. One thing is different, though, which is that in the winter you will want to draw supply air from the ceiling of the exchange chamber. Refer to Figure 7.7 for details.

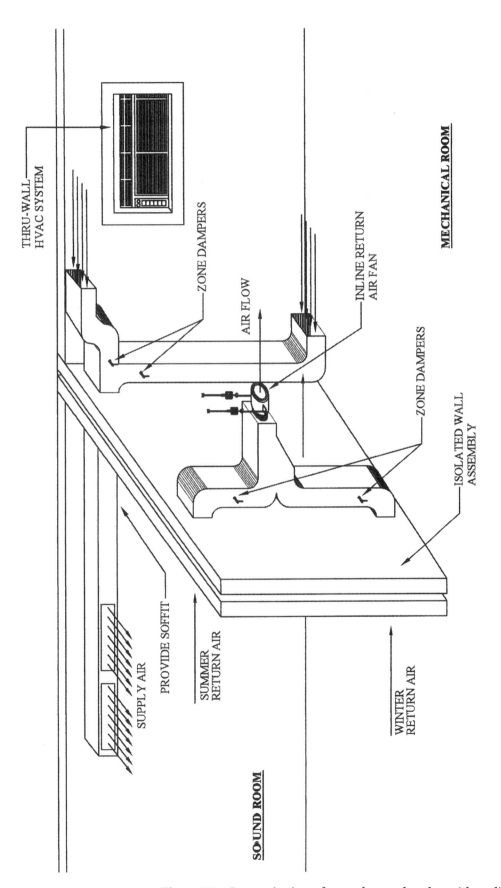

THRU-WALL
HVAC SYSTEM

ZONE DAMPERS

AIR FLOW

INLINE RETURN
AIR FAN

MECHANICAL ROOM

ZONE DAMPERS

ISOLATED WALL
ASSEMBLY

SUPPLY AIR

PROVIDE SOFFIT

SUMMER
RETURN AIR

WINTER
RETURN AIR

SOUND ROOM

Figure 7.7   Isometric view of an exchange chamber with cooling/heating.

The reason for adding the ability to pull air from the ceiling of the chamber rather than the floor (in winter) is due to simple convection. Heat rises, so the warmest air in the space will be at ceiling level, and this is the air you want to feed into your working room.

Separate Systems

You also have the option of using totally separate systems for your heating and cooling needs. This can be very beneficial if your existing systems can handle the additional loads.

For example, if you have central air conditioning now, and it can handle your needs (which may well be the case, if it is as overdesigned as a lot of home systems are), then adding some duct and a few motorized dampers to handle flow may well be just what the doctor ordered. It is a lot cheaper than a new system by far. You should realize that most home systems do not have the fresh air that you will need for your room, and that you will probably require some additional dehumidification. However, this way is still cheaper in the long run.

The same goes for heat. If your boiler can handle the additional load, it's pretty easy to add some more heating to the space. If you do this, I would recommend that you consider the installation of an under-floor heating system. These systems utilize low temperature water—using PEX (cross-linked Polyethylene) tubing. They produce heat that is uniform through the room, is much less of a drain on your existing system, and is more energy efficient than standard convection systems (i.e., baseboard heat).

Another benefit to these systems is that they are quiet. Typical hot water baseboard and electric element heaters go through an expansion process when warming up and can cause quite a bit of noise in your room. Although you could work through this in the case of a control room, it's possible that mics could pick up the noise in a tracking room and destroy an otherwise perfect take.

With standard convection heating systems, the heating is accomplished by building up thermal layers beginning at the ceiling of the room and working down from there. Eventually, the temperature set at thermostat height (typically 5' above finish floor) is reached. It isn't unusual to have temperatures 10° to 20° warmer at ceiling height than they are at the thermostat. Also, temperatures at floor level are much cooler than they are 5' in the air.

But with radiant floor heat, the starting temperature at the floor is the controlling factor, with the air cooling off as it rises, and the output from the floor continuing until the thermostat is satisfied.

Not having to develop the thermal layer at the ceiling (before satisfying the needs of the room) means that lower water temperatures can be used, and not having to heat an area of the room that no one comes in contact with (by this I am thinking about the couple of feet directly below the ceiling) means that heating costs are lower. Radiant-floor heating systems typically use water temperatures of 85–140°F (30–60°C), compared with baseboard hydronic systems that operate at 130–160°F (54 to 71°C) or sometimes 160° to 180° (71 to 82°C) with older boilers.

Radiant floor systems require special hardware and valve assemblies to work, and they cost more than standard baseboard to install. But if you can afford the initial investment, then the added comfort and slight savings in operating costs would be well worth it.

Oh, one other benefit with these systems—they don't eat up any wall space, so your walls are completely open for placement of furniture, casework, gear, or whatever your *heat* desires.

Endnotes

[1] Mosteller RD: Simplified Calculation of Body Surface Area. *N Engl J Med* 1987 Oct 22;317(17):1098 (letter)

[2] November 1997 ASHRAE Journal 37, Lewis G. Harriman III, Dean Plager, Douglas Kosar

CHAPTER 8

Room Testing

OK, you've built your room—gone in and pounded around a bit on some drums—or played some music (very loudly) and are happy with the isolation—but not happy with the way it sounds inside the room. This chapter is going to teach you how to understand what is happening within your room, so that you can make the decisions you need to "treat" the room intelligently.

This is also the chapter you are going to begin with if you live in an apartment or condo and can't do a whole lot of isolation construction, but have neighbors who will accommodate you with your music, or who have schedules that you can work around. Even if you can't do isolation construction, you can treat your room to make it sound better inside.

In fact, a lack of sound isolation will probably help you in this regard, because the more sound that escapes the room, the fewer problems you will have relating to modal issues.

Toward that end, this chapter is going to focus on one piece of software that exists specifically for this purpose: determining room modes, peaks and nulls, reverb time, etc. Understand that there are a lot of different programs out there that will work; however, covering all of them would be impossible. Plus, some of them are made with professional acousticians in mind and carry a price that reflects that fact.

Before we begin, let me stress to you that regardless of what software you use, you cannot take a single reading and trust that data. There is a reason that institutes require (not recommend) a minimum number of test readings to provide the data that will be analyzed. It's the only method of measurement that will provide you with enough statistics to verify that the data is good. Anomalies in readings can take place without your knowing anything about it, and they will "screw up" your data. However, if you take 10 readings, the statistical probability that the same anomaly happened in each reading—at exactly the same point in time—at exactly the same amplitude—is so improbable as to be non-existent. For example, if you all of a sudden have one or two readings that differ from the remaining eight or nine, then you can feel pretty confident that they have bad data in them. So, make it a point not to settle for one or two test readings.

The software you are going to examine here is ETF by Acousti Soft, Inc[1]. It is a very reasonably priced package. I purchased it with all the bells and whistles, including their recommended hardware, and it only set me back the cost of a decent (not great) guitar. Another great thing about this package is that the manufacturer is only a phone call away, answers his own phone, and is right there to help you if you have any issues or questions.

Let's begin with an understanding of what exactly it is you will need to measure and treat to make your room correct, and how you can go about determining this with the software.

The Basics

As you examined in Chapter 3 when learning about room modes (and other acoustical room effects), there are a number of fairly significant issues you need to deal with that are created by the room you constructed.

Probably the greatest challenge you are facing is dealing effectively with modal issues. Remember that these problems relate to frequencies below 200 Hz, and tend to create waves of peaks and nulls within your room.

Being able to measure what exactly is occurring with the frequencies in this range will go a long way towards telling you what treatments you are going to need and (as you apply them to your room) just how effective they are in helping you achieve your goal.

One other thing you have to picture clearly in your mind is this: With the exception of narrow band bass traps, whenever you apply a treatment to your room, it will tend to affect a fairly wide band of frequencies, not just one frequency. So, if you have a peak at 600 Hz and a null at 830 Hz, a broadband treatment will help to alleviate both problems at the same time. For this reason, the focus here (for the most part) will be towards utilizing broadband treatments.

THE USE OF EQ AND IN ROOM TREATMENTS

You need to spend a little bit of time on the concept of EQ as a method of treating sound within your room. EQ is the term for an equalizer designed to cut and boost individual frequencies of an audio signal using a series of filters. You see them on your stereo systems, and some of your PA systems incorporate them as a part of their design.

There is an ever growing movement to use EQ as a method of treating room modal issues. Some newer speaker assemblies (being manufactured by leading companies in the field of studio monitors) incorporate narrow-band (parametric) EQ as a part of the product. Literature explaining how to use these products to "fix" low frequency room modes is included in the owner's manuals. Some of these products come with specialized software for room testing to help you achieve this goal.

This is a very attractive proposition to someone who has just finished his room. After spending the kind of money required to properly isolate your home studio, not to mention the time involved, it seems like a great idea to forgo spending more money on room treatments, and the additional time involved in getting that done, when you can just buy new monitors, or a multiband pEQ, and get right to making music.

After all, you need good quality monitors anyway, so why not just kill two stones with one bird?

Let's begin by looking at your tracking room. In this room, you will be placing microphones in a wide variety of locations, with the goal being to capture accurately the sound being produced there. This means that inside the control room, you will have to use EQ to deal with two totally different sets of problems when mixing. The first problem is a correction of what you recorded; the second problem is how your tracking room is coloring that sound. Plus, you have the issue of nulls in the tracking room, and you can't possibly add into the mix something that wasn't recorded. This is due to the fact that a microphone was not picking up particular notes being played by your bass guitarist because of a null in that location.

Achieving this goal is an impossible dream, thus the tracking room needs to be treated, regardless of what you do in the control room. So you're going to treat the tracking room to tame it down and make the sound in the room an accurate representation of what's coming out of the musician's instruments. For the same reasons as above, a combination control/tracking room will have the same requirements.

OK, let's look at a stand-alone control room.

In the control room, you want to hear an accurate representation of what you captured on your recording media. This is your starting point for determining what you need to do in the mix. It's from here that you will determine what needs reverb and how much to add, where compression is needed, etc. You want this representation to be reasonably flat and for the room to have just slightly less reverb than the average living room.

The "flatness" that you want to achieve is the reason that you spend good money on studio monitors instead of using stereo speakers to mix with.

Suppose for a moment that you could take these new speakers and deal with peaks and dips, go through your whole setup with them, and adjust the frequencies you need to deal with, to get an accurate representation of your recordings. What happens to the nulls? Yes, the nulls—remember looking at those in Chapter 2?

This question has been asked (by myself and others) with the following answer: "You boost the nulls."

Great answer, but unfortunately it doesn't work. Although you might be able to do this to a dip, a null (by it's very nature) is 0dB, and you can boost 0dB 100%, and it will still be 0dB. Even dips in amplitude can't be boosted by greater than 6db without creating additional issues related to ringing.

So if you've gone all the way through the entire process of EQ'ing your speakers to correct anomalies in your room, then you have to add treatment to deal with nulls and dips.

But the minute you start treating those nulls (through the use of physical room treatments), you begin affecting peaks right along with them. Suddenly, the EQ settings that you so carefully adjusted, all the work that you spent testing and tweaking—over and over again—painstakingly working to make your room "right"—is gone. Yes, sir, just like magic—it disappeared, and here you've been told that magic doesn't exist.

The same is true with flutter echo, reflections destroying stereo imaging, and comb filtering—none of these issues can be dealt with through the use of EQ in a room. So what do you do?

Begin by dealing with your room first: testing, determining what your problem areas are, and treating those areas. Get your room as good as it can be. And then—only then—if need be, use EQ. Not to treat the room, but rather to treat the speakers and to tweak them. Let that be the finishing point (rather than the starting point) to clean things up.

There is one more thing you need to know about the use of EQ if you're trying to use this method to treat a room, and that is that it is truly location specific.

By this I mean that instead of attempting to smooth out the response throughout a room (as industry standard room treatment methods tend to do), this method is much more location specific. Thus, if you boost a signal so that its amplitude is correct in one room area, then its amplitude in other areas will be excessive. The same is true (in reverse) if you decrease amplitude on a peak.

In all fairness to those involved in this, I would point out that with a very sophisticated pEQ (parametric EQ) that has the capability of providing a filter making use of an inverse signal, you can smooth out a room resonance by about 6dB; however, this still does not make the null disappear. Ultimately, it's your decision to make. There is obviously conflicting information and advice regarding this issue, with some speaker manufacturers (major ones at that) heading in a particular direction, and a lot of industry professionals supporting the concept.

However, due to the issue with nulls—which has never been answered to my satisfaction—I view this as not yet solving the modal issues within a room. Therefore, until the point where someone—somewhere—finds a method of treating the last part of this equation, my recommendation is going to be to treat the room.

FREQUENCY RESPONSE

What is the frequency range you need to deal with? It's the frequency within the human hearing range, namely 20 Hz to 20 kHz. So with that in mind, what actually is your goal when treating your room? A flat frequency response from 20 Hz to 20 kHz, right?

Well, let's begin by clarifying what exactly a flat response is.

If you were to use a tone generator to produce a series of 80dB tones (let's say outside, so modal problems weren't an issue)—rising from 20 Hz to 20 kHz—you would probably be surprised to find that the tones did not sound the same in amplitude. In fact, the higher the range of the tone (to a point), the more bright and loud you would perceive it to be. That's because the human ear is not flat by nature. What this means is that you don't hear every frequency at the same volume.

The human brain is engineered to hear most clearly at the frequency range of speech. Thus, there is a fairly narrow band of frequencies that is clearer to us than others. The generally accepted range for this is from around 500 Hz to 5k Hz. Above and below this range—although we can hear—we do not perceive the amplitude to be the same as within the speech range.

The tone generator would be producing sound on a linear scale, but the ear hears sound based on a logarithmic scale. Due to this, people don't listen to music (for example) with what would actually be a flat response. They boost (or cut) frequencies until they suit the individual's taste. This is entirely subjective. If you were to set up a sound system for what your mind said was flat, and then took measurements of the actual amplitudes for each of the various frequencies from 20 Hz to 20 kHz, you would be amazed at just how un-flat it really was.

Over the years, different types of test signals have come into popularity, such as pink noise excitation, time delay spectroscopy, and periodic impulse excitation (among others). Each in turn has made improvements in measurement quality and ease of use. Pink noise was designed to emulate the human perception of sound, and thus is logarithmic in nature. White noise (on the other hand) is linear in nature.

ETF employs one of the current "state-of-the-art" measurement techniques, called MLS. MLS is an abbreviation for Maximum Length Sequence. MLS measurements are fairly standard in many different applications today, one of which is room acoustics. It is basically a pseudo-random sequence of white noise pulses. It utilizes the measurement of white noise transmissions and transforms this data into equivalent logarithmic sound levels, equating to human hearing.

One big advantage of MLS techniques over other means is that it is possible to perform quasi-anechoic measurements of loudspeakers without having to place them inside an anechoic chamber. The impulse responses of these speakers can be easily windowed in the time domain, in order to analyze the direct signal and reject reflections from the walls of the room. What is more important (for our purposes) is that the room impulse response itself (and related parameters such as reverberation time) can be measured as well.

The MLS method can also be used to analyze and obtain information about the impedance or the absorption coefficient of a surface. As you add treatment to the room, you can directly measure its effect on the room.

Let's look at the results you can get from this testing method and how they may (or may not) be useful to suit your purposes.

A SIMPLE IMPULSE RESPONSE
Impulse response is the response of a space to an impulse. An impulse is a very short duration sound. Some examples are a gunshot, a clap, or the click of a switch.

Walk into your room and clap your hands. The resulting action is the sharp sound of the clap itself (the impulse) and then a series of reflections, slight echoes, coming at you from (possibly) all sides. This is the "response" side of the equation.

Impulse response is simply defined as the sounds in the room after the initial impulse. Understand that this not only is determined by the room, but also by whatever produces the sound, the location of the sound source within the room, and the location of the listener.

To clarify "whatever produces the sound," in a perfect world, the sound in your room would be totally uncolored, i.e., a perfect reproduction of what you recorded. However, reality is that two different speakers, from different manufacturers (or even speakers from the same manufacturer) in exactly the same location in the room, can produce a different sound from the same exact signal. By this, I mean both in tonal nature as well as intensity. No speaker, amplifier, pre-amp, etc. is perfectly flat; they all color the sound to some extent. Different speakers will produce varying levels in amplitude from exactly the same source. So the response to each will be somewhat different.

Likewise, exactly where the receiver (for example, the listener or the microphone) is located within the room will change not only the perceived intensity of the initial impulse, but also the length and intensity of the response.

All of this ties back into what you examined in Chapter 2 when you looked at room modes and other issues with boundary interference. An example of impulse response can be seen in Figure 8.1 below.

Figure 8.1
Impulse response chart.

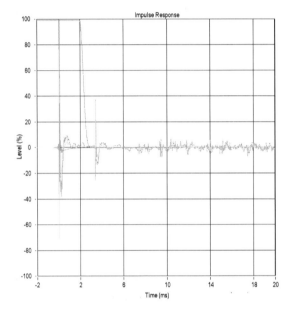

The vertical axis of this chart shows the amplitude of the sound waves. On the horizontal axis is time, measured in milliseconds (1/1000 of a second). The initial "spike" on the graph, at 0ms, is caused by the sound of the impulse itself reaching a recording microphone. The oscillations and spikes that follow are echoes, as the sound reverberates through the room and, to a lesser extent, within the speaker itself.

Although it's possible to present the data accumulated in this manner, it really isn't very useful information for you. Knowing only the reflection time for an event doesn't help you determine what treatments your room requires, but the same information that produced that chart is data that can be used to produce any number of charts with this software.

For example, that same information can be used to provide a frequency response curve.

FREQUENCY RESPONSE CURVE

A frequency response curve is generated by applying a mathematical operation known as the Fourier Transform to an impulse response.

A Fourier series is an expansion of a periodic function $f(x)$ in terms of an infinite sum of sines and cosines. A Fourier series makes use of the orthogonality relationships of the sine and cosine functions. The computation and study of Fourier series is known as harmonic analysis and is extremely useful as a way to break up an arbitrary periodic function into a set of simple terms that can be plugged in, solved individually, and then recombined to obtain the solution to the original problem or an approximation of it to whatever accuracy is desired or practical.

The Fourier series, which is specific to periodic (or finite-domain) functions f(x) (with period 2π), represents these functions as a series of sinusoids:

$$f(\mathbf{x}) = \sum_{n=-\infty}^{\infty} F_n \, e^{inx},$$

where Fn is the (complex) amplitude.

Now, having read the paragraphs above, you're thinking that a promise has been broken—that being the promise to not bury you in math. Nope, not true. I'm giving you just the very basics here, but am happy to say that the program can do all this for you. For example, it can deliver the information you need without you having to worry about any of the math.

Figure 8.2 is an example of a frequency response curve for a sub-woofer placed in eight different locations within a room. (without changing the listening position). What you are looking for here is the placement that develops the flattest response. In this case, position 5 was the flattest of the group's response locations and would be the best location in the room for that sub-woofer.

In order to produce a chart like this, you have to be able to overlay the results from one test to another. This is a capability that you have with this software.

Figure 8.2
Frequency response curve.

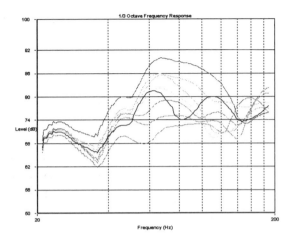

Notice that there are two obvious differences between this and the impulse response graph. First, the horizontal axis now represents frequency, not time. This representation tells us nothing of when the sounds arrived. Instead, it adds up the amount of sound energy of each frequency that arrived at the microphone over a given period of time, known as the gate time. Usually, this gate time is set long enough to include the first big spike you see in the impulse response (the sound coming directly from the speaker), but short enough that all the subsequent spikes (the echoes from around the room) are ignored. For this reason, the frequency response, as shown in Figure 8.2, is primarily the response of the speaker, with room effects ignored. This is valuable in that it allows comparisons of different speakers, independent of the rooms they happen to be measured in.

The other thing you will notice is that frequency response doesn't oscillate back and forth from positive to negative the way that the impulse response does. It is in the nature of waves to oscillate. As a more direct measurement of the sound waves, this oscillation is seen in the impulse response. As already mentioned, however, the frequency response sums the amount of energy of each frequency that arrives at the microphone over a given time interval, rather than displaying the state of the sound wave at a given time. For this reason, no oscillation is observed.

This is one of the more useful tools you can have when first setting up your room—getting the speakers into a position where they exhibit their flattest response is a great first step in room setup.

The procedure you use for this is shown in Figure 8.3

Frequency Response Measurement

Figure 8.3
Frequency response measurements.

Step 1: The impulse response of a speaker / room is measured

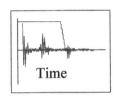

Step 2: A gating or windowing function is applied to the data to remove reflections.

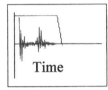

Step 3: The portions outside the gating curve are erased (set to zero).

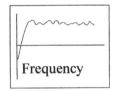

The Fourier Transform (FFT) is applied to calculate the frequency response

LINEAR FREQUENCY RESPONSE

Figure 8.4 is a graph of a linear frequency response. Look how jagged it is. That's not unusual because it indicates the normal comb filtering that occurs in all listening rooms. Note that the overall response is gently sloping down, decaying as the frequencies become higher. There's a little more energy at the lower octaves relative to higher octaves.

Figure 8.4
Linear frequency response.

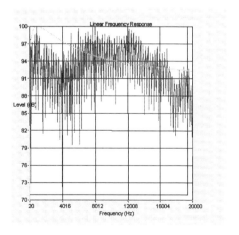

As you treat your room to correct for comb filtering, you will see this graph smooth out.

LOW FREQUENCY RESPONSE

This is an extremely useful piece of information for you.

When you review a Low Frequency Response Chart, what you are doing is examining an initial impulse and then a series of resonances following that signal. It is useful to use long gate times with only one slice to pinpoint resonant frequencies, but it is also useful to use time slice calculations to visually identify the location of resonance. This software can provide time slice calculations for up to eight slices, with a time domain from 10ms to 160ms between slices (selective as either 10, 20, 40, 80, 160ms). The first slice at t=0 shows the loudspeaker and room response. Later slices tend to show only the resonant decay of the room.

Long gate times are chosen to include the part of the impulse response that includes the room response, so that low frequency room resonance can be included in the frequency response calculation. Long gate times provide greater frequency resolution and finer detail in the frequency response calculations.

Let's take a minute here to look at and understand gate times—how to use them effectively and how to understand what they do for you.

The gating curves are applied to the impulse response to calculate frequency response slices. With a setting of 40ms with a gate time of 100ms, you provide the following information:

slice 1 t=0: -25–100ms

slice 2 t=40: 40–140ms

slice 3 t=80: 80–180ms

slice 4 t=120: 120–220ms

slice 5 t=160: 160–260ms

slice 6 t=200: 200–300ms

slice 7 t=240: 240–340ms

slice 8 t=280: 280–380ms

Each curve will begin 40ms beyond the start time of the previous and will show you the resultant data curve for 100 ms of that time hack.

The later slices, such as the 280–380ms slice, will contain mainly background noise in small rooms. There is some truncation with the gate curves. An example of a 0–10ms gate curve can be viewed from the impulse response to see this truncation. The impulse response shows a

0–10ms gate by default when a new measurement is created. The effect of truncation can be viewed in the impulse response measurement.

This method of looking at room resonance is popular, but it is just as useful to have one slice with a very long gate time. A single slice with a long gate time will show the modes that most clearly influence room response. The rate of decay of the resonance is indicated by its sharpness on the frequency response curve. The sharper the resonance, the longer it will take for it to decay to an inaudible level.

A method of determining the effect of noise on the results is to take two or three measurements and compare them. Differences in measurements are due to background noise when all else is equal.

One other point—as you begin to lengthen the gate time, you'll find it necessary to adjust the graphic coordinates in order to see the low end of the decay.

Let's begin with an example of a single line wave, showing you the difference between a short and long gate time (which results in the definition of the signal with sharper resolution). Figure 8.5a, with a gate time of 40ms, would suggest a fairly smooth, rounded signal, with the exception of a sharp dip at 173.61 Hz, which dropped to 74.72dB. Note that between 20 and 48.4 Hz, the amplitude of the signal is below 80dB.

Figure 8.5a
Low frequency response—low gate time.

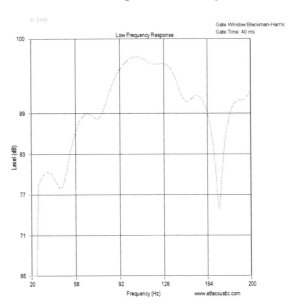

However, take that same data, push it out the gate time, and you'll see a completely different picture. Figure 8.4b is charted from the same data, but at a 400ms gate.

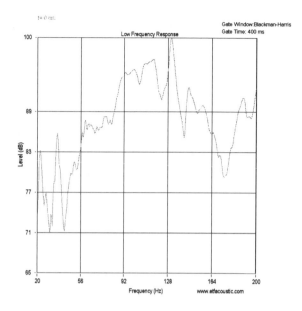

Figure 8.5b
Low frequency response—400ms gate time.

Suddenly, there are conditions that you never would have guessed existed with the original setting. 22.7 Hz just peaks its head above 83dB, with 36.33 Hz at 86dB. There are dips at 30.28 Hz and 42.39 Hz that didn't show up before. At 130.54 Hz, there's a peak that hits 100dB, nowhere to be seen in the original.

Add another piece to this picture— one more slice. Use a 40ms splice spacing setting for this. Figure 8.4c shows almost no change at 22.7 Hz, 30.28 Hz, or 36.33 Hz. The dip at 42.39 Hz, though, has dropped another 4 1/2dB. There is a fairly consistent decay from there through 126.5 Hz of roughly 2dB, and then at 130.54, you again are back to less than 1dB. What's also interesting is that instead of decay at the 173.61 Hz measurement, it rose over 2dB to 81.49 Hz. A room mode has been excited and is building up at the microphone position.

Figure 8.5c
Low frequency response—40ms slice time.

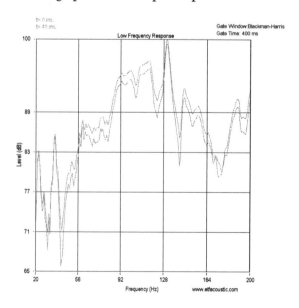

Add two more slices, Figure 8.5d, and you're looking at four slices total now. When you do this, you'll find that the bottom drops below the starting point of 65dB, so you'll have to lower the bottom coordinates to allow for this.

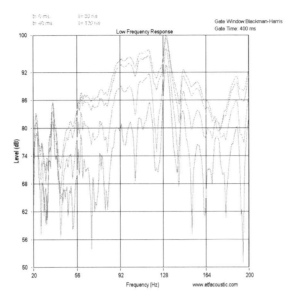

Figure 8.5d
Low frequency response—view of four time slices.

The large drops are where you're viewing normal decay of the source. We're reading (at the fourth slice) from 120 to 520ms. Note that again, you see a fairly well balanced drop-off from 48.44 through 126.5 Hz, roughly from 15 to 25dB in decay. However, the peaks you've been watching haven't decayed along with those frequencies. At 22.7 Hz, decay of the source is only 3.8dB. Likewise for the following: 30.28 Hz—3 1/2dB, 36.33 Hz—4.3dB, 130.54 Hz—6.4dB, and again at 173.61 Hz—1.3dB of decay.

This is a perfect example of room modal activity at work. You should continue to view this through all eight slice levels (not here though). Jump right to the last step—you'll probably be surprised at the results.

Figure 8.5e is the eight-slice plot of this data. The areas that were apparently modal in nature won't surprise you at all, but in some areas that appeared to be decaying at a fairly normal rate, things changed.

For example, at 68 Hz, you'll see a fairly consistent decay through the first four slices—with readings of 85.79dB (initial reading), 83.82dB (second slice), 76.34dB (third slice), and 53.99dB (fourth slice) for a 32dB (rounded) decay. The last four readings are 63.68dB (fifth slice), 64.75dB (sixth slice), 64.03dB (seventh slice), and 62.81dB for the final slice, meaning that in the 160ms between those readings the amplitude of that frequency rose 10dB.

Figure 8.5e
Low frequency response—view of
eight time slices.

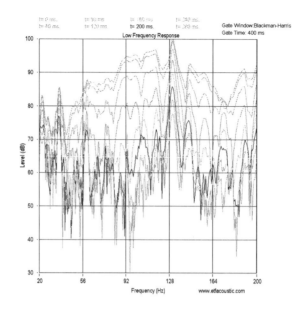

Once again, as you see these anomalies taking place, it's great being able to click on the area in question and get an accurate readout of actual decay at any particular frequency. By now you should be able to see why this is such a valuable tool in this arsenal. It's much more effective than just using a waterfall plot, although not quite as attractive. Using this tool to test the effectiveness of your low frequency treatments is a must.

Data presented in this manner can be used not only to evaluate low frequency room response, but also loudspeaker response. This graph is slightly less intuitive, but much more versatile and powerful than most 3D waterfall-type displays.

One of the features that is highly useful in this chart (and others) is the capability to provide accurate information for both amplitude and frequency of peaks and dips with a simple point and click on the chart with the mouse cursor. You just place the mouse cursor over the point you want information on and click. Then the information is portrayed on your screen (upper right-hand side of the chart) for both frequency and amplitude. If you have multiple slices on the screen, then the amplitude of each slice is displayed as well.

REVERBERATION TIME

Reverberation time (RT) is the amount of time it takes for an initial sound to decay by a certain number of decibels. This is typically referred to as RT/60, which represents the amount of decay time (in milliseconds) for a total reduction of 60dB. This represents 1/1,000,000 of the initial sound pressure level. You can also work with variants of this with the software, specifically RT/20 and RT/30. Understand that although the RT20 and 30 examine (initially) a smaller segment of the data (i.e., a 20 or 30dB reduction rather than the full 60dB), in the end the calculation extrapolates this data to the full RT/60.

The reverb time desired for a room differs based on room size. You'll see plenty of places on the Internet where people quote "RT60 for a control room should be .25 seconds" (or .33–.27, etc.), but reality is that there isn't any one number that's the right one. As with everything else in acoustics, there is a calculation for this, a rather simple one at that.

The ITU[2] recommendation is "tm = 0.25 *(Vm3/100)^1/3", which would translate (in imperial measurements) to "tm = 0.25 *(V cf / 3531.34)^1/3(raised 1/3 power)". The "V cf " notation refers to the proposed room volume in cubic feet. This recommendation is based on room sizes of floor area (for monophonic or two-channel stereophonic reproduction) of 20-60m². or (for multichannel stereophonic reproduction) of 30-70m².

So for a standard stereo control room that would be from 215'² to 645'². Right in the ballpark of home recording studios.

Understand that this is a recommendation, but when it finally comes down to treating your room, getting it to work for you is all that matters. For a lot of people the outcome of this calculation makes the room a bit too "dry" for them.

By the way, this isn't the same as when you examine RT/60 for large rooms (which is really where the decay time formulas are applicable). Sabine's formula states that reverberation time rises in direct proportion to a room's cubic volume and in inverse proportion to the amount of sound-absorbing material. To understand this, you have to spend a few minutes looking at factors that contribute to this.

The limiting distance (D_L) is a parameter associated with truly reverberant spaces (such as gyms, churches with little absorption, concert halls, i.e., truly large spaces). In spaces like these, there is a reverberant sound field (L_R), which is fairly uniform throughout the space, and there are reflections that are not.

When the space is excited (acoustically) through the use of a loudspeaker (as an example), there will be a localized sound field (L) from that device for those in close proximity to it. In other words, you can clearly identify the source directionally. If you have a steady sound source (such as a sine wave), as the listener moves farther away from the source, the direct sound level will drop, but the reverberant level will remain steady. The distance at which the two sounds are equal is referred to as the "critical distance" (D_C).

At roughly three times the critical distance, the sound from the original source is almost completely masked by the reverberant field, to the point that it is just about impossible to identify the origin of the source.

In a room the size of most home studios (or listening rooms), you don't ever get all that far from the source of the sound, not the way you would (say) at a large stage for a performing big name band (a show you and your friends are sharing with 40,000 other people), at a large church, or even at your local school auditorium. Nor do you get very far away from what that source influences—all of those modes and nodes and reflections that you've read about earlier. Most home recording studios are not large enough to have reverberant fields (by strict definition), yet your measurements would suggest otherwise.

So what is it that you're seeing when you look at this information? It's the decay of the room's modal activities.

In a room that's fair sized (by home studio standards), let's say with 9' high ceilings, 14'–6" wide by 21'–0" in length. (That's a ratio of 1: 1.62: 2.33, which is very close to the good room mode of 1: 1.60: 2.33 reported by L. W. Sepmeyer:[3].) If you're sitting roughly 38% back from the front of the room, you'll be sitting 8' from the front wall, only 13' from the back wall, 7'3" from the side walls, and your head would be about 5 1/2' from the ceiling (3 1/2' from the floor).

Not a whole lot of distance from those surfaces when you think about it, and in that (relatively) small space, acoustically there's a lot going on. For example, sounds in this room will travel only an average of 8' before reflecting from a surface. So if the time for a 60dB decay was .33 seconds, then there would be at least 46 reflections during that period, and without treatments the decay time would be a lot more than .33 seconds.

The 8' average distance (mentioned above) is based on something called "Geometrical Ray Acoustics" (GRA), which states that the mean free path is equal to 4 V/S—where V= the room volume and S= the room surface area. It is from this theory that Sabine's equation for determining the reverb time of a room grew.

The calculation for the (46 reflections) is the speed of sound, multiplied times the decay rate, divided by the average distance before reflection (1130 * .33 / 8).

Let's look a little more deeply at what's involved with RT/60 itself.

RT/60

RT/60 is the time required, within an enclosed space (partially or fully), for the initial sound pressure level to decay a total of 60dB (= 1,000,000 of the initial RMS sound pressure).

In accordance with ASTM[4] C 423, Standard Test Method for Sound Absorption and Sound Absorption Coefficients by the Reverberation Room Method, you test for decay rate as follows.

The level of the background noise in each measurement band, which includes both the ambient acoustical noise in the reverberation room and the electrical noise in the measuring instruments, shall be at least 15dB below the lowest level used to calculate decay rate

Turn on the test signal until the sound pressure level in each measurement band is steady. Turn off the test signal and start measuring sound pressure level in each measurement band either immediately or after a delay in range of 100 to 300. (Data collected before the first 100 to 300ms have elapsed may be viewed or retained for informational purposes, but these data are not used in the calculation of decay curves.)

The reason that the delay time period in the range of 100 to 300ms is not used for calculations is because this ensures that the data collected includes no distortions or transients caused by turning off the test signal. Viewing the decays on an oscilloscope, computer screen, or paper chart can help avoid a number of problems, such as those related to transients, but you do not use this information to calculate the decay itself.

You then measure and store the sound pressure level in each measurement band until the level is about 32dB below the steady state level. After storing the measured levels, repeat this procedure 10 times for a stationary microphone. (This assures the reliability of the readings.)

The sound pressure level produced when the source is on and the sound in the reverberation room is in the steady state will be at least 45dB above the background noise in each measurement band. The value of 45dB is the minimum value required by this method. In fact, the steady state may need more than 45dB above the background noise to satisfy the requirements of other sections of this standard.

Once you have gathered this data, it's an easy task to chart this in the ETF software to see the initial state of the room you've constructed.

If you want, you can also perform calculations prior to beginning construction of your room to help you get a rough idea of what you'll need for treatments in order to help you establish your budget.

The formula for calculating RT/60 for a space is really not all that deep mathematically. Take a look at Figure 8.6 and then walk through the explanation of the formula.

Figure 8.6
RT/60 calculation.

$$RT60 = \frac{0.049V}{Sa}$$

Where:
   RT60 = the reverb time in seconds
   V = the room volume
   Sa = the total absorption in sabin units

This calculation is really rather easy. RT60 equals 0.049 * the volume of the room (V) in cubic feet * times the total Sabin units (Sa) in the room. One note of interest, this formula works for metric measurements as well, if you simply substitute 0.161 for the 0.049 value. Understand one thing: this formula is perfect for rooms that have reverberant fields, which small home studios do not. However, it's a tool that will give you a fair idea of what's going to happen in your room. So, although it isn't perfect, it will help you get at least a rough idea of what you're up against.

Everything that exists absorbs some frequency to some extent. Since you're building a room (or multiple rooms), it gets a little easier because you only have to deal with construction materials. You do not have to worry about the absorption coefficients of rocks, trees, frogs, UFO's, or bad karma.

There are many lists of absorption coefficients for materials used in the construction industry and plenty of books you can buy. If you are in doubt about a particular material's properties, you can always contact the manufacturer of that particular material. Their engineering department can provide you with the information you need.

Another great source for data is a Web site by a gent named Bob Golds. Bob has researched hundreds, if not thousands, of materials, providing a very comprehensive listing of materials broken out by manufacturer, product name, density, and absorption coefficient. It's one of the sites on my favorites list.

The Web site is http://bobgolds.com. When you visit there, go to the link called "Fiberglass and Rockwool Absorption Coefficients." Bob also has some other interesting things to look at while you visit, so feel free to enjoy.

Yet another source for a spreadsheet with a lot of construction materials, and their absorption values, is located at http://forum.studiotips.com. Once on the site, go to III Treatments, open the thread entitled: "Sabin numbers for various materials," and (finally) download the file entitled: "Copy of Sabin Data_sorted.xls." This data was put together by Scott R. Foster, a site administrator at the studiotips Web site.

Figure 8.7 is a list of some common materials with their associated absorption coefficients.

Coefficients Of General Building Materials And Furnishings						
MATERIALS	ABSORPTION COEFFICIENT					
	125 Hz	250 Hz	500 Hz	1000 Hz	2000 Hz	4000 Hz
Brick	0.03	0.03	0.03	0.04	0.05	0.07
Carpet (heavy) on concrete	0.02	0.06	0.14	0.37	0.6	0.65
Carpet with heavy pad	0.08	0.24	0.57	0.69	0.71	0.73
Carpet with Impermeable backing	0.08	0.27	0.39	0.34	0.48	0.63
Concrete block (course)	0.36	0.44	0.31	0.29	0.39	0.25
Concrete block (painted)	0.1	0.05	0.06	0.07	0.09	0.08
Concrete (Poured Smooth)	0.01	0.01	0.02	0.02	0.02	0.03
Light fabric	0.03	0.04	0.11	0.17	0.24	0.35
Medium fabric	0.07	0.31	0.49	0.75	0.7	0.6
Heavy fabric	0.14	0.35	0.55	0.72	0.7	0.65
Concrete, terrazzo, marble or glazed tile	0.01	0.01	0.015	0.02	0.02	0.02
Wood	0.15	0.11	0.1	0.07	0.06	0.07
Heavy glass	0.18	0.06	0.04	0.03	0.02	0.02
Ordinary glass	0.35	0.25	0.18	0.12	0.07	0.04
Gypsum board 1/2"	0.29	0.1	0.05	0.04	0.07	0.09
Plaster	0.013	0.015	0.02	0.03	0.04	0.05
Water surface	0.008	0.008	0.013	0.015	0.02	0.025
Air, sabins/1000 cubic feet					2.3	7.2
People	4 sabins					
dB Reduction Guideline Using Absorption						
To get a 3 dB reduction: add enough absorption to equal the existing absorbtion in the untreated room.						
To get a 6 dB reduction: add enough absorption to equal three times the existing absorption in the untreated room.						
To get a 9 dB reduction: add enough absorption to equal seven times the existing absorption in the untreated room.						

Figure 8.7   Construction material coefficients.

And finally, Figure 8.8 shows you one way to put this together into a format that will be useful to you.

Looking at this chart, it's easy to see that you identify the room areas by their locations, for example, walls, floors, ceilings, and then insert the square foot area for each component. Place the material absorption coefficient value (a) in the proper column for each frequency. The coefficient is then multiplied by the area to achieve the value of "Sa". So the concrete floor, which has a (a) value of 0.01 (at 250 Hz) and an area of 304.5sf, has a total Sabin value (Sa) of 3.045. Once you add up all of the values for each frequency (total Sabin units), you multiply the total room volume (in this case 2740.5 cf) times 0.049 and then divide that sum by the total Sabins for the final RT60 for that particular frequency.

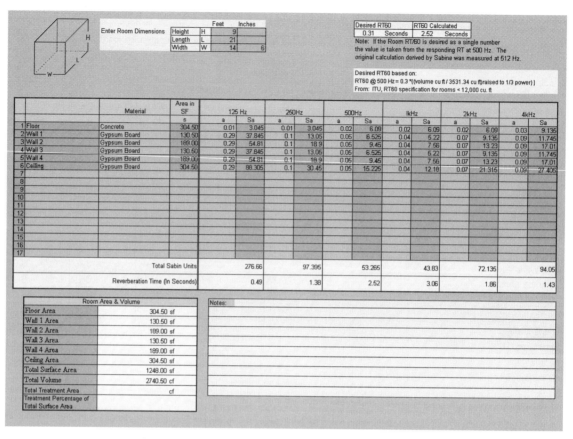

Figure 8.8   RT/60 calculator for sample room.

This is pretty easy if it's all set up in a spreadsheet. By the way, looking at the chart you'll see that the reverb times for the 500 Hz to 1 kHz frequencies are really long—over three seconds at 1 kHz. You'd really need to smooth things out for this room to sound right when mixing (or recording for that matter).

You'll look at this chart again in a couple of chapters to see how you can use it to anticipate your room treatments in advance. You also have this chart available on the companion Web site. It's in Microsoft Excel format, once again, keeping you free from the math.

Let's take a look at the options you have for viewing data relating to Reverb Time with ETF.

Energy Time Curves

Figure 8.9
Schroeder integration plot.

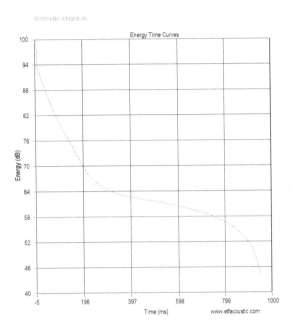

Figure 8.9
Schroeder integration plot.

In the above Figure 8.9, you can see an energy time curve, based on the Schroeder Integration Curve[5]. Note that you have to adjust the coordinates properly to enable you to capture the full 60 decibels of decay. Not surprisingly, after the initial almost vertical drop-off, you see a less steep decay from 310ms through 850ms before the final drop to the end. The overall RT/60, in this case taking 947ms, is much too long for a small room.

However, this plot, although helpful, still does not give you any data that is relevant to frequency issues in your room. ETF uses the Schroeder integration over 1/3 octave bands to determine RT/60 (this is why it is so slow).

It also does not deal with issues relating to low frequencies; the above plot is a full range Schroeder integration for frequency bands between 500 Hz and 5 kHz. So this curve is more useful as a reference for choosing time intervals of calculation for reverberation time.

Early decay can be determined by choosing an early time interval, for example, 2ms–60ms (the time for a 10dB decay in Schroeder plot). This can be found by using RT/20, RT/30, or RT/60.

Note that in the above graph, a linear portion exists between nearly 0 and 200ms. A safe time interval would be 50ms to 200ms to calculate reverberation time in this space.

Reverberation Time

The next step after examining energy time curves would be examining the actual reverberation time.

ETF calculates RT/60/30/20 using Schroeder integrations over 1/3 octave bands with 1/3 octave spacing. The energy time curves provide a Schroeder plot from which to decide time intervals for the calculation. The rate of sound decay in a room is determined by applying a "linear least squares fit" to the Schroeder integration, over each (fractional) octave band, over the specified time interval. Confusing isn't it? Well, it's not really that bad—a "linear least squares fit" is just a mathematical method of finding the best-fitting curve to a given set of points by minimizing the sum of the squares of the offsets ("the residuals") of the points from the curve. There, now doesn't that make more sense?

Let's try it this way: ETF applies a mathematical procedure to the data it gathers for each frequency band, which determines the best fitting curve to display the decay rate of that frequency within the room.

Don't worry about the math involved. ETF does it all by itself. You just have to input the time interval for the decay and let the software produce the results. I'm still trying to avoid burying you in the math.

Reverberation start and finish times of 50–150ms are typically chosen for small room acoustics. Early decay time can be determined by selecting the appropriate time interval, as chosen from a Schroeder integration in the energy/time curves measurement. Look at Figure 8.10 for a sample of this chart.

Figure 8.10
Reverberation time.

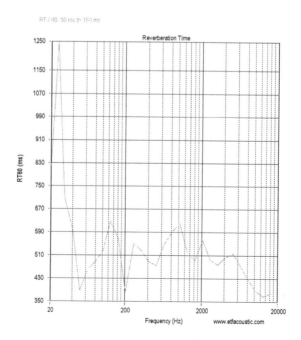

One of the things that jumps out at you right off the bat here is the extraordinary decay time for low frequencies (those below 200 Hz).

It is important to realize that most of the low frequency energy in rooms is not reverberant energy. The RT/60 curve has limited accuracy below a few hundred Hz. That lower energy (as you have already examined in the explanation of RT/60 above) will, for the most part, be controlled by excited room modes. Again, in rooms this size, you never really develop a true reverberant field.

A nice feature of this function is the capability to view a fairly wide range of mid and higher frequencies. Ignoring those below 200 Hz (for the reasons stated above, although the software will allow you to see this, should you choose, as witnessed in Figure 8.8), you can select the following frequency ranges:

▶ 200Hz to 2kHz

▶ 200Hz to 20kHz

▶ 1Khz to 10kHz.

Figure 8.11 is an example of the data with a 50ms to 150ms time slice and 200 Hz to 20 kHz display.

Figure 8.11
Reverberation time plot.

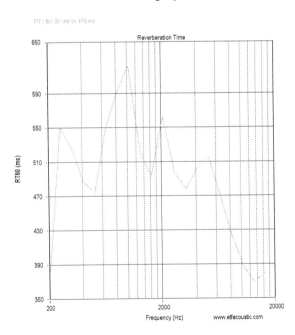

This plot indicates that you still would have a ways to go to achieve the average RT/60 of .31 seconds for our test room above, but also remember that we are dealing with raw data here for an untreated room, and the treatments to create an RFZ (Reflection Free Zone) for the listener will smooth this out considerably.

The switches for sound quality measurements seen in the "Gating" options for this chart are large room parameters and are not used in typical applications of this software. A brief description of these follow:

▶ **Definition**: Definition is the ratio of the sound energy over a specified time period in ms to the total sound energy.

▶ **Clarity**: Clarity is definition expressed as: 10*Log (Definition/1-Definition).

WATERFALL PLOTS

There are quite a few people out there missing the boat on this use of your data. Waterfall plots are not only nice looking, but can also be quite helpful once you understand what you're looking at. ETF gives you a couple of different options for waterfall plots, both low and high frequency.

Low Frequency Waterfall Plot

Figure 8.12 is a pretty good 3D snapshot of what's going on, and although you cannot use the cursor to identify a particular frequency or amplitude, you can get a pretty good idea of where your problem areas will be by using this chart.

Figure 8.12
Low frequency waterfall plot.

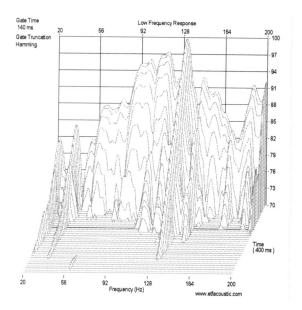

Look at the sharp ridges and how they extend out into the time domain. Those indicate excited room modes. The same goes for the valleys between them. From peaks to null, you can see it all here. What you're looking for (when you're finished with room treatments) is a nice boring picture. Fairly even crests gently falling down and ending in a reasonably straight line across. Yup, boring, that's the ticket.

High Frequency Waterfall Plot

With a high frequency waterfall plot, setting the gate time and coordinates properly, to present the data in a useful manner, is again important. Figure 8.13 is an example of this plot.

Figure 8.13
High frequency waterfall plot.

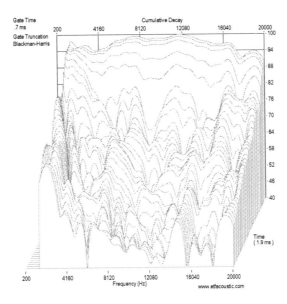

Once again, you can clearly see the effects of room modes (and other boundary effects) by viewing the areas of decay that climb in amplitude. Room modes are visible and identified by the sharper peaks and valleys.

PSYCHO-ACOUSTICAL RESPONSE CURVE

This is a highly debated, some might even say controversial, subject, but it can really be a useful tool. There are certain acousticians who will say that the steady state response is all that you need, and for trained acousticians, people who work in this field on a daily basis, this may well be the case. However, for those who don't, for the people who don't understand how actual sound translates to the human ear, this can be a huge help.

The basic premise of a psycho-acoustical response curve is that it mimics (in a 2D graph) what the ear perceives, relative to frequency response. If there is a resonant mode, it will be displayed as a peak at that frequency. The human ear has longer integration times at lower frequencies than at higher frequencies. So the gate time for the psycho-acoustical response curve is longer for lower frequencies than higher frequencies. Figure 8.14 is a psycho-acoustical response curve of the low frequency waterfall plot seen previously.

Figure 8.14
Psycho-acoustical response curve.

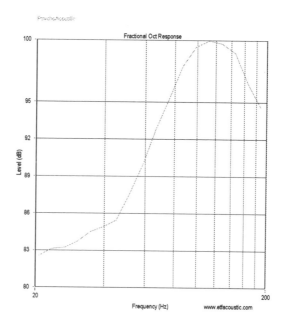

The most useful purpose of this tool is for the final setup of your room, tweaking your monitors (EQ adjustment) after completion of your room treatments. Take a series of final readings and then use the psycho-acoustical curve to shape your EQ to arrive at what the ear will view as a flat response.

Well, that's the last ETF feature we will look at in this chapter. Actually, it's more of a tool than you've witnessed at this point, but you'll look at the rest when you're actually testing after treatments. You don't need that information right now.

Once again, I cannot stress enough that when taking readings, you should take multiple readings. Look them over and select one from a group of matching measurements to work with. This will protect you from having some anomaly (be it a transient spike, outside noise, a cricket in the room chirping, etc.) from affecting the readings and winding up with erroneous data that screws you up in the end.

Endnotes

[1] At the time of this writing, Acousti Soft, Inc. was in the process of modifying their product named RPlusD with the intent that it will replace the EFT software. The R+D package will provide the same features as EFT, plus add some bells and whistles EFT doesn't have.

[2] Rec, ITU-R BS. 1116-1

[3] Computed Frequency and Angular Distribution of the Normal Modes of Vibration in Rectangular Rooms. Journal of Acoustic Society of America Volume 37 No. 3, pages 413-423 (1965)

[4] American Society for Testing and Materials

[5] M. Schroeder, "New method of measuring reverberation time", Journal of Acoustical Society of America, 37, 409-412 (1965)

CHAPTER 9

Room Treatments

In this chapter, you'll examine "do it yourself" (DIY) room treatments, as well as learn about some of the options for manufactured units. (These suggestions are from companies that I have dealt with and know the people who make things work.)

If you're working your way through this book while you're constructing your studio, then it's probably been a while since you read Chapter 2. It might not be a bad idea to browse briefly through that chapter as a refresher before reading this one.

First, to make a room sound the best it can possibly sound for the purposes of recording, mixing, and critical listening, acoustical treatments are a necessity. The three key needs are low frequency control, control of early reflections, and control of sound decay. Thanks to the explosive growth of the personal studio industry over the last few decades, many different types of effective acoustical treatments in many different decorative styles are now commercially available. From DIY to design-build, not only the sound of a room, but also the look and feel— the "vibe"—can be customized.

Low Frequency Control

"Bass traps," or (more technically correct) "low frequency control devices," are one of the most important considerations for small room acoustics. Without good low frequency control, mixes might sound "muddy" (too much bass) or "thin" (not enough bass—often described as "suck-out"). Recordings could have weird resonance "bumps" or cancellation effects (sometimes described as "hollowness").

Effective low frequency control can smooth things out. After treating with effective bass traps, the bass that is heard is the true bass from the recording or mix. In mixing, the guesswork is minimized, and mixes translate to other systems much better.

Most good, commercial bass traps are designed to address a wide range of the low frequency spectrum. The only limitations tend to be space and money. The latter is less of an issue since there are a lot of DIY approaches that can cost next to nothing. Space, however, can be a limiting factor. Low frequencies have long wavelengths and higher energy in a room (relative to higher frequencies). This usually means that the best low frequency control devices are going to be large. Since these devices are typically being considered for small rooms, we have a classic "Catch-22" situation. The best low frequency control could take up more space in a room than all of the gear (and people) combined!

But don't lose hope. Clever designers, manufacturers, and acousticians have been working for years on methods to control low frequency sounds that don't take up acres of precious studio space. Commercial devices available typically take on one of three forms: pressure devices, velocity devices, and hybrid devices that employ a combination of pressure and velocity control. Let's take a look at these.

Pressure Devices

Pressure devices tend to be placed directly in the room corners or directly on the walls and ceiling of a room. The corners of a room are always the areas of high pressure. For certain axial modes, the areas of high-pressure buildup extend to include the entire surface, including the corner. Placing devices designed to control the pressure buildup directly in or near corners is a very common approach to low frequency control. Placing devices designed to control velocity buildup can also be used near the corners and surfaces of a room, but should not necessarily be placed directly in the corner or on the wall.

Pressure control devices are the more active types of devices—resonating devices, such as solid panel absorbers, or Helmholtz devices, such as perforated panel absorbers and "slat" absorbers. These devices typically control a fixed range of low frequency sound dictated by design parameters, such as the size of perforations, the depth of porous cavities, the surface weight of a panel, and so on. In general, a solid or perforated panel, or slats, placed over an empty airspace will be an extremely efficient narrowband absorber. The absorption will be very high at and around the center frequency, but will not affect more than about 1/12–1/6 of an octave around the design frequency. If a porous material is used in the cavity behind the solid panel, perforated panel, or slats, the overall absorption will decrease, but the bandwidth tends to cover about an octave centered at the design (resonant) frequency of the device.

In general, resonant absorbers can be tricky to implement. Care must be taken that the certain higher frequencies aren't reradiated into the room by a resonating panel or cavity. Good advice is to have professional assistance, which means an acoustician to help with the design and a carpenter to help with the construction.

Velocity Devices

Velocity devices can be as simple as thick, porous material placed on the wall with airspace behind them. The thicker the material and the deeper the airspace, in general, the more control you will have at lower frequencies. These devices tend to be quite efficient, absorbing sound at and above the lowest frequency predicted, and usually offering some benefits at even lower frequencies. An example of a good velocity absorber is a 4" thick piece of mineral fiber, typically around 3 lb/ft^3 density, over an equally sized airspace.

Hybrid Devices

There are also quite a variety of devices that work as both pressure and velocity absorbers. These are the more common corner devices offered from many manufacturers. The behavior of a dense, porous material in or over a corner tends to yield benefits both in the pressure and velocity domains. Dense foam absorbers, designed to be placed in corners, can yield control down to 50–100 Hz, depending on the size. Spacing the devices away from the corner can offer even greater low frequency control.

Dense fiber panels placed over a corner, with or without porous backfill, are also becoming more common. These are a hybrid, combining velocity absorption—it's a wide porous panel placed over a corner—and pressure absorption—it's also a rigid, resonant panel absorber (the density of the porous panel here tends to be more like 6 lb/ft^3 or more) with an air cavity behind it. Filling the space behind the rigid panel with less dense fiber or foam improves the performance even more.

There are guidelines for choosing various devices. The first thing that should be considered is the effective frequency range of the loudspeakers or other sound sources in a room. Placing loudspeakers that roll off below 60 Hz in a 12'x10'x8' room means that controlling the first axial mode at 47.1 Hz will probably not be necessary. (Remember that calculating room modes is discussed in Chapter 2.) Placing a bass amp in the same room and recording the performance will require addressing that first mode, since a bass guitar can easily produce frequencies lower than 30 Hz if it's of the five- or six-string variety.

After the range of control has been determined, choosing, installing, or building bass traps can begin. Table 9.1 gives some very general guidelines for choosing appropriate low frequency control for a room.

Table 9.1
Room treatment options[1].

Lower Limit	Typical Room Volume	Example Treatments
60-80 Hz	<1,000 ft³	"Standard" corner foam devices Panels across the corner; 1" thick (min.), 12" wide (min.) Small "Helmholtz" resonators
40-60 Hz	1,000 to 2,000 ft³	Large corner foam devices Panels across the corner 2" thick (min.), 24" wide (min.) Porous, resonant, or hybrid devices near corner; e.g., 12" diam. tubular "traps" Free-standing porous or hybrid devices around the room Small- to medium-sized "Helmholtz" resonators Porous absorbers (min. 4" thick) on walls and/or ceiling with airspace behind (min. 2" deep)
<40 Hz	>2,000 ft³	Larger corner foam devices spaced out from corner (min. 6") "Tuned" panel or membrane devices directly on walls and/or ceiling Deep porous devices (min. 8" thick) on walls and/or ceiling with airspace behind (min. 4" deep) Large "Helmholtz" resonators Passive, electronic damping <u>not</u> in-line with audio signal (i.e., <u>not</u> "room-correction")

Early Reflection Control

To control early reflections, absorption is generally the preferred method. Since the frequency range of these reflections is higher—typically 300–500 Hz and up—thinner materials can be used, which means many more aesthetic choices for room finishes. Absorption for recording studios is typically one of the three "F's:" fiber, foam, or fabric.

▶ **Fiber:** These are usually 3–8 lb/ft³ mineral (including glass) fibers, as well as other natural (e.g., wood, cotton) or synthetic (for example, polyester) fiberboards. The mineral fiber panels are often covered with an acoustically transparent cloth for aesthetic purposes. Most acoustical ceiling tiles also fall into this category, although very few common ceiling tiles are absorptive enough to consider for recording studios. If a ceiling tile grid is going to be included in a recording studio design, careful attention should be paid to the absorption of the proposed tiles in each frequency band (i.e., don't just compare "NRCs"), including the low frequencies. There are many varieties of ceiling tiles available from companies such as Armstrong and USG—some of which have very good absorption characteristics. Ceiling tiles glued directly to a flat wall or ceiling should generally be avoided. The minimum thickness for a flat, fibrous absorber for recordings studios is 1".

▶ **Foam:** These are usually 1.5–2.5 lb/ft³ acoustical foam panels (avoid "packing" or "bedding" foams). There is a wide variety of flat and sculpted designs available for aesthetic purposes. The minimum overall thickness for a sculpted foam absorber for recording studios is 2".

▶ **Fabric**: Curtains are the most common in this genre. Heavy drapes (typically greater than 18 oz/yd) with greater than 100% "fullness" might be worth considering. ("Fullness" defines the folds in the drape; 100% fullness means that a drape that is 20' when fully extended with no folds covering 10' of wall.) This type of absorber—a moving blanket would be another example—is more effective with an airspace behind it, and it is most effective in multiple layers with airspaces between. The overall thickness of the fabrics + airspace should be at least 3" for recording studios, although this approach is typically much less effective than fiber and foam equivalents.

For all of the above, thicker is generally better, at least up to about 4" to 6". If more low frequency absorption is a desired byproduct of early reflection control, absorbers as thick as 12" would be appropriate. If space on the walls has already been taken up with resonant absorbers for low frequency control, foam or fiber panels can usually be attached to the faces of them to control high frequency early reflections. Care should be taken not to add too much mass to a resonant absorber because that could affect the frequency range at which it's most effective. Perforations or slats should generally not be covered up for the same reason. If you decide to take this approach, then experiment with it for a bit before making the attachments permanent. If you damp the face panel too much, you will reduce its ability to effectively vibrate at its center frequency and thus defeat its ability to perform.

Care should also be taken to choose the absorber that is going to offer the best possible reduction of the early reflection. For the smaller control rooms, angles of incidence between loudspeaker, wall, and listener can be quite high. For flat absorbers, the maximum absorption is observed when sound strikes the panel perpendicular to it; usually referred to as "normal" incidence. A sound source and listener in a small room are usually positioned so that the incident angle of early reflection is not even close to perpendicular. For a flat absorber, the absorption decreases when sound strikes it off-axis (see Figure 9.1). This means that flat absorbers—particularly fibrous absorbers with a 3–8 lb/ft^3 density and a stretched fabric wrap—can actually reflect high frequency sound. Lower density fibers and foams, particularly sculpted foams, do not exhibit this variation in absorption for angles of incidence. In fact, some newer absorbers have been optimized so that a maximum thickness of material can be positioned to "face" the incident sound and maximize broadband absorption.

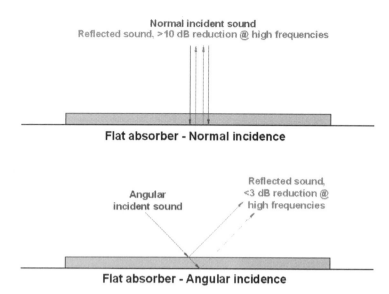

Figure 9.1
Incidence effect at panels[2].

Next, you need to have a basic understanding of what it is you are looking at when you review the data from manufactures of products you will use to construct traps or manufacturers who provide finished products for your use.

Absorption Coefficient

Understanding the absorption coefficient of the treatments you are going to install in your room is critical for you to effectively treat that space. It is not as difficult as it may seem.

Reported absorption coefficients are based on an area of the material that measures one square foot in area. A reported absorption of 0.00 means the material did not absorb any of the related frequency. The frequency was either reflected or passed through (and back) with no change in levels. A reported absorption of 1.00 means that the frequency was absorbed 100%. For example, 0.45 represents 45% absorption, 0.17 = 17%, etc. An easy way to picture this is that an absorption coefficient of 1.0 represents a 1' square window (in the open position) through the wall of the room, allowing all of that particular frequency to escape the room; however, for some frequencies the window closes party—perhaps completely.

What is even more interesting is that it is possible for the value to be greater than 1. Yup, you can actually capture more sound than 100%. Although this might sound impossible, it's not (impossible), and it is (true). ASTM c-423 (Standard Test Method for Sound Absorption and Sound Absorption Coefficients by the Reverberation Room Method) does not tell us how to interpret the data when this occurs; in fact, it's completely silent on the subject. So the numbers are just reported as measured.

But apparently this exists due to the fact that the measurements (in sabins) for total absorption are then divided by the area of the absorber, without taking into account the edge effect, or the back of the absorber if it is not mounted directly to a surface.

Thus, if you have an absorber mounted on a wall, the front and edges will absorb. If at a particular frequency that absorption measured 10 sabins, with a product that measured 2'x4' in size, the reported absorption coefficient would be 1.25 sabins.

Measurement of a Sound Absorption Coefficient

This description is from ASTM":[3] "The absorption of the reverberation room is measured as outlined in 4.1 both before and after placing a specimen of material to be tested in the room. The increase in absorption divided by the area of the test specimen is the dimensionless sound absorption coefficient. In inch-pound units, it is reported with the dimensionless "unit" sabin per square foot, Sab/ft^2."

OK, so exactly what is a "sabin?"

A sabin is a unit of acoustic absorption equivalent to the absorption by one square foot of a surface that absorbs all incident sound. The unit honors Wallace Clement Ware Sabine (1868–1919), an American physicist and Harvard University professor who founded the systematic study of acoustics about 1895. Sabine used this unit, which he called the open window unit (owu)[4], as early as 1911.

That's where that picture of a one-foot window (mentioned earlier) in the open position comes from—the particular frequency in question would just escape the room. Totally escape = totally absorbed. Pay attention to the fact that I keep repeating "the particular frequency." Remember that it's a special window, because when you open it fully, only some frequencies are able to escape fully, while still others might not escape at all, and others might escape to only varying degrees. Magic, methinks.

Now, let's take a look now at some treatment methods you might use.

DIY Treatments

One important thing to consider with DIY treatments is that the products you use have been tested and certified as being safe (from a flame perspective) in the manner that you will use it.

For example, ASTM E-84 is a fire test standard for construction materials, including wall coverings. This test standard is used for fabrics, vinyls, and so on that are installed directly over a wall surface, and they must be in touch with that surface. This standard does not certify the fabric as being safe when installed with an airspace between it and the surface that it is covering.

The test standard used in that condition (for example, for draperies, table cloths, etc.) is NFPA 701.

So, for panel traps, which are constructed with the fabric tightly installed to the fiberglass, ASTM E-84 is an acceptable standard, while NFPA 701 is not. Likewise, for the mid and high bass traps, Helmholtz Resonators, etc., NFPA 701 is used, and ASTM E-84 is unacceptable. Some products are treated, tested, and approved for both standards. This is the best of all possible worlds when it comes to your safety.

The same goes with foams. Acoustic foams are products that have been tested and approved for use under ASTM E-84 (which is similar to NFPA #255 and UL #723). These products do not develop smoke or have a flame spread index (how quickly the flame spreads on the material) that overly endangers life and limb. For example, Red Oak flooring has a flame spread index of 100, with a developed smoke index of 100. Auralex 2" Studio Foam has a flame spread index of 35, and a developed smoke index of 350.

Maximum smoke index allowed for interior finish use is 450.

However, standard packing foams (like the foam placed for acoustic treatment that was involved in some of the nightclub fires in recent years) flash and burn like wild fire, with developed smoke well in excess of 450. So keep it safe and only use materials that have been certified to conform to these standards.

Now that this has been said, understand that DIY treatments can be anything from extremely easy to painstakingly exasperating to construct. Some of the easiest treatments you can use are through the use of rigid fiberglass panels. So let's begin by looking at those.

FIBERGLASS PANELS
Products such as Owens Corning 703 and 705 rigid fiberglass panels can be used to create some very effective broadband attenuators. These products (and products manufactured by other manufacturers with the same, or very close, absorption values) can be wrapped in fabric to create not only effective, but also attractive attenuators.

Table 9.2 is an absorption chart for the 703 and 705 products manufactured by Owens Corning. Although the test data only lists frequencies as low as 125 Hz, you can see the low frequency trends with this material as the density (thickness) and mounting changes.

OWENS CORNING 703/705 Rigid Fiberglass										
PRODUCT	THICKNESS	MOUNTING	DENSITY	1/3 Octave Band Center Frequency (Hz)						
				125hz	250hz	500hz	1000hz	2000hz	4000hz	NRC
703, plain	1" (25mm)	Type "A"	3.0 pcf (48 kg/m3)	0.11	0.28	0.68	0.9	0.93	0.96	0.7
705, plain	1" (25mm)	Type "A"	6.0 pcf (96 kg/m3)	0.02	0.27	0.63	0.85	0.93	0.95	0.65
703, plain	2" (51mm)	Type "A"	3.0 pcf (48 kg/m3)	0.17	0.86	1.14	1.07	1.02	0.98	1
705, plain	2" (51mm)	Type "A"	6.0 pcf (96 kg/m3)	0.16	0.71	1.02	1.01	0.99	0.99	0.95
703, plain	3" (76mm)	Type "A"	3.0 pcf (48 kg/m3)	0.53	1.19	1.21	1.08	1.01	1.04	1.1
705, plain	3" (76mm)	Type "A"	6.0 pcf (96 kg/m3)	0.54	1.12	1.23	1.07	1.01	1.05	1.1
703, plain	4" (102mm)	Type "A"	3.0 pcf (48 kg/m3)	0.84	1.24	1.24	1.08	1	0.97	1.15
705, plain	4" (102mm)	Type "A"	6.0 pcf (96 kg/m3)	0.75	1.19	1.17	1.05	0.97	0.98	1.1
703, plain	6" (152mm)	Type "A"	3.0 pcf (48 kg/m3)	1.19	1.21	1.13	1.05	1.04	1.04	1.1
703, FRK	1" (25mm)	Type "A"	3.0 pcf (48 kg/m3)	0.18	0.75	0.58	0.72	0.62	0.35	0.65
705, FRK	1" (25mm)	Type "A"	6.0 pcf (96 kg/m3)	0.27	0.66	0.33	0.66	0.51	0.41	0.55
703, FRK	2" (51mm)	Type "A"	3.0 pcf (48 kg/m3)	0.63	0.56	0.95	0.79	0.6	0.35	0.75
705, FRK	2" (51mm)	Type "A"	6.0 pcf (96 kg/m3)	0.6	0.5	0.63	0.82	0.45	0.34	0.6
703, FRK	3" (76mm)	Type "A"	3.0 pcf (48 kg/m3)	0.84	0.88	0.86	0.71	0.52	0.26	0.75
705, FRK	3" (76mm)	Type "A"	6.0 pcf (96 kg/m3)	0.66	0.46	0.47	0.4	0.52	0.31	0.45
703, FRK	4" (102mm)	Type "A"	3.0 pcf (48 kg/m3)	0.88	0.9	0.84	0.71	0.49	0.23	0.75
705, FRK	4" (102mm)	Type "A"	6.0 pcf (96 kg/m3)	0.65	0.52	0.42	0.36	0.49	0.31	0.45
703, ASJ	1" (25mm)	Type "A"	3.0 pcf (48 kg/m3)	0.17	0.71	0.59	0.68	0.54	0.3	0.65
705, ASJ	1" (25mm)	Type "A"	6.0 pcf (96 kg/m3)	0.2	0.64	0.33	0.56	0.54	0.33	0.5
703, ASJ	2" (51mm)	Type "A"	3.0 pcf (48 kg/m3)	0.47	0.62	1.01	0.81	0.51	0.32	0.75
705, ASJ	2" (51mm)	Type "A"	6.0 pcf (96 kg/m3)	0.58	0.49	0.73	0.76	0.55	0.35	0.65
703, plain	1" (25mm)	Type E-405	3.0 pcf (48 kg/m3)	0.65	0.94	0.76	0.98	1	1.14	0.9
705, plain	1" (25mm)	Type E-405	6.0 pcf (96 kg/m3)	0.68	0.91	0.78	0.97	1.05	1.18	0.95
703, plain	2" (51mm)	Type E-405	3.0 pcf (48 kg/m3)	0.66	0.95	1.06	1.11	1.09	1.18	1.05
705, plain	2" (51mm)	Type E-405	6.0 pcf (96 kg/m3)	0.62	0.95	0.98	1.07	1.09	1.22	1
703, plain	3" (76mm)	Type E-405	3.0 pcf (48 kg/m3)	0.66	0.93	1.13	1.1	1.11	1.14	1.05
705, plain	3" (76mm)	Type E-405	6.0 pcf (96 kg/m3)	0.66	0.92	1.11	1.12	1.1	1.19	1.05
703, plain	4" (102mm)	Type E-405	3.0 pcf (48 kg/m3)	0.65	1.01	1.2	1.14	1.1	1.16	1.1
705, plain	4" (102mm)	Type E-405	6.0 pcf (96 kg/m3)	0.59	0.91	1.15	1.11	1.11	1.19	1.1

0.00 = no absorbtion.
1.00 = 100% absorbtion.
Type "A" Mounting - Material is placed directly against a solid backing.
Type E-405 Mounting - Material I splaced over a 16" air space. Facing (if noted) is exposed to sound source.

Table 9.2   Owens Corning absorption coefficients.

As you can see from this chart, you generally have a slight advantage when using 703 (3pcf density), compared to the 705 (6pcf density), pretty much across the board. Note also that the 6" of 703 product using a Type "A" mounting exhibits absorption coefficients greater than 1.00 at all reported frequencies—a perfect example of edge effect in play.

For this reason, understand that installing this material inside of a wood frame (which will make the cleanest looking finished product) will result in slightly lower sound attenuation than you might expect based simply on the numbers available. This decrease is due to the fact that the frame will take the edges of the panel out of the equation.

Although you are looking at Owens Corning products as examples here, there are a multitude of manufacturers around the world that produce rigid fiberglass panels, and the test data tend to make them fairly equal. As long as you stick with the same densities as the OC products, you will always be in the ballpark.

Don't get too hung up on small variances in numbers between manufacturers because a variance of 15% is virtually meaningless.

If you have problems obtaining rigid fiberglass in your area, you can substitute "Fire-Safing" (also known as Rockwool® and Thermafiber®) for this purpose. Note that Fire-Safing is more prone to breaking up than rigid fiberglass, and it will require a frame for longevity's sake.

Figure 9.2 is a simple 1"x 4" wood frame constructed for a 2'x 4' panel using 2" rigid fiberglass. Note the corner blocking installed to keep this square. The corner blocking is simply 3/4" pine let into the routed back of the frame. The use of this material helps you to maintain a square frame for your fiberglass. It also gives you a place to mount the stand-off brackets, which will keep this away from your wall, giving you greater sound attenuation. Note the line struck two inches from the outside face and the nails tacked in along that line. With rigid insulation, you can use this method to hold the fiberglass panel in place.

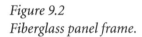

Figure 9.2
Fiberglass panel frame.

Figure 9.3 is the frame with insulation installed.

Figure 9.3
Fiberglass panel—frame with insulation.

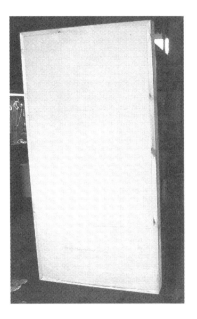

Figure 9.4 shows the back fabric installed. Be careful not to pull too tightly when installing the fabric, or you'll bend the frame. You want the material snug without creases, but not too tight. Experiment with it, and you'll get used to it in no time.

Figure 9.4
Fiberglass panel backing installed.

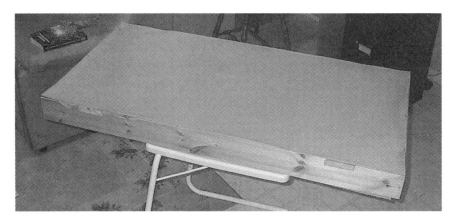

The face fabric is then installed—just wrapped and stapled to the back of the panel frame. Take your time with the folds to keep them clean and neat.

Figure 9.5
Fiberglass panel facing.

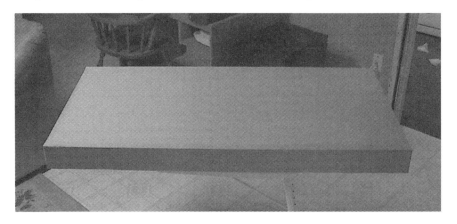

In Figure 9.6, the finished product has simple hangers and 2" standoffs to maintain an airspace between the wall and the back of the panel when installed. (Remember that you gain efficiency with greater airspace behind the panel.)

Figure 9.6
Panel standoffs and hangers.

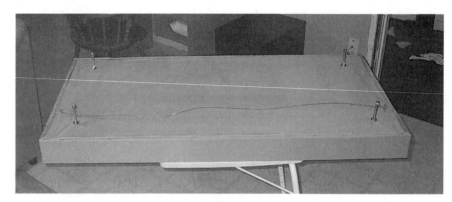

Figure 9.7 is the finished panel in place. Pretty nice looking for a homegrown remedy. Also, in this installation, there is actually a thermostat mounted on the wall behind the panel. The thermostat was installed off-center of the wall and always looked out of place. The panel hides it effectively, but the clearance off the wall allows the free flow of air, so it will still operate properly.

Figure 9.7
Completed fiberglass panel.

Something you have to consider, for this type of panel, is the cloth covering that you use.

In order for these panels to be effective, air has to be able to pass freely through them. This means that you need to have a fabric that "breathes easily." In other words, if you put the fabric tight against your face, then you should be able to breathe easily through the fabric.

One thing of importance I would point out to you—do not go to your local fabric store and pick up just any old fabric for this. Once again, make certain that the fabric you purchase is fire retardant; otherwise, you have to fire treat it prior to its use. Remember what you learned previously about testing and rating standards.

An excellent source for fire retardant fabrics is Guilford of Maine Fabric (see note below).

Features of Guilford of Maine Fabric

Material is available by the linear yard in a 66" width.

48 standard colors to choose from.

Other Guilford of Maine fabric charts are available for special orders.

Fabric is 100% Terratex polyester.

Pattern is non-directional.

PRODUCT DATA

Flammability: Class 1 Fire Rated per ASTM E-84

Weight: .5oz per linear yard

Tensile Strength: 150 lbs. minimum

Tear Strength: 30 lbs. minimum

Colorfastness to Light: 40 hours

Colorfastness to Crocking: Class 4 min.—dry; Class 4min.— wet

Moisture Regain— .5% maximum

Acoustical Solutions, Inc.

Ph: 800-782-5742 Fax: 804-346-8808

Web site: http://www.acousticalsolutions.com

Note that the above product is fire rated per ASTM E-84, which makes it acceptable for this use.

If you choose to use materials that have not been previously treated, then you must purchase fire-retardant materials to properly treat the fabric. There are a lot of companies that manufacture these products, one of which is Flame Stop Inc. Figure 9.8 lists their applicable products, and the materials they can treat.

Figure 9.8
Flame Stop products.

Flame Stop, Inc.		
MATERIALS	**TESTING STANDARDS**	**PRODUCT**
Draperies, Wallpaper, Carpet, Furniture, Decorative Woods, Paper, Straw, Most Synthetics, Acoustical Ceilings, Indoor	ASTM-3 84, NFPA 255, 701 UL 723	**FLAME STOP I ™**
Fabrics with at least 25% Natural Fiber, Drapes, Bedding, Carpets and Wall Coverings, Silk	TITLE 19, UL 723, ASTM E-84, NFPA 255, 701, FAR 25.853	**FLAME STOP I-C ™**
Open Cell Foams, Airline Fabrics, Foam Rubber	TITLE 4, FAA 25.853-C	**FLAME STOP I-D ™**
Open and Closed Cell Foams, Synthetic Fabrics, Plastics, Hay Barriers, Thatching, Bamboo, Tough to Penetrate Materials (Our Most Concentrated Product)	ASTM E-84, NFPA 255, 701, UL 723, FAR 25.853	**FLAME STOP I-DS ™**

Flame Stop, Inc.
924 Bluemound Rd.
Fort Worth, TX 76131
Tel. 817-306-1222
Fax. 817-306-1733
Toll Free: 1-877-397-7867
Website: http://www.flamestop.com/

LOW BASS PANEL TRAPS

A panel absorber is manufactured by constructing a sealed compartment with a rigid panel face. Typically, your existing wall will create the back of this bass trap, although you can create movable panels, as well utilizing a 3/4" plywood or MDF back surface.

One advantage to a panel absorber is that they are able to be "tuned" fairly closely to specific frequencies. If after treating your space with broadband sound attenuation, you find that you have one problem frequency "hanging around," then you can deal with that through the use of this type of treatment.

This trap's strength is also its weakness because it cannot be used as a wide broadband treatment. Therefore, it should be used as a last resort and not a starting point.

Figure 9.9 shows plan details for construction of a 2'x 4' panel trap using 1/4" plywood.

Figure 9.9
Panel trap plan.

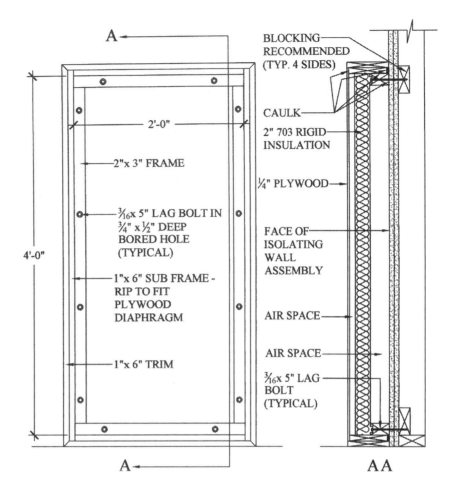

The factors determining the trap's center frequency are the mass (density) of the panel and the depth of the trap.

The formula for calculating the trap frequency is shown in Figure 9.10

Figure 9.10
Panel trap formula.

f = 170/sqrt(m * d)

Where:
 f = resonance frequency
 m = surface density of the panel in lb./sq. ft.
 d = depth of airspace in inches

Note that there's no deep math here. This is an easy calculation you can program into a spreadsheet to examine different material properties and panel depths.

Figure 9.11 is a chart of typical plywood sizes and their corresponding densities. Note that these numbers are per design, but you should really accurately measure the panels you purchase due to the fact that different core material and facings, as well as different manufacturers, can provide materials of the same thicknesses with different densities.

Typical Plywood Densities						
3.3 mm	=	4.85 kg/sheet	1/8	=	10.70 Lbs/sheet =	0.33 psf
6.5 mm	=	9.71 kg/sheet	1/4 in.	=	21.40 Lbs/sheet =	0.67 psf
7.5 mm	=	11.20 kg/sheet	5/16 in.	=	24.69 Lbs/sheet =	0.77 psf
9.5 mm	=	14.10 kg/sheet	3/8 in.	=	31.09 Lbs/sheet =	0.97 psf
12.5 mm	=	18.60 kg/sheet	1/2 in.	=	41.01 Lbs/sheet =	1.28 psf
15.5 mm	=	23.10 kg/sheet	5/8 in.	=	50.93 Lbs/sheet =	1.59 psf
18.5 mm	=	27.50 kg/sheet	3/4 in.	=	60.63 Lbs/sheet =	1.89 psf
25.5 mm	=	38.00 kg/sheet	1 in.	=	83.78 Lbs/sheet =	2.62 psf
Information from the Canadian Plywood Association.						

Figure 9.11   Typical plywood properties.

The panel shown previously in Figure 9.9 has a center frequency of 88.64 Hz, based on the densities calculated in Figure 9.11. If you were to deepen the trap by 2" (substitute 1x8 for the 1x6 frame), the center frequency would drop to 75.84 Hz. Likewise, if you were to leave the frame as is and substitute 1/8" plywood for the 1/4" plywood, the center frequency would raise to 126.18 Hz. Also, understand that the placement of the insulation behind the panel gives you attenuation that covers about one octave around the center frequency (half above—half below). If you do not install the insulation, the panel frequency tightens to roughly one half octave (one quarter above and below).

Note: there is an apparent error above if you use the two-digit density numbers shown in the chart in Figure 9.10. This is due to rounding down to double digits from the actual conversion done in a spreadsheet. So, although you should set up your own spreadsheet, if you were to use the above figures, the center frequency of the panel would calculate as 88.56 (rounded to two digits). This is not a really large problem. Seeing as how these panels affect about an octave around the center frequency, you'll capture what you need regardless. However, if true accuracy is what you want, then set up that spreadsheet.

Be careful when you build one of these to maintain the airspace between the panel and fiberglass as shown. If the fiberglass is allowed to touch the back of the panel, it will damp the panel, and the trap will not perform as designed. It is equally important that this trap be 100% sealed against air movement. The trap works on an air-spring principle: any air leakage will cause the trap to fail. So caulk in all locations indicated thoroughly. Allow caulk to cure for a minimum of 24 hours (or as recommended by the manufacturer) for complete curing before testing the trap.

Testing of the trap can be performed easily with the use of sine waves. Begin with a continuous wave at the designed center frequency of the panel. You should be able to feel the vibration of the panel face. Slowly raise and lower the frequency to find the panel's actual center frequency. The center frequency of the trap will be the one where its vibration is greatest. You can use this information to help adjust panel design, if necessary.

HELMHOLTZ TRAPS

Helmholtz traps are a type of membrane trap that does not rely on sealed spring cavities. There are many different types of these traps, some utilizing wooden slats, while others use hardboard panels with holes drilled into them. We're going to focus on Helmholtz slot resonators in this book.

A slot resonator is constructed by using members to frame off the wall surface, similar to the panel traps, which then have insulation placed inside. This is then covered with flame-retardant fabric, and finally slats of particular widths are placed with a slot in between each piece.

The width in the slot opening is a critical piece of the puzzle when it comes to these working properly—with smaller slots, greater board widths, deeper slots, and deeper boxes lowering the frequencies. Thus, a disadvantage to this method is the painstaking attention to detail required to really get it right. A variance of even 1/16" can drastically change the center frequency on these traps. However, these traps can also be constructed with a box depth that varies, making them a very good means of achieving broadband low frequency attenuation.

Figure 9.12 gives you the formula for calculating a slot resonator. Once again, there is no deep math involved here. The formula is another easy one to program into a spreadsheet or to perform on a calculator (assuming it has a square root function key). There are also a ton of online calculators for these traps as well. Just do a search for "slot resonator calculators," and you'll find plenty of them.

Figure 9.12
Helmholtz slot resonator calculation.

$$f = 2160 \times \text{sqrt} \, (r \, / \, ((d \times D) \times (r + w)))$$

Where:

> f = Resonant Frequency in Hertz (Hz)
> r = Slot Width
> w = Slat Width
> d = Effective Depth of Slot (1.2 times the actual slat thickness)
> D = The depth of box to the inside face of the slat.
> 2160 = c / (2 x π) rounded
> c = Speed of Sound in inches/sec.

Be careful if you choose to go this route. Sometime, back a ways, there was an error in this calculation that made its way through the Internet. See Figure 9.13 for a side-by-side comparison of the correct and incorrect formulas to make certain the one you use is correct.

Figure 9.13
Helmholtz slot resonator formula correction[5].

$$f = 2160 * sqrt (r / ((d * D) * (r + w))) \quad \text{Correct}$$

$$f = 2160 * sqrt (r / ((d * D) + (r + w))) \quad \text{Incorrect}$$

└─ That is the problem

OK, on to how one goes about building one of these.

Figure 9.14 is a plan for a slot resonator. Note that one of the differences between this and a panel trap is that the insulation is placed touching the back of the slats. This helps to keep the slats from creating a vibrating noise when the panel is excited. Note also that you maintain airspace behind the insulation. This, too, is important for the trap to work effectively.

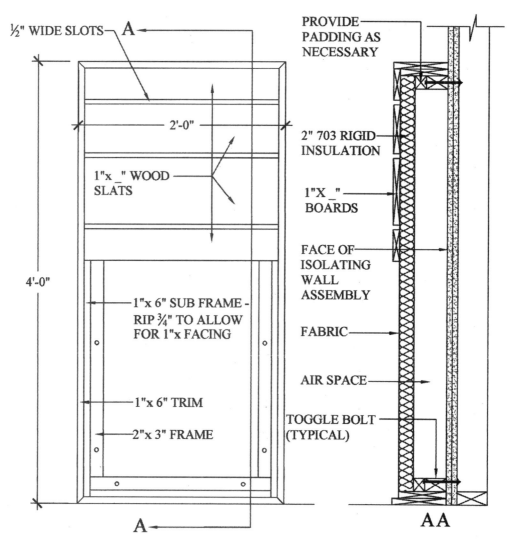

NOTE: THE USE OF ALTERNATING 1"X 4" / 1"x 6" / 1"x 8" IS EQUAL TO THE USE OF 1"x 6" FOR THE PURPOSE OF CALCULATING THE CENTER FREQUENCY.

Figure 9.14   Helmholtz slot resonator plan.

Figure 9.15 is an example of a broadband slot resonator built into a corner in a room.

Figure 9.15
Helmholtz corner slot resonator.

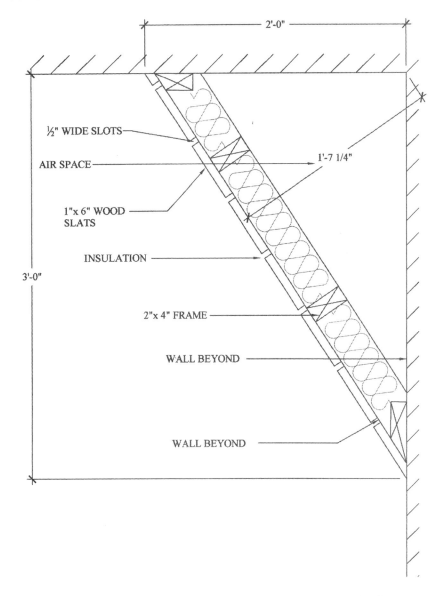

This resonator is fairly broadband in nature and will handle frequencies ranging from about 66.44 Hz to 155.82 Hz.

Once again—pay attention to the cloth being used for treatment. Guilford of Maine also has fabrics suitable for this work. Their style 2100 (for one example) is tested and approved for both FM 701 and ASTM E-84.

Figure 9.15a is a 3D view of this slot resonator in the room corner. If the unit is constructed as shown (from floor to ceiling), it will be a reasonably effective unit. This is because it covers not only the corner (remember looking at bass buildup in corners earlier in the book), but also because it covers two trihedral corners. Recall that a trihedral corner is where a floor/wall/wall or ceiling/wall/wall meet, and it is the location of the greatest bass buildup in the space.

Figure 9.15a
Helmholtz corner slot resonator
isometric view.

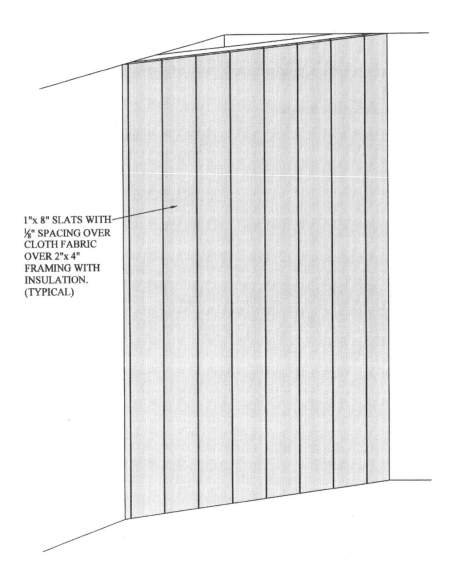

1"x 8" SLATS WITH
⅛" SPACING OVER
CLOTH FABRIC
OVER 2"x 4"
FRAMING WITH
INSULATION.
(TYPICAL)

MID/HIGH BASS ABSORBERS

Mid/high bass absorbers can be made to complement a series of low frequency bass traps. Figure 9.16 is a plan for a typical 2'x 4' mid/high absorber. These traps are manufactured similarly to the bass panel traps and will fit side by side with them, but they do not utilize a rigid panel for the face. Rather, this is a cloth finish and thus breathes air freely.

Figure 9.16
Mid/high bass absorber plan.

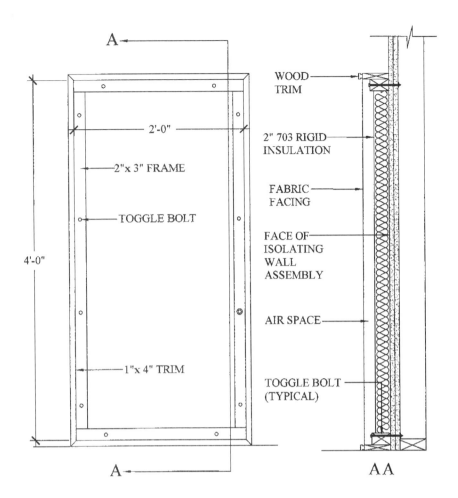

DIFFUSORS

You won't spend a lot of time on this—not here anyway. Just enough time to become familiar with the subject.

Acoustic diffusion is created through a series of non-flat shapes that have enough dimensional variation to scatter the sounds that strike them. By the use of the term "non-flat," you should understand that this refers to flats in multiple planes, as well as non-flat shapes in general (for example, convex and concave surfaces). Acoustic diffusion comes in quite a few different forms—the common pyramids and partial barrel forms, along with quadratic shapes.

In the 1970s Schroeder's designs [6][7] were the stepping-off point for the widespread use of diffusion for acoustic control of room boundary issues. Schroeder presented methods of designing concert hall ceilings that could avoid direct reflections into the audience. In 1975, he provided a way of designing highly diffusing surfaces based on binary maximum-length sequences, and showed that these periodic sequences have the property that their harmonic amplitudes are all equal.

He later extended his method and proposed surface structures that give excellent sound diffusion over larger bandwidths. This is based on quadratic residue sequences of elementary number theory, investigated by A. M. Legendre and C. F. Gauss.

Dr. Peter D'Antonio[8] (AKA Dr. Diffusor), took this to another level in the 1980s with his studies, and when he formed RPG Diffusor Systems and developed the Reflection Phase Grating Diffusor.

Suffice it to say that there is no easy way to break this down from a mathematical point of view. It took D'Antonio and Konnert 14 pages just to describe the workings of the RPG Diffusor and that's done with the understanding that engineers were reading the paper—thus they had no reason to simplify.

If this is something that you really want to pursue, I would suggest that you either purchase a kit (if you really want to construct it yourself), or turn to a company like Auralex or RPG to purchase something you know is going to work.

Figure 9.17 is a kit you can purchase from a company called Decware for their Model P1324 Quadratic Residue Diffuser.

Figure 9.17
P1324 Quadratic Residue Diffuser kit.

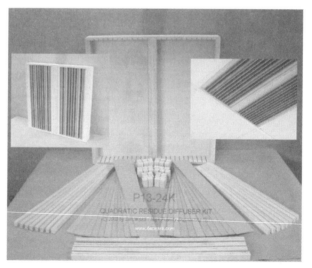

Their product is designed based on a prime 13 sequence, which is repeated twice in their 24x24x3 inch diffuser. This gives you diffusion over three octaves! 1125 Hz ~ 12,000 Hz. These units are made from solid wood and are available in kit form (as shown in Figure 9.17) or assembled (as shown in Figure 9.17a).

Stands and other accessories will be available soon from this manufacturer. These modular units are designed to be used in groups. They can be fastened to wall surfaces, ceilings, or used with legs as freestanding units. They're a perfect fit in drop ceilings, as shown in Figure 9.17b.

Figure 9.17a
P1324 Quadratic Residue Diffuser
preassembled.

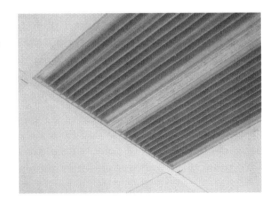

Figure 9.17b
P1324 Quadratic Residue Diffuser
in ceiling grid.

You can finish these by painting them, applying stain, or with clear finishes. In some cases, you can cover them with speaker cloth. To treat an area, no less than two units are recommended.

Finally, a note about diffusor performance data: Until very recently (October 2005), there were no independent testing labs capable of measuring diffusion/scattering performance of diffusor products. As of this writing, a new standard to outline the measurement and quantification of diffusion/scattering performance—ISO 17497 Part 1—has just been released, and a new laboratory in California is finally available to conduct independent testing of diffusors and sound scattering surfaces.

Manufactured Treatments

When discussing manufactured treatments, the two most popular methods of treatment are either high-quality acoustic foams or products utilizing specialized acoustic fiberglass. You are going to examine products here from three different manufacturers without any judgments being made (by the author) as to who makes the best (or even better) products.

Because I know the products from these manufacturers and enjoy a personal relationship with parties in each firm that are involved in the design of these products, I am not showing you anything that I have not personally experienced. I do not, however, own stock in any of these companies, nor do I have any other vested interest in any of these firms.

Two of the companies spend money on acoustic research and product development, and their products are at the forefront of product development in the industry. They are constantly looking for new ideas and methods for improving their products and the industry as a whole.

The third company is a small one; however, the owner provides a service, rather than a unique product. This company provides some very nice-looking versions of the DIY broadband rigid glass products I discussed earlier. They have recently had their products tested at Riverbank, so there is no guessing what their products will provide. If you do not feel that your skills are up to making a professional looking product at home, but your budget cannot afford products from either of the other two firms, this company is well worth considering.

The products from these firms work. I've seen them in studios. I've examined before and after conditions using products from both manufacturers, and they both impress me. However, there are also other manufacturers out there who make similarly good products, and also some whose products I would not recommend. (I will not list those firms here.)

I do not list these other firms (who make similar products), not because their products are inferior, but rather because I do not have personal knowledge of their products. Thus, I can neither recommend nor warn against their products. As to the firms that I would not recommend, if you spend even a few minutes looking them over carefully, you will come to the same conclusions I did, which is why I do not need to name them. They have not invested the time or expense to have their products tested at a recognized facility, and therefore cannot back up any claims to their products' performance.

When looking at companies who have claims that test data proves their products to equal those shown here, look carefully for the actual test reports and request them if they are not published. If they cannot (or will not) produce reports for you, or if those reports are not from a recognized, reputable testing laboratory, then do not even consider their products. Any reputable manufacturer will provide copies of the actual test data to make the sale (if that's what it takes).

If you decide to shop for yourself with unknown firms, then remember the old saying: *Caveat emptor—Let the buyer beware.* Because in the end, the only person really responsible to protect you from getting ripped off is you.

AURALEX

The two most commonly used sound absorption materials (for manufactured treatments) are high-quality acoustic foam and specialized acoustic fiberglass. Generally, acoustic foam is just referred to as foam, although there are some very dramatic differences in cell structure and density between acoustic foam and the thousands of other types that are manufactured. This is why you can't just buy mattress pads with which to acoustically treat your studio.

In addition to the two most popular types of acoustic absorption materials, Auralex offers a Class A, fire-resistant, natural fiber panel called SonoFiber. SonoFiber acoustic panels are the perfect solution for those budget-conscious projects requiring a Class A fire rating without the aesthetic demands of designer treatments such as fabric-covered panels.

Let's look at some of the options available at Auralex.

SpaceArray

For audio professionals seeking to maximize the acoustical performance of their recording spaces, pArtScience™ SpaceArray™ diffusors evenly and randomly disperse sound waves to provide a consistent acoustical environment in any room. Unlike other high-end diffusors, the SpaceArray employs a quasi-random array using state-of-the-art engineering techniques and carefully selected, high-quality materials for superior sound diffusion. It has the following qualities:

▶ **Outstanding performance**: Eliminates flutter echoes and other acoustical anomalies without removing acoustical energy from the space.

▶ **Quasi-random array**: Randomization of reflections evenly distributes sound in a space, taking the guesswork out of microphone placement and mixing. It just sounds better.

▶ **Modular**: 2' by 2' panels used in a variety of applications and placement options, including "T-Bar" grids.

▶ **Beautiful solid wood construction**: Widely used for musical instruments and decorative finishes for over 1,000 years, Paulownia wood has one of the highest strength-to-weight ratios of any wood in the world.

Figure 9.18 is an example of this diffusor.

Figure 9.18
SpaceArray™ diffusors

Space Coupler

The pArtScience™ SpaceCoupler™ is an acoustical treatment that creates a natural "large sound" within a small room footprint. Unlike current alternatives, which involve custom design and remodeling, the SpaceCoupler works within the current room footprint for a fraction of the cost. Here are some of its features:

▶ **Loosely couples spaces**: Creates a natural "large sound" in an otherwise small room.

▶ **Waveguide design**: Redirection of sound energy offers an attractive alternative to traditional absorptive and diffusive surface treatments.

▶ **Modular**: 2' by 2' panels used in a variety of applications and placement options, including "T-Bar" grids.

▶ These units are made with the same beautiful wood used for the SpaceArray™ diffusors. Check out Figure 9.19 to see one of these treatments.

*Figure 9.19
SpaceCoupler™.*

Audio Tile

For audio professionals looking for aesthetic alternatives to acoustical absorption treatments, pArtScience™ AudioTile™ ShockWave delivers maximum broadband absorption for a pleasing, well-controlled sound without being perceived as too dry. Unlike traditional products, the patent-pending AudioTile offers unlimited design possibilities for one-of-a-kind personalization and a custom designed look. Here are some of its features:

▶ **Maximum broadband absorption**: 0.81 absorption coefficient @ 125 Hz. Max. NRC = 1.00 to 1.05, depending on installation.

▶ **Varying thicknesses**: Foam thicknesses from 1" to 4" are built into each pattern, providing varying degrees of absorption at varying frequencies. Greater thicknesses can be achieved with alternative layouts.

▶ **Unlimited tessellation design patterns**: Allows a unique means of blending absorption, diffusion, and reflection.

▶ **Easy Installation**: Mount by using Foamtak™ spray adhesive, Tubetak Pro™ liquid adhesive, or Temp•Tabs™ Studiofoam® mounting kits.

Figure 9.20 is an example of the AudioTile™ ShockWave

Figure 9.20
AudioTile™ ShockWave.

Studiofoam™ Acoustic Panels

The term "Studiofoam Acoustic Panels" covers a wide variety of acoustic absorption products manufactured by Auralex. They are a series of foam room treatments with a specific target (acoustically) for each product. Let's walk through a brief description of each one.

Studiofoam Wedge—1 , 2 , 3 , 4

This is perfect for those environments that demand good sound control, but where complete acoustic absorption isn't required or desired. One-inch Studiofoam Wedge works most effectively on mid and high frequency sound waves and may be used to acoustically treat walls, or, more commonly, ceilings (especially if they aren't parallel to the floor), even when the walls are treated with thicker acoustic Studiofoam. One-inch acoustic Studiofoam Wedge absorbs as well as some competing two-inch products, so if your budget is a bit "thin," then use this.

Two-inch Studiofoam Wedges are used to treat small- to medium-sized areas, including vocal booths, control rooms, and sound studios. They effectively kill standing waves and flutter echoes and, when used in conjunction with low frequency absorbers, can effectively help to tame the full frequency bandwidth in virtually any room. Two-inch acoustic Studiofoam is quite simply one of the workhorses of the industry and is a safe bet if you're tuning your room yourself without the help of a professional acoustician. Figure 9.21 is an example of one- and two-inch Studiofoam Wedges.

Figure 9.21
Studiofoam Wedge 1", 2".

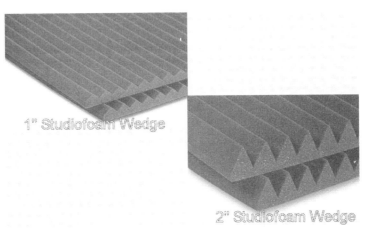

Twice as absorbent as two-inch at 125 Hz, three-inch Studiofoam Wedges can even do many of the same things that four-inch ones can do (especially when used with LENRD or Venus Bass Traps). They also can provide a well-controlled, more accurate sound in any size room.

Three-inch acoustic Studiofoam Wedges are recommended for rooms with higher SPLs (sound pressure levels) or lower frequencies (such as drum or voiceover booths). There are rooms that have more low-end problems than some folks acknowledge. So if you step up from two-inch to three-inch, you will benefit from the extra low-end sound absorption. Figure 9.22 is an example of the three-inch Wedges.

Figure 9.22
Three-inch Studiofoam Wedges.

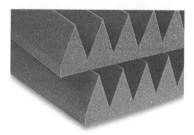

Four-inch Studiofoam Wedges are recommended for medium to large areas, such as concert halls, gymnasiums and churches, rooms with pronounced low frequency problems, or where sonic accuracy is mandatory and maximum acoustic absorption is required (for example, voiceover or drum booths, forensic audio labs, and mastering rooms).

Four-inch acoustic Studiofoam Wedges provide three times the low-end control of two-inch wedges and can effectively tame even the worst sonic anomalies. In some instances, using four-inch acoustic Studiofoam can lessen the need for significant dedicated bass trapping.

Figure 9.23
Four-inch Studiofoam Wedges.

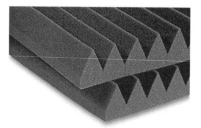

Studiofoam Pyramids—2", 4"

Two-inch acoustic Studiofoam Pyramids treat small- to medium-sized areas, including iso booths, control rooms, and sound studios. They effectively kill standing waves and flutter echoes, and when used in conjunction with the LENRD or Venus Bass Traps or the Sunburst Broadband Absorbers, can effectively tame the full frequency bandwidth in virtually any acoustic environment.

Two-inch Studiofoam Pyramids offer a bit of extra sound diffusion and slightly less sound absorption than two-inch Studiofoam Wedges, so they yield a less dry-sounding space with a bit more "air." You can see the Pyramids in Figure 9.24.

Figure 9.24
Two-inch Studiofoam Pyramids.

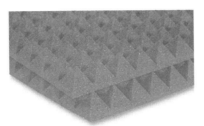

As with four-inch Studiofoam Wedges, four-inch Studiofoam Pyramids are recommended for larger spaces, rooms with pronounced low frequency problems, or where sonic accuracy is mandatory and stronger acoustic absorption is required.

Having four sides exposed on each pyramid also yields more sound wave diffusion, which is desirable in some spaces. So four-inch acoustic Studiofoam Pyramids will yield less overall dryness than four-inch Studiofoam Wedges. Take a look at Figure 9.25 to see the four inch Pyramids

Figure 9.25
Four-inch Studiofoam Pyramids.

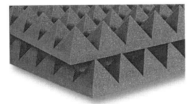

Studiofoam Metro—2", 4"

The differing heights of protrusions on the acoustic Studiofoam Metro products serve to spread sonic energy out in the time domain, as well as each one absorbing a slightly different slice of the frequency spectrum. You see, it takes slightly different amounts of time for sound waves to travel through the different sections of the Metro, strike the mounting surface, and travel back through the Metro into the room, so wavefronts are, in effect, softened rather than just being absorbed.

This is why a two-inch Studiofoam Metro room will retain a bit more "feel" than a room that's treated with a stronger acoustic absorber and why, when coupled with a judicious amount of MetroFusors and Metro LENRDs, a well-controlled, natural-sounding acoustic space will result.

Studiofoam Metro blurs the line between those products that work well acoustically and those that yield the aesthetics that some users desire. Figure 9.26 is an example of this product.

Figure 9.26
Studiofoam Metro.

Studiofoam Wedgies

Studiofoam Wedgies are one-inch squares of two-inch thick Studiofoam, and they are a great solution for spot treating sound studios, home listening rooms, iso booths, and more. With slightly more wedges per square foot than two-inch acoustic Studiofoam, Wedgies feature maximized surface area for greater exposure to sound waves. Studiofoam Wedgies are a great solution for small flutter echo problem areas, and, when spread apart, yield beneficial sound diffusion off their exposed edges. You can see the Wedgies in Figure 9.27.

Figure 9.27
Studiofoam Wedgies.

Studiofoam Sonomatt

Sonomatt acoustic foam panels are cut in the industry standard "egg crate" style to keep the price low, and they absorb almost as well as two-inch Studiofoam Wedges. Due to the manufacturing process used, Sonomatt's dimple pattern will not be square to the edges of the panels, so installing them side-by-side may not be advised from a visual consistency standpoint. However, it may be a good choice if you intend to cover your sound control materials with acoustical cloth. Look at Figure 9.28 for an example of this product.

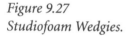

Figure 9.28
Studiofoam Sonomatt.

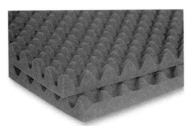

SonoFlat Panels

SonoFlat Panels are 2" x 2' x 2' panels made of the same materials used in Studiofoam. They offer good absorption of mid to high frequencies. The edges are beveled, contributing to an elegant look not normally associated with acoustic foam. The panels can be installed easily and arranged in a multitude of attractive patterns.

SonoFlats are equally at home in a recording studio or a home theater, offering a unique, sophisticated look and a cost-effective choice for accurate sound. This product is pictured in Figure 9.29.

Figure 9.29
SonoFlat Panels.

LENRDs

In 1996, Auralex® introduced the very first acoustical foam corner device specifically designed to control low frequency problems in small rooms: The LENRD® Bass Trap. The LENRD is a 24" tall, triangular acoustical foam absorber, 12" wide along each flat edge and 17" wide across the face. It is specifically designed to address low frequency mode problems in the 80 to 300 Hz range. The device can be placed in any 90° corner, preferably the vertical, wall/wall corners first, to control modal anomalies. When used as a corner treatment, the overall contribution of modal energy to what is heard at a mix position (for example) is lessened. The most characteristic difference is the reduction of modal decay. Sonically, treatment with LENRDs will help give more "punch" to the bass and less "mud" in the finished mix.

Figure 9.30 is a view of the LENRD bass trap.

Figure 9.30
LERND bass trap.

MegaLENRDs

Like the LERND, the MegaLENRD is also 24" tall, but is twice as deep, making it 24" along each flat edge and 34" wide across the face. The extra mass of foam in the corner gives good control down to about 50 Hz. Since the MegaLENRD is large enough to free-stand in the room, control down to the 30 Hz range is not unrealistic, if spacing the devices out from the corner is feasible in a larger room. Check out Figure 9.31 to see the MegaLENRD.

Figure 9.31
MegaLENRD bass trap.

TruTrap Genesis

The TruTraps Genesis system is a hybrid product solution that combines broadband absorption with quadratic diffusion to give you the tools you need to accurately treat the sound in your room.

Genesis consists of four three-inch TruPanels and four Q'Fusors, and adheres to the principle of utilizing an air gap behind a passive absorber to provide significant broadband absorption and increased low frequency control. Using the three-inch TruSpacers provides a 50% increase in absorption at 125 Hz (.4 to .62 NRC), and even more when the TruPanels are placed diagonally in corners.

Mount the Q'Fusors to the front of the TruTraps for a combined coverage of 32 sq. ft., or mount the Q'Fusors directly on the wall for an additional 14 sq. ft. of coverage. The Q'Fusors expand the sweet spot, while the TruPanels continue to trap low to mid frequencies.

Using one or more Genesis systems provides a low profile broadband solution that allows great functional and design alternatives, creating a professional look for your room. Everything you need is provided, including the TruSpacers and TubeTak Pro adhesive, making the TruTraps an easy, turnkey answer for great acoustical control, and the best value of any "off-the-wall" alternative anywhere. (See Figure 9.32.)

Figure 9.32
TruTraps Genesis.

Venus Bass Traps

The Venus Bass Trap achieves a prodigious level of low frequency sound control at your room boundaries, where low frequency problems begin, at a price that allows it to fit into most budgets. Venus Bass Traps ship in a 2'x4"x12" size, but are often cut in half to 2'x2', and then paired with a 12" Auralex CornerFill, as shown in Figure 9.39.

While the Venus Bass Trap can provide serious low frequency sound control and broad bandwidth absorption that's literally second to none in all rooms, it really shines in larger rooms like gymnasiums, houses of worship, and multipurpose rooms (see Figure 9.33).

Figure 9.33
Venus Bass Trap.

VersaTile

This next generation absorber combines a visually attractive acoustic foam absorption panel with specially engineered air cavities to yield extraordinary sonic benefits.

The VersaTile design allows it to be implemented in a variety of ways. It can be positioned to bridge a corner, creating a sizable air pocket that gives you some great low frequency absorption. It can also be placed on walls and ceilings with either side out, allowing for some sophisticated looks, while offering superior absorption characteristics versus thinner, flat acoustic foam panels (see Figure 9.34).

Figure 9.34
VersaTile.

SonoFiber Panels

For the professional needing an aesthetic yet cost-effective alternative to full-wall custom fabric systems, Auralex ELiTE ProPanels cover the spectrum. ProPanels are fabric-covered, acoustic absorptive panels, designed to absorb slap and flutter echoes, providing a more pleasing and accurate listening environment.

B22 ProPanels

B22 ProPanels are one-inch thick, beveled edge absorptive panels in a 2'x2' size. They are available in four standard fabric choices, and are normally in stock for immediate shipment.

The 2'x2' size expands design and placement options, providing unlimited aesthetic appeal (see Figure 9.35).

Figure 9.35
B22 ProPanels.

B24 ProPanels

These one-inch thick, 2' by 4' beveled-edge panels have a 0.80 Noise Reduction Coefficient (NRC), making them the perfect choice for absorbing slap and flutter echo in a wide array of applications. Their four available colors provide both extensive design options, as well as the ability to fit attractively within most room environments (see Figure 9.36)

Figure 9.36
B24 ProPanels.

Figures 9.37 through 9.40 are a sampling of Auralex Product installed in some of their clients' facilities.

Figure 9.37
Acoustically treated live recording room (courtesy of the Fender Museum).

Figure 9.38
Acoustic treatments in control room.

Figure 9.39
Acoustic treatments in control room.

Figure 9.40
B24 ProPanels in a live room.

Auralex Product Data

Figures 9.41 through 9.41l are a listing of the Auralex products test data for the products listed here.

Figure 9.41
AudioTile test data.

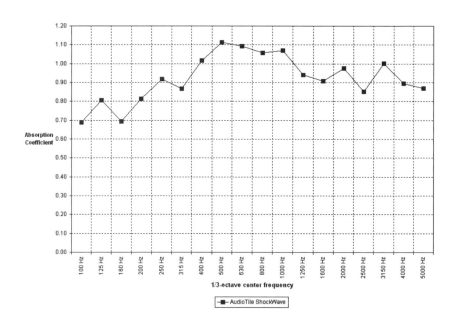

Figure 9.41a
TruTraps test data.

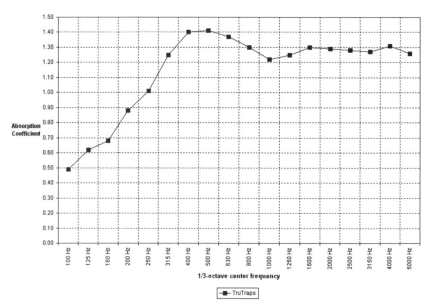

Figure 9.41b
LENRDs test data.

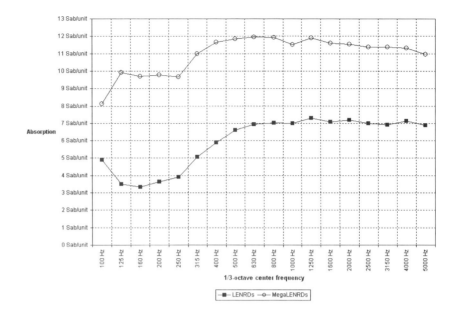

Figure 9.41c
Sonofiber Panels test data.

Auralex Products	
Frequency	SonoFiber 2'x2'x1" Natural fiber panel (no facing)
100 Hz	0.05
125 Hz *	0.09
160 Hz	0.12
200 Hz	0.19
250 Hz *	0.2
315 Hz	0.42
400 Hz	0.54
500 Hz *	0.72
630 Hz	0.84
800 Hz	0.93
1000 Hz *	0.97
1250 Hz	1.02
1600 Hz	1.04
2000 Hz *	1.04
2500 Hz	1.04
3150 Hz	1.02
4000 Hz *	1.01
5000 Hz	1.01
NRC	0.75
Mounting	A
* Values reported as octave-band absorption coefficients in accordance with ASTM C423.	

Figure 9.41d
StudioFoam Metro test
data

Auralex Products - Absorption Coefficients		
Frequency	2" Studiofoam Metro 2'x4'x2" Foam Panel	4" Studiofoam Metro 2'x4'x4" Foam Panel
100 Hz	0.08	0.24
125 Hz *	0.13	0.31
160 Hz	0.09	0.4
200 Hz	0.18	0.56
250 Hz *	0.23	0.72
315 Hz	0.35	0.98
400 Hz	0.47	1.13
500 Hz *	0.68	1.19
630 Hz	0.82	1.23
800 Hz	0.9	1.24
1000 Hz *	0.93	1.26
1250 Hz	0.96	1.26
1600 Hz	0.92	1.24
2000 Hz *	0.91	1.22
2500 Hz	0.89	1.2
3150 Hz	0.87	1.19
4000 Hz *	0.89	1.2
5000 Hz	0.92	1.2
NRC	0.7	1.1
Mounting	A	A
* Values reported as octave-band absorption coefficients in accordance with ASTM C423.		

Figure 9.41e
StudioFoam Pyramids
test data.

Auralex Products - Absorption Coefficients		
Frequency	2" Studiofoam Pyramids 2'x4'x2" Foam Panel	4" Studiofoam Pyramids 2'x4'x4" Foam Panel
100 Hz	0.11	0.21
125 Hz *	0.13	0.27
160 Hz	0.09	0.28
200 Hz	0.13	0.37
250 Hz *	0.18	0.5
315 Hz	0.27	0.7
400 Hz	0.34	0.85
500 Hz *	0.57	1.01
630 Hz	0.73	1.09
800 Hz	0.9	1.13
1000 Hz *	0.96	1.13
1250 Hz	1.05	1.13
1600 Hz	1.07	1.12
2000 Hz *	1.03	1.11
2500 Hz	0.98	1.12
3150 Hz	0.96	1.09
4000 Hz *	0.98	1.12
5000 Hz	1.05	1.13
NRC	0.7	0.95
Mounting	A	A
* Values reported as octave-band absorption coefficients in accordance with ASTM C423.		

Figure 9.41f
StudioFoam Sonomatt test data.

Auralex Products - Absorption Coefficients	
Frequency	2" Sonomatt 4'x8'x2" Foam Panel
100 Hz	0.08
125 Hz *	0.13
160 Hz	0.14
200 Hz	0.2
250 Hz *	0.27
315 Hz	0.35
400 Hz	0.47
500 Hz *	0.62
630 Hz	0.75
800 Hz	0.85
1000 Hz *	0.92
1250 Hz	0.96
1600 Hz	1.01
2000 Hz *	1.02
2500 Hz	1
3150 Hz	1.02
4000 Hz *	1.02
5000 Hz	1.06
NRC	0.7
Mounting	A
* Values reported as octave-band absorption coefficients in accordance with ASTM C423.	

Figure 9.41g
StudioFoam Wedgies test data.

Auralex Products - Absorption Coefficients	
Frequency	2" Wedgies 1'x1'x2" Foam Tile
100 Hz	0.15
125 Hz *	0.15
160 Hz	0.1
200 Hz	0.19
250 Hz *	0.21
315 Hz	0.36
400 Hz	0.45
500 Hz *	0.7
630 Hz	0.9
800 Hz	0.99
1000 Hz *	0.99
1250 Hz	1.05
1600 Hz	1.05
2000 Hz *	1.05
2500 Hz	1.01
3150 Hz	1.03
4000 Hz *	1.05
5000 Hz	1.08
NRC	0.75
Mounting	A
* Values reported as octave-band absorption coefficients in accordance with ASTM C423.	

Figure 9.41h
SonoFlat Panels test data.

Auralex Products	
Frequency	2" SonoFlats 2'x2'x2" Flat, beveled Foam Panel
100 Hz	0.12
125 Hz *	0.16
160 Hz	0.28
200 Hz	0.36
250 Hz *	0.46
315 Hz	0.69
400 Hz	0.85
500 Hz *	0.99
630 Hz	1.07
800 Hz	1.12
1000 Hz *	1.12
1250 Hz	1.15
1600 Hz	1.12
2000 Hz *	1.14
2500 Hz	1.14
3150 Hz	1.13
4000 Hz *	1.13
5000 Hz	1.1
NRC	0.95
Mounting	A
* Values reported as octave-band absorption coefficients in accordance with ASTM C423.	

Figure 9.41i
Venus bass traps test data.

Auralex Products	
Frequency	Venus Bass Traps 2'x4'x12" Foam Panel
100 Hz	1.19
125 Hz *	1.63
160 Hz	1.3
200 Hz	1.31
250 Hz *	1.34
315 Hz	1.32
400 Hz	1.36
500 Hz *	1.29
630 Hz	1.25
800 Hz	1.25
1000 Hz *	1.26
1250 Hz	1.2
1600 Hz	1.22
2000 Hz *	1.25
2500 Hz	1.21
3150 Hz	1.18
4000 Hz *	1.2
5000 Hz	1.24
NRC	1.3
Mounting	A
* Values reported as octave-band absorption coefficients in accordance with ASTM C423.	

Auralex Products			
Frequency	VersaTile Convex 24"x16"X2" Foam Panel	VersaTile Concave 24"x16"X2" Foam Panel	VersaTile Corner 24"x16"X2" Foam Panel
100 Hz	0.45	0.32	0.95
125 Hz *	0.36	0.26	0.88
160 Hz	0.27	0.36	0.85
200 Hz	0.34	0.38	0.88
250 Hz *	0.48	0.52	1.01
315 Hz	0.67	0.67	0.99
400 Hz	0.75	0.74	0.95
500 Hz *	0.84	0.9	0.99
630 Hz	0.84	0.92	1.05
800 Hz	0.84	0.91	1.1
1000 Hz *	0.8	0.92	1.12
1250 Hz	0.84	0.91	1.13
1600 Hz	0.86	0.9	1.11
2000 Hz *	0.9	0.92	1.13
2500 Hz	0.94	0.99	1.14
3150 Hz	0.97	1.01	1.14
4000 Hz *	0.99	1	1.17
5000 Hz	0.99	1.06	1.19
NRC	0.75	0.8	1.05
Mounting	A	A	A
* Values reported as octave-band absorption coefficients in accordance with ASTM C423.			

Figure 9.41j   VersaTile test data.

Auralex Products - Absorption Coefficients				
Frequency	1" Studiofoam Wedges 2'x4'x1" Foam Panel	2" Studiofoam Wedges 2'x4'x2" Foam Panel	3" Studiofoam Wedges 2'x4'x3" Foam Panel	4" Studiofoam Wedges 2'x4'x4" Foam Panel
100 Hz	0.09	0.17	0.17	0.24
125 Hz *	0.1	0.11	0.23	0.31
160 Hz	0.1	0.16	0.19	0.36
200 Hz	0.1	0.24	0.31	0.62
250 Hz *	0.13	0.3	0.49	0.85
315 Hz	0.16	0.45	0.71	1.09
400 Hz	0.2	0.64	0.87	1.21
500 Hz *	0.3	0.91	1.06	1.25
630 Hz	0.43	1.01	1.1	1.17
800 Hz	0.59	1.06	1.05	1.16
1000 Hz *	0.68	1.05	1.04	1.14
1250 Hz	0.77	1.02	1.03	1.08
1600 Hz	0.85	1.03	0.97	1.06
2000 Hz *	0.94	0.99	0.96	1.06
2500 Hz	1.01	0.97	0.98	1.11
3150 Hz	1.03	0.95	1.01	1.09
4000 Hz *	1	1	1.05	1.09
5000 Hz	1.03	1.05	1.03	1.1
NRC	0.5	0.8	0.9	1.1
Mounting	A	A	A	A
* Values reported as octave-band absorption coefficients in accordance with ASTM C423.				

Figure 9.41k   StudioFoam Wedgies test data.

Figure 9.41l
ProPanels test data.

Frequency		Auralex Products	
		B22/B24/X24 ProPanels 1" thick, 6# FG panel with GoM fabric facing	C24/C44/CT45 ProPanels 2" thick, 6# FG panel with GoM fabric facing
100	Hz	0.16	0.28
125	Hz *	0.07	0.42
160	Hz	0.11	0.41
200	Hz	0.22	0.66
250	Hz *	0.29	0.89
315	Hz	0.36	0.99
400	Hz	0.48	0.98
500	Hz *	0.8	1.12
630	Hz	0.92	1.12
800	Hz	0.94	1.11
1000	Hz *	1.01	1.07
1250	Hz	1.03	1.1
1600	Hz	1.02	1.09
2000	Hz *	1.05	1.1
2500	Hz	1.03	1.12
3150	Hz	1	1.1
4000	Hz *	0.99	1.09
5000	Hz	1.02	1.12
NRC		0.8	1.05
Mounting		A	A
* Values reported as octave-band absorption coefficients in accordance with ASTM C423.			

More Information

Auralex also carries products for sound isolation and some attenuation products not listed here. Please visit their Web site.

http://auralex.com

Auralex Acoustics, Inc.
6853 Hillsdale Court
Indianapolis, IN 46250
PHONE: 317-842-2600
FAX: 317-842-2760

REALTRAPS

The RealTraps product line is based on membrane bass traps that also absorb mid and high frequencies. This makes them a total solution for recording studios, listening rooms, home theaters, auditoriums, and anywhere economical, but very high performance acoustic treatment is required.

All RealTraps panels may be hung from the walls, installed straddling corners, mounted on inexpensive microphone stands, or mounted on RealTraps stands.

All of their products are small and lightweight, easy to handle, and can be shipped economically. They mount easily with one screw or hook, just like a picture, without glue or permanent wall damage. They can be mounted vertically or horizontally as space permits, or installed at the top of a wall where they're out of the way. Since RealTraps products are made with rigid fiberglass and metal, they're non-flammable with a Class A fire rating, so they can be installed with confidence in public venues.

MiniTraps

MiniTraps are 2'x 4', 3-1/4 inches thick, and weigh 18 pounds. Despite their small size, these are real performers that have exceptional specs, especially at low frequencies. Figures 9.42 through 9.42e show MiniTraps installed in a wide variety of spaces. From studio control rooms to string rooms to entertainment rooms in the home, these traps can get the job done.

Figure 9.42
MiniTraps in control room.

Figure 9.42a
MiniTraps in Nile Rodgers's control room[9].

Figure 9.42b
MiniTraps in tracking room.

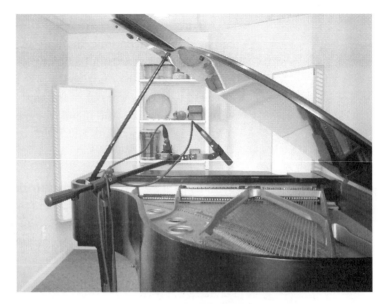

Figure 9.42c
MiniTraps installed in living room.

Figure 9.42d
MiniTraps installed in living room.

Figure 9.42e
MiniTraps in combo tracking/
control room.

When mounted in corners, MiniTraps absorb very well to below 80 Hz, and are still effective (0.30) to as low as 40 Hz. One reason MiniTraps are so effective is the air gap behind the panels. When mounted on a wall with a spacer, sound gets behind a MiniTrap so its rear surface can also absorb. This air gap increases absorption as much as 50 percent, and also extends absorption to lower frequencies when compared with flat wall mounting. When placed straddling a corner, the absorption is even greater, especially at lower frequencies, which works not only because sound waves can get to the back of the trap, but also because the air gap is so large there.

In addition to the 2'x 4' size, MiniTraps are available in a 2'x 2' model meant specifically for mounting in tri-corners where two walls meet the ceiling or floor. This provides further improvement beyond treating the regular wall-wall and wall-ceiling corners (again, the buildup in trihedral corners).

MiniTraps are also available in a high-frequency model that absorbs more at mid and high frequencies. Where standard MiniTraps are intentionally semi-reflective at higher frequencies, the HF type trades slightly less low-frequency performance for maximum absorption above 250 Hz. This is useful for reducing echoes and overall ambience, or for treating first reflection points in a listening room.

Although MiniTraps cost more per unit than lesser treatments, they are *far* more effective, so you can use fewer of them. And since the front surface of a MiniTrap is semi-reflective at mid and high frequencies, you can install enough of them to truly solve low-frequency problems, but without making the room too dead, as happens with foam or plain fiberglass.

MondoTraps

MondoTraps are a fairly recent addition to the RealTraps family. As you can see in the product data, they absorb twice as much as MiniTraps below 100 Hz, and proportionally more above 100 Hz . When very high performance at low frequencies matters more than anything else, MondoTraps are an obvious choice—they'll get the job done.

MondoTraps are two feet wide by 4'-9" tall by four inches thick and weigh 28 pounds. Because of their large size and weight, an optional stand is available, so you can avoid permanent wall mounting, and can easily move them around as desired. See Figure 9.43.

Figure 9.43
MondoTrap mounted on optional stand.

MicroTraps

MicroTraps are similar to MiniTraps, except thinner, and their absorption does not extend to as low a frequency. MicroTraps are ideal for placing at the first reflections points in a listening room, or wherever general mid- and high-frequency absorption is needed. For example, you can use them to tame reflections in a vocal booth or for an overall reduction at speech frequencies in large live spaces, such as noisy bars, restaurants, and factories.

Figure 9.44
MicroTraps mounted on mic stands for temp vocal isolation.

MicroTraps are 2x4 feet by 1-1/4 inch thick and weigh eight pounds. They attach easily to standard microphone stands or can be mounted on RealTraps Stands described below. This is a great solution for apartment dwellers who can't mount anything to the walls permanently. Stand mounting also lets you create a temporary vocal booth, or use the same traps in different places within a room to change the acoustics, or use the same traps in different rooms. Figures 9.44 and 9.44a show you some of the options with MicroTraps.

Figure 9.44a
MicroTraps installed in music room.

GoboTraps

The GoboTrap system consists of a metal carriage with wheels that accommodates either standard or "Gobo" MiniTraps. The traps are stacked sideways on the carriage to create a gobo that's four feet wide, and two or three traps can be attached for a total height of either four or six feet. The GoboTrap carriage hovers *very low* to the floor to minimize sound leakage under the traps, and the wheels are large enough to roll easily on thick carpet or over wires.

You can use either standard MiniTraps or GoboTraps, depending on the application. To create an acoustically dead-sounding area or an enclosed booth within a larger space, or for use as a large portable absorber to change the "liveness" of a room, you'll use standard MiniTraps. For more isolation, perhaps to surround a drum set or loud amplifier, you'll use GoboTraps instead.

GoboTraps are the same size and weight as a MiniTrap, and are available in standard and HF versions. Standard GoboTraps are absorbent on the rear and reflective on the front, where the HF type is absorbent on both sides. Both are built with an internal barrier to block sound from passing through.

GoboTraps are sold in a variety of configurations, as a package that includes two or three MiniTraps or GoboTraps, as GoboTrap panels only, or you can buy just the carriage for use with existing MiniTraps (see Figure 9.45).

Figure 9.45
GoboTraps in tracking room.

SoffitTraps

Unlike conventional bass traps that intrude visually in a living room or home theater setting, SoffitTraps are designed to mount high up in the ceiling corners and look just like a built-in soffit. SoffitTraps can be painted using standard latex paint to match the walls and ceiling, and like all RealTraps products, they're based on a damped membrane to provide very high performance down to the lowest bass frequencies.

SoffitTraps are 12-1/2 by 16-1/4 inches by four feet long and weigh seven pounds. Since rooms are rarely multiples of exactly four feet, custom lengths are available at no additional charge. Seams between sections are easily hidden using standard drywall tape and joint compound, and the traps can be painted to match the rest of the room.

SoffitTraps can also be installed vertically in wall-wall corners, or disguised as a table (top not supplied) to serve as plant holders or as stands for loudspeakers up to 50 pounds. When used as speaker stands, they effectively decouple the loudspeaker cabinet from the floor, in addition to offering bass trapping. Note that SoffitTraps are designed as bass traps only and absorb up to around 500 Hz. Figure 9.46 is a soffit trap disguised as a corner table. Figure 9.46a is a series of soffit traps installed at the wall/ceiling juncture. Note how they blend into the room.

Figure 9.46
SoffitTrap as corner table.

Figure 9.46a
SoffitTrap installed at wall/ceiling.

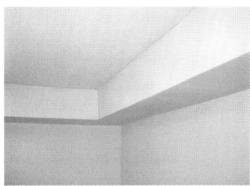

RealTraps Stands

RealTraps stands offer an attractive way to mount any RealTraps product for easy portability, and they're more stable than standard microphone stands. The stand base is designed to align the trap perfectly into a corner, just touching the walls, or you can space the trap five inches away when parallel to a wall.

RealTraps Room Kits

RealTraps also offers two discounted room kits. The regular room kit includes eight standard MiniTraps for bass trapping, plus three MicroTraps to control early reflections. The Mondo room kit comes with four MondoTraps, four standard MiniTraps, and three MicroTraps.

RealTraps Product Data

Figures 9.47 through 9.47f show a listing of the RealTraps product test data.

Figure 9.47
RealTraps test data—MiniTrap
mounted on wall.

MiniTrap On Wall		
Frequency	Absorbtion Coefficiency	Units in Sabin
50 Hz	0.05	0.42
63 Hz	0.07	0.53
80 Hz	0.16	1.24
100 Hz	0.6	4.83
125 Hz	0.82	6.59
160 Hz	0.91	7.28
200 Hz	1.5	11.97
250 Hz	1.56	12.44
315 Hz	1.53	12.26
400 Hz	1.86	14.86
500 Hz	1.71	13.7
630 Hz	1.47	11.79
800 Hz	1.4	11.23
1000 Hz	1.43	11.45
1250 Hz	1.43	11.45
1600 Hz	1.41	11.26
2000 Hz	1.38	11
2500 Hz	1.33	10.66
3150 Hz	1.28	10.2
4000 Hz	1.24	9.92
5000 Hz	1.21	9.76
6300 Hz	1.17	9.37
8000 Hz	1.2	9.6
10000 Hz	1.22	9.77

Figure 9.47a
RealTraps test data—MiniTrap
mounted in corner.

MiniTrap In Corner		
Frequency	Absorbtion Coefficiency	Units in Sabin
50 Hz	0.31	2.48
63 Hz	0.42	3.35
80 Hz	0.93	7.44
100 Hz	1.73	13.82
125 Hz	1.66	13.24
160 Hz	1.13	9
200 Hz	1.3	10.4
250 Hz	1.1	8.82
315 Hz	1.19	9.51
400 Hz	1.31	10.48
500 Hz	1.19	9.55
630 Hz	1.2	9.62
800 Hz	1.12	8.95
1000 Hz	1.1	8.83
1250 Hz	1.03	8.24
1600 Hz	0.99	7.93
2000 Hz	0.98	7.58
2500 Hz	0.91	7.24
3150 Hz	0.89	7.13
4000 Hz	0.86	6.88
5000 Hz	0.8	6.42
6300 Hz	0.76	6.06
8000 Hz	0.66	5.28
10000 Hz	0.62	4.92

Figure 9.47b
RealTraps test data—SoffitTrap
mounted in corner.

Frequency	SoffitTrap In Corner	
	Absorbtion Coefficiency	Units in Sabin
50 Hz	0.96	5.19
63 Hz	0.98	5.29
80 Hz	1.83	9.91
100 Hz	4.39	23.81
125 Hz	4.3	23.31
160 Hz	2.41	13.06
200 Hz	1.92	10.41
250 Hz	1.67	9.05
315 Hz	1.63	8.83
400 Hz	1.13	6.11
500 Hz	1.04	5.66
630 Hz	0.84	4.56
800 Hz	0.73	3.95
1000 Hz	0.6	3.27
1250 Hz	0.49	2.65
1600 Hz	0.45	2.46
2000 Hz	0.38	2.05
2500 Hz	0.3	1.6
3150 Hz	0.24	1.29
4000 Hz	0.17	0.93
5000 Hz	0.15	0.81
6300 Hz	0.02	0.15
8000 Hz	0	0
10000 Hz	0	0

Figure 9.47c
RealTraps test data—SoffitTrap
mounted mid-wall.

Frequency	SoffitTrap Mid-Wall	
	Absorbtion Coefficiency	Units in Sabin
50 Hz	0.73	3.93
63 Hz	1.36	7.38
80 Hz	1.05	5.67
100 Hz	1.8	9.77
125 Hz	2.49	13.52
160 Hz	2.75	14.89
200 Hz	1.83	9.92
250 Hz	1.5	8.12
315 Hz	1.54	8.33
400 Hz	1.19	6.46
500 Hz	0.97	5.28
630 Hz	0.9	4.9
800 Hz	0.62	3.35
1000 Hz	0.53	2.86
1250 Hz	0.51	2.75
1600 Hz	0.43	2.34
2000 Hz	0.38	2.04
2500 Hz	0.33	1.78
3150 Hz	0.28	1.53
4000 Hz	0.21	1.15
5000 Hz	0.15	0.82
6300 Hz	0.13	0.7
8000 Hz	0	0
10000 Hz	0	0

Figure 9.47d
RealTraps test data—MicroTrap
mounted on wall.

MicroTrap On Wall		
Frequency	Absorbtion Coefficiency	Units in Sabin
50 Hz	0.04	0.33
63 Hz	0.04	0.33
80 Hz	*0.00	*0.00
100 Hz	0.03	0.27
125 Hz	0.07	0.56
160 Hz	0.15	1.23
200 Hz	0.27	2.12
250 Hz	0.51	4.08
315 Hz	0.83	6.63
400 Hz	0.87	6.97
500 Hz	1.06	8.45
630 Hz	1.17	9.35
800 Hz	1.29	10.33
1000 Hz	1.29	10.28
1250 Hz	1.33	10.65
1600 Hz	1.27	10.18
2000 Hz	1.25	10.01
2500 Hz	1.23	9.86
3150 Hz	1.25	9.98
4000 Hz	1.22	9.78
5000 Hz	1.21	9.67
6300 Hz	1.18	9.45
8000 Hz	1.16	9.26
10000 Hz	1.15	9.17

* Test averaging sometimes yields values of zero for very small numbers.

Figure 9.47e
RealTraps test data—MondoTrap
mounted in corner.

MondoTrap In Corner		
Frequency	Absorbtion Coefficiency	Units in Sabin
50 Hz	0.56	5.34
63 Hz	0.64	6.07
80 Hz	1.55	14.72
100 Hz	1.45	13.79
125 Hz	2.04	19.4
160 Hz	1.56	14.81
200 Hz	1.39	13.16
250 Hz	1.26	12
315 Hz	1.32	12.57
400 Hz	1.5	14.21
500 Hz	1.72	16.31
630 Hz	1.56	14.84
800 Hz	1.3	12.32
1000 Hz	1.22	11.57
1250 Hz	1.08	10.23
1600 Hz	0.98	9.3
2000 Hz	0.99	9.41
2500 Hz	0.98	9.34
3150 Hz	1.01	9.61
4000 Hz	0.97	9.23
5000 Hz	0.96	9.08
6300 Hz	0.96	9.13
8000 Hz	0.96	9.13
10000 Hz	0.92	8.74

Figure 9.47f
RealTraps test data—MondoTrap
mounted on wall.

MondoTrap On Wall		
Frequency	Absorbtion Coefficiency	Units in Sabin
50 Hz	0.24	2.25
63 Hz	0.52	4.91
80 Hz	0.3	2.89
100 Hz	0.68	6.47
125 Hz	1.22	11.56
160 Hz	1.21	11.49
200 Hz	1.52	14.41
250 Hz	1.6	15.18
315 Hz	1.79	16.97
400 Hz	1.93	18.35
500 Hz	2.03	19.29
630 Hz	1.81	17.19
800 Hz	1.51	14.31
1000 Hz	1.5	14.28
1250 Hz	1.42	13.53
1600 Hz	1.36	12.94
2000 Hz	1.32	12.52
2500 Hz	1.34	12.74
3150 Hz	1.35	12.84
4000 Hz	1.27	12.11
5000 Hz	1.27	12.03
6300 Hz	1.25	11.88
8000 Hz	1.25	11.86
10000 Hz	1.21	11.46

All RealTraps products are tested at IBM's Hudson Valley Acoustics Laboratory in Poughkeepsie, NY. During testing, the MiniTraps were mounted exactly as we recommended—in one test they were spaced four inches away from the mounting surface, and for the other they were placed in the room corners. Note that these tests yield absorption data as sabins.

More Information
RealTraps co-owner Ethan Winer is well known in the industry for his many articles in popular audio magazines, and all of his recent articles about acoustics and room treatment are available on the RealTraps site.

RealTraps
34 Cedar Vale Drive
New Milford, CT 06776
860-210-1870
www.realtraps.com

GIK ACOUSTICS
GIK Acoustics is a small firm that offers a good-looking range of broadband treatments for a very reasonable price. If you want entry-level treatments, but cannot produce a professional looking product at home, this is a company worth considering.

GIK 244—2 x 4 Acoustic 4" Panel

There is nothing on the market that can compare with the GIK 244 acoustic panel when it comes to simple cost/performance. Check out Figure 9.48 for a sample of this product. With hundreds of them sold, studio and home theater owners all agree that the GIK 244 is the number one choice for clear sound when you don't feel up to doing it yourself. The GIK 244 leaves the room very natural sounding, tightening up the bass so that every note can be heard. Cymbals ring, while bass kicks! Four-inch thick, 8 pounds per cubic foot acoustic mineral treatment is the product provided in these panels. The panels are fitted inside a 5 1/2" deep wood frame, so even if you mount them tight to a wall, you gain the advantage of having 1 1/2" of airspace behind the insulation.

Figure 9.48
GIK 244 acoustic panels.

GIK 242—2 x 4 Acoustic 2" Panel

The GIK 242 panel is manufactured with the intent of providing an RFZ (reflection free zone) for the listening position in the room. Additionally, the GIK 242 can be used in combination with the GIK 244. The manufacturer recommends mounting GIK 244 panels in each corner and troubled low-end spots in the room (to deal with the bass buildup taking place there), while mounting the GIK 242 at the first and secondary reflection points. This combination is an effective way to fine-tune a room. The GIK 242 panels are manufactured of two-inch thick 8pcf mineral wool mounted inside of a two-inch deep wood frame. Additional benefits can be had by mounting these panels off the wall. Although there is no laboratory test data provided by the manufacturer on these panels, there is no reason to believe that the absorption coefficients of these products would be any different than those reported by manufacturers on comparable products.

Figure 9.49
GIK acoustics 242 acoustic panels.

So, if you don't feel qualified to build a professional looking panel yourself, but don't have the budget to play with the "big boys," or even if you do, but would rather use your time more productively, GIK Acoustics is the company to turn to for entry level products at a reasonable price.

Figures 9.50 through 9 .50f show you some of the GIK products in various setups.

Figure 9.50
GIK panels in drum booth.

Figure 9.50a
GIK panels in control booth.

Figure 9.50b
GIK panels in vocal booth.

Figure 9.50c
GIK panels in control room.

Figure 9.50d
GIK panels in tracking room.

Figure 9.50e
GIK panels in control room.

Figure 9.50f
GIK panels in control room.

GIK Acoustics Product Data
Figure 9.51 is a listing of the GIK 244 Acoustic Panels.

More Information
Check out this company's Web site to find additional information.

www.gikacoustics.com

GIK Acoustics
404 486 8996
Fax 770 234 5919

Frequency	GIK 244 Broadband Bass Trap 24" x 48" x 5.5"	GIK 244 Broadband Bass Trap 24" x 48" x 5.5"	GIK 244 Broadband Bass Trap 24" x 48" x 5.5"
50 Hz	0.58	0.26	0.47
63 Hz	0.78	0.23	0.45
80 Hz	2.02	0.46	0.66
100 Hz	1.85	0.63	0.89
125 Hz *	1.64	0.89	0.93
160 Hz	1.48	1.02	0.84
200 Hz	1.40	1.62	1.05
250 Hz *	1.75	1.84	1.00
315 Hz	1.67	1.79	1.09
400 Hz	1.78	1.79	1.17
500 Hz *	1.65	1.63	1.12
630 Hz	1.49	1.40	1.03
800 Hz	1.30	1.23	0.84
1000 Hz *	1.08	1.07	0.69
1250 Hz	0.92	0.96	0.58
1600 Hz	0.79	0.85	0.51
2000 Hz *	0.70	0.80	0.46
2500 Hz	0.64	0.73	0.43
3150 Hz	0.58	0.68	0.41
4000 Hz *	0.57	0.68	0.40
5000 Hz	0.53	0.63	0.41
Mounting	Non-Standard / 45° Straddle Corner	Non-Standard / 5" Off Wall	A

GIK Acoustic Panels - Absorption Coefficients

* Values reported as octave-band absorption coefficients in accordance with ASTM C423.

Figure 9.51   GIK acoustics 244 absorption coefficients.

Endnotes

[1] Provided by Jeff D. Szymanski, PE

[2] Provided by Jeff D. Szymanski, PE

[3] ASTM C 423 – 02a, Standard Test Method for Sound Absorption and Sound Absorption Coefficients by the Reverberation Room Method

[4] University of North Carolina at Chapel Hill, "How Many? A Dictionary of Units of Measurement" Russ Rowlett PhD,

[5] This error was first noted, and reported by Scott Smith, Newsgroups: alt.sci.physics.acoustics, 02-02-2004 and was further verified by Eric Desart on Thu Feb 19, 2004 at http://forum.studiotips.com

[6] Schroeder, M.R., "Diffuse Sound Reflection by Maximum Length Sequences", J. Acoust. Soc. Am. 57, No. 1, 149-150 (January 1975)

[7] Schroeder, M.R., "Binaural Dissimilarity and Optimum Ceilings for Concert Halls: More Lateral Sound Diffusion", J. Acoust. Soc. Am. 65, 958-963 (1979)

[8] D'Antonio, Peter; Konnert, John H. "The Reflection Phase Grating Diffusor: Design Theory and Application", J. Audio Eng. Soc., Vol. 32, No. 4, pp. 228-238; 1984 April

[9] Nile Rodgers–Le Crib Studios in Westport, CT

CHAPTER 10

Putting It All Together

In this chapter, you're going to work with studio design, anticipating treatments, and looking out for design problems that are going to cost you something big down the road. You'll learn how to think your way through a design from start to finish, using information you've gathered from the various chapters of this book along the way. Don't hesitate to go back to those chapters for reference as you work your way through this material.

This chapter is also the one you want if you're living in a condo or apartment and can't alter the structure, but need to do treatments. If you fit into that category, then skip down to the subheading "Studio Treatments" and begin your reading from there (unless, of course, you just find this so fascinating that you have to read it all).

If you are going to design a studio for yourself, you'll examine situations that work, as well as situations that would have worked except…oh well….

Yes, you'll examine some options in here that could have better outcomes if you're careful. As has been pointed out to you throughout this book, it's pretty sad when you get to the end of a project and have to say, "I forgot _____." (Let's hope you never have to fill in that blank.)

This chapter is going to walk you one step at a time through the entire design process and show you how to think your way through what's facing you. It will help you develop a feel for how you need to plan and what's involved with each step of the process.

Please take the time to study this carefully, because this will make the difference between your having "smooth sailing" through the construction process, or spending a long, long, time trying to work your way out of problems. A few extra days, or even weeks, of planning on your part is going to save you more than that in productivity (and money) in the long run. The intent here is not to design a studio for you (although if something here works for you, then by all means feel free to use it); rather, it is meant for you to learn to think your way through the process. It's also meant to teach you how to look at something you want to build, i.e., picture the pieces involved and then determine how you will assemble your studio at each particular location when you come to it. All this with the goal being a studio that you can be proud of and that gives you everything you paid for, namely, isolation with good acoustics.

Obviously, this book cannot cover every possible condition that you might encounter, nor will it try to do so. In fact, it shouldn't have to. Each of the conditions you'll examine will also work with other situations; it's all a matter of scale. For example, if you have a sanitary pipe that runs below your ceiling against a wall, the detail for a duct chase below the ceiling will work for your needs. Just scale it down to meet the size of the pipe. By the same token, should that pipe run through the middle of the room below the ceiling, the detail for the dropped beam will be perfect to enclose it. Again, it's just a matter of scale.

Remember, this exercise is intended to help you think your way through the process. So lay out your room, and then take a deep breath and look at each item in the space that will affect you. Determine before-hand how you will deal with that particular item; then put it down on paper and study it. Make sure that you have taken all of the pieces that make up that item into consideration. Like the pipe in the room—does your plan take into account the hangers or the bell size? It won't do you any good to design and construct your chase to fit the pipe and then have to thin out your drywall to accommodate the fittings.

Yes, it's going to take you time to work your way through this, but hey, you've waited this long to have your studio, so an extra week or two of proper planning isn't going to kill you.

Let's begin by taking a look at a layout inside of the basement of a 24'x42' ranch.

Studio Design and Detailing

Begin by planning to keep your surround walls a minimum of 1" clear of the inside face of the foundation. This should allow the walls to be completely free from touching the existing structure, even if there are slight variations. If you have an older stone foundation—one that wasn't built with anyone worrying about the inside face being nice and true—the best you'll be able to do is to stay as close as you can.

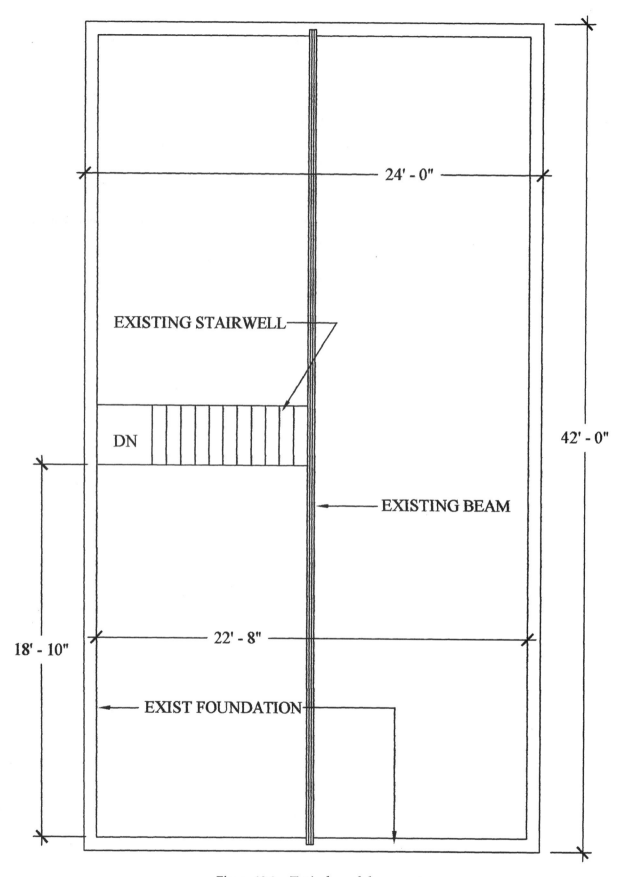

Figure 10.1   Typical ranch basement.

Figure 10.1 shows you a typical layout of a ranch basement, with a center stair that's built off the face of the carrying beam (which is typically constructed at the centerline of the house lengthwise).

Hopefully, your electrical service, boiler (furnace?), and washer/dryer are all located on one end of the house, which gives you the opposite half of the basement for your studio. If not, you wouldn't want to move your boiler, but it shouldn't be a killer of a deal to relocate your washer/dryer. And, if your electrical service is located in the other half (your half) of the basement, you can live with this.

One of the things that will be important during the design phase of the work is that you accurately delineate your existing structure. To do this create an as-built drawing. That means that you really do want to know exactly where your floor joists are in relation to the real world. The same goes for structural beams, columns, piping—anything that might interfere with your plans during the construction process, etc.

Figure 10.2 shows an example of an as-built of the deck and structural support members for this home. This is an exercise well worth doing. You'll use this information later in the process.

There are a lot of fairly inexpensive (and free) CADD programs out there. CADD programs are architectural drawing programs that let you accurately put in the computer what exists in the real world. The learning curve for these isn't all that bad. It would be worth your while to find one and play with it until you're reasonably proficient. You'll be glad you did in the end. You do (of course) have the option of doing this the "old fashioned" way—drawing with pencil and paper—drafting is what we used to call it.

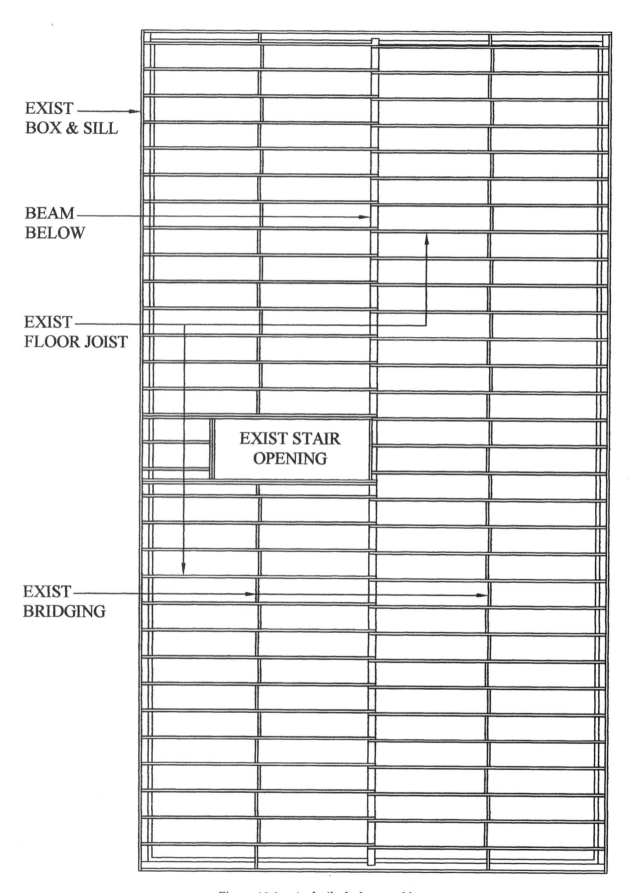

EXIST
BOX & SILL

BEAM
BELOW

EXIST
FLOOR JOIST

EXIST STAIR
OPENING

EXIST
BRIDGING

Figure 10.2   As-built deck assembly.

For the sake of argument, let's assume that the bottom half of this drawing is your half, (which would give you 22'-8"x18'-10" of space to work with). What, exactly are your options? Well, that's 427 sf of space, which would allow you enough room to build either a great combo room, or a comfortable little multi-room studio containing the following:

▶ Iso-booth—32 sf

▶ Control room—101 sf

▶ Main room—180 sf

▶ Cord/mic/gear storage—21 sf

▶ Vestibule to control room—19 1/2 sf

OK, now you're thinking that something must be wrong. Those numbers only add up to 353.5 sf, what happened to the other 73 sf? Well, as with everything else in the world, "We deals with what we gots ta deal with." The advantage to multiple rooms is isolation while recording. The disadvantage is that all those isolating walls eat up a lot of good square footage of real estate. In this case, the equivalent of a room that's slightly over 8'x9' in size.

Picture that with double wall assemblies and a 1" air space, you have two rows of 3 1/2" studs, plus the 1", plus at least four layers of 5/8" drywall total, so 10 1/2" of total wall thickness. And if you add another layer of drywall on each side, then 11 3/4".

That's almost one square foot of floor space for each linear foot of wall.

Also, a single room wouldn't have the entire area available either. You still need the perimeter wall (the one adjacent to the foundation) and a double assembly by the stairway, which would give you 385.5 sf of clear floor space with one open room, so the multiple rooms only really cost you 32 sf. Let's look at the pros and cons for each approach.

Pros for an open combination studio/control room:
▶ Larger room size generally means minimizing the amount of room modal activity. Remember that the smaller the room is, the easier it is to excite modes.

▶ A larger room allows more usable wall space and floor space for setup of gear. Many fewer windows and doors.

▶ If you're recording yourself (or you as a part of the band), then you're in the same room as the recording gear, which makes control of the gear easier.

▶ If this room doubles as your practice room, a larger space is always more comfortable.

Cons for the same room:

▶ No isolation during the act of recording. Even with headphones on, bleed-through colors the mix.

▶ It's difficult to isolate vocals from other microphones in the space, and any vocals captured from instruments' microphones make it difficult to re-dub vocal sections.

Pros for separate rooms:

▶ You can easily isolate vocals from the band.

▶ Monitoring a live recording can be done without the need for headphones.

▶ It just looks more "pro," and if you become proficient at this, you might want that if you pick up some work with local bands.

Cons for separate rooms:

▶ If you are part of the recording (i.e., guitarist, drummer, etc.), then running back and forth to turn gear on/off is a pain, and a remote control for the recorder becomes a necessity.

▶ It's difficult to set up and monitor levels, etc. if you're not near the gear (once again when recording yourself).

▶ A smaller room means greater modal activity. The smaller the room, the more treatment will be required to correct for this.

Now, this is all a personal thing. For example, I prefer a single larger multipurpose room. Not to say that I haven't thought about just how nice it would be to have a "real" studio, but my real estate dictates (to me) what I can and can't do.

In a multipurpose room, if you don't mind monitoring with head-phones, you can set your vocalist's levels so that she/he can almost whisper into the mic, eliminating the problems with bleed-through into other mics. Just cut the vocals in later. Besides, if you're accustomed to being recorded, you're used to wearing headphones anyway.

You can DI the bass and guitar for the initial recordings if you choose, so you just capture the percussion (with mics on the room) and dub the other instruments back in later. But, in the process of this, you also tend to lose some of the spontaneity that takes place when recording a band live.

So with a series of smaller rooms (still large enough for "the band"), you can set up some gobos, record live, isolate your vocals, and just go for it. Ultimately, it's your decision to make.

ON TO OPTIONS

For the purpose of this exercise, let's take a look at a multiroom space constructed within your basement, based on the original basement you looked at in Figure 10.1. Figure 10.3 is a layout of a multiroom studio set within the space. Not a bad little layout—nice control room, small vocal booth, main room large enough for a four-piece band.

By the way, the drumset you see sitting by the corner of the main room is used in this chapter just to give you a decent perspective of room size. It's a fairly large kit—24" bass—14" snare—toms are 8",10", 12", 14" (mounted) with a 16" floor tom. Brass includes a 14"HH, 14" crash, 10" splash, 12" splash, 18" crash, and a 20" ride.

This is drawn accurately to scale, so you can picture what else fits into the space.

So you just finished designing this, brought it to an acoustic Web site for review, and are awaiting comments.

The comments come back as follows:

"The concept is nice. I like the fact that you've maintained symmetry in the control room. The storage room is a good use of a space that probably would be wasted otherwise and works well with creating that airlock entry into the control room for added isolation."

"The same goes for the airlock into the room—a little extra isolation from the remainder of the house. Mom can do laundry while you're down there making music."

"But…" (don't you just hate it when that happens—when someone says "but" after saying all those nice things?) "I don't think that you've thought through all of your other needs with this layout."

"For example, your HVAC requirements."

"Let's take a few minutes to work this through. You obviously need to learn to think like a designer."

Picture for a moment here what would be involved with getting HVAC ducts from the area above the stairway to the control room and vocal booth. If you tried to do a duct run through the space at the bottom of the stairs, you would find that it creates a headroom problem, and you would not have code compliant stairs when you finished. This would be a bad thing.

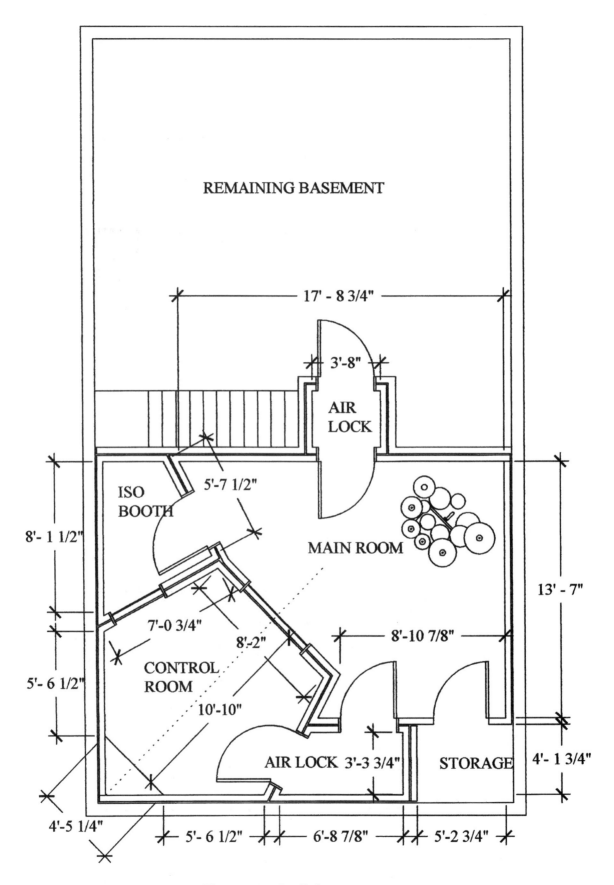

Figure 10.3 Studio layout.

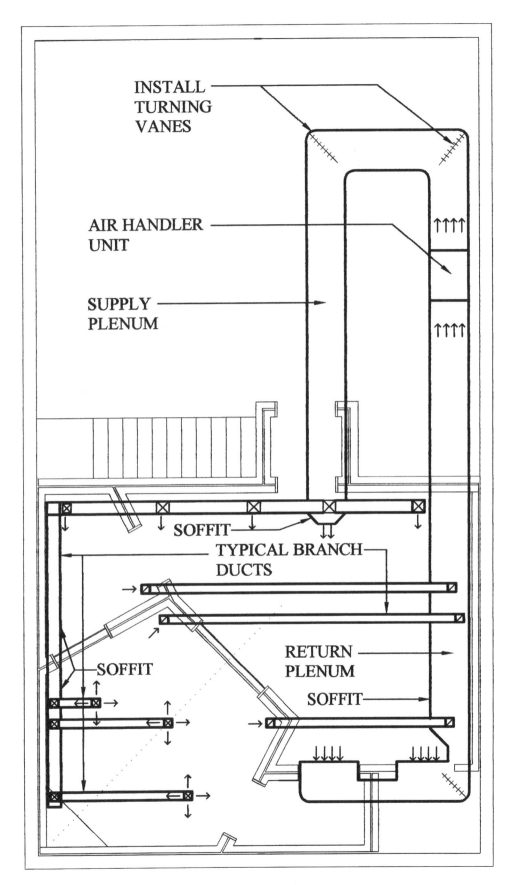

Figure 10.4   HVAC duct layout.

Ducts tend to take up quite a bit of space, and for that reason, you want them to stay away from running through the bodies of your rooms to the best of your abilities. Take a look at Figure 10.4. This is what you would end up designing for duct runs with this layout.

Look carefully at the way the duct runs through the space. At the right-hand wall of the main room, you have a return air duct run, which requires a chase to box it in. Note that in order to get enough fresh air back into that duct from the main room, you'll have to create the funny little jog you see down by the storage room. Plus, the supply duct has to poke out into the room (right above the entrance door) far enough so that you can create the takeoffs from that to the rooms adjacent to the main room. So you'll have this funny little "box out" that you'll have to build below the ceiling, which exists for this duct as well.

You can provide a push (of air) across the room from the end of that duct as shown, but that leaves a couple of dead spots in the room that won't receive air flow, so you have to add some supply registers left and right of the main plenum as well.

The supplies for the iso-booth and main room can run above the ceiling until they hit the left-hand wall, and then the duct has to drop down below ceiling height to continue. This requires a duct chase in both the iso-booth and control room. You can (as shown) install top takeoffs from that supply duct, so that the remainder of your duct in those rooms is above the ceiling.

Your total duct material requirements within the room itself will be the following:

▶ Main plenums—supply and return—25'-10"

▶ Branch duct runs—91'-9"

▶ Supply registers required—8

▶ Return grilles required—5

That's quite a bit of materials for this small space. Let's see if we can shorten that list up a bit and clean up the rooms at the same time.

One other comment regarding this layout. The beam that carries the floor above cuts directly through the window and door openings into the control room. While the window is located in such a position that there can be a work-around developed for this (more on that a little later in the chapter), the door is another story.

The beam cuts directly through the jamb on one side of the door and does not allow you enough room to install all of the isolation required.

Picture that on the door side of the beam, you have to install framing and drywall, which can't touch the beam itself or you lose the isolation between the room and the existing building's structure. Also, for the door, you need gasketing and the door itself to be free and clear of the beam, not to mention that you also need a door jamb (frame). None of this is possible with this beam, thus you are going to need to find a way to install your door without the beam being a part of the equation.

Here are the options for this situation. Working within the same footprint, you can try flipping the room layout around to see if something might work. Since you worked very hard to get a layout you liked, why throw it away if you don't have to? Because it fits within the space, there are four possible layouts that work with this floor plan. Let's look at one of them.

Figure 10.5 is basically the same layout, but oriented differently within the space. This is simply a mirror image of the original plan drawn on the W-X axis of the room (left to right) directly through the room center, with the exception that the door into the control room has been rotated so that it's completely free from the beam. This also required a modification of the wall adjacent to the iso-booth to maintain symmetry in the control room.

What about the other options? Well, one of them you already worked through and discarded due to issues. Another would be to mirror that layout with a flip from left to right, but that would leave you in the same position as the original. The third would place the studio entrance through the control room, which would be less than desirable from both the entrance point of view and the lower ceilings (in the control room) due to duct runs. So the option we're examining now is really the best of the four.

Note how the gear closet and airlock now create a passageway into the space for the main HVAC supply plenum. If the ceiling heights in those spaces are lower than the main rooms, it is not a big deal. Let's add some ductwork to this to see how you make it from "A" to "B."

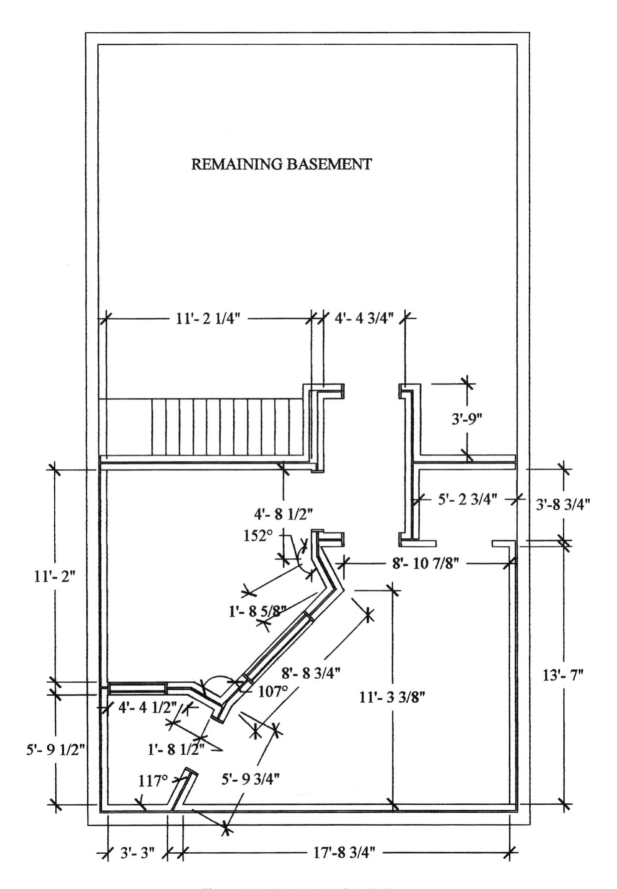

Figure 10.5   Reorientated studio layout.

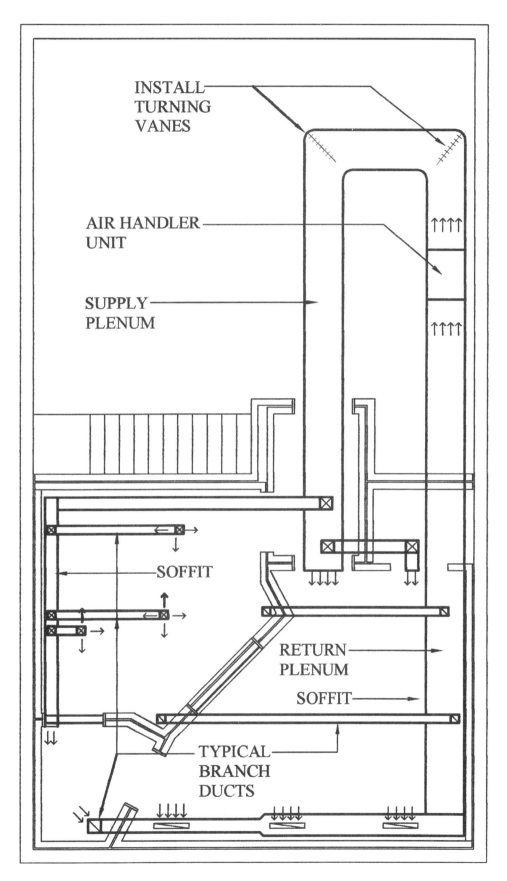

Figure 10.6   Modified HVAC duct layout.

HVAC SYSTEMS

Figure 10.6 adds a duct layout for this space. The air handler is still sitting in the house side of the basement. By the way, make sure to use isolation hangers for that equipment. The main room now has a duct chase (for the main return plenum) located at the right-hand side wall only. The main supply ends inside of the entrance air lock.

You will have a couple of small soffits required in the control room. None are required in the iso-booth, and the body of the main room is clean.

Note how the lateral runs with this layout all step up inside the space within the existing floor joist. This maximizes the ceiling heights in your studio. You can tell this because they show up as top takeoffs from the main plenums.

Note also the layout of the supply/returns. In the main room, you have one supply that ends at the face of the wall for the air lock entering the room and one small branch to the right. The two supplies that you needed on the left are now gone. On the opposite side of the room are a smaller series of return grilles (located in the ceiling), which are intended to draw the air evenly through the space.

The supply in the iso-booth ends at the face of the wall, while the return grilles are located in the ceiling.

Your new total material requirements within the room itself are the following:

▶ Main plenums—supply and return—31'-0"

▶ Branch duct runs—78'-10"

▶ Supply registers required—6

▶ Return grilles required—6

With this layout, you require an additional 5'-2" of main plenum; however, you save 12'-11" of branch duct. Plus, you save two supply registers (which are more expensive than the one extra return grille that you need with the new plan).

The layout in the control room (in either case) is perfectly symmetrical within the space. Yes, it is. It's just hard to envision with an angled drawing. Create a reflected ceiling plan (as if the floor were a big mirror), rotate the room 45°, and you'll see it clearly.

Figure 10.7 is a reflected ceiling plan (RCP) of the studio.

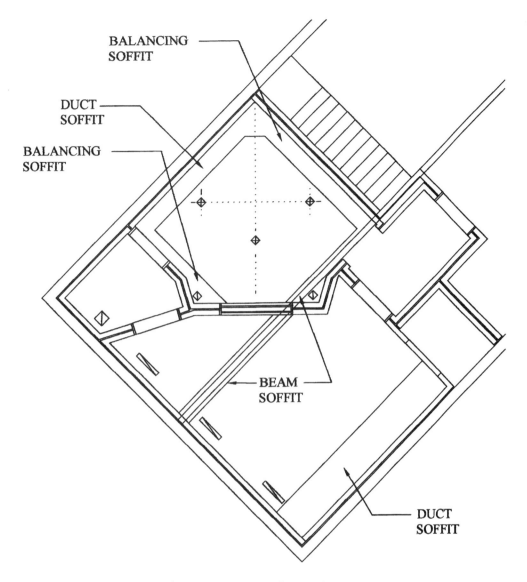

Figure 10.7   Rotated control room RCP.

Remember that inside the control room, symmetry is everything. The HVAC layout here gives good air distribution throughout the room and places air directly above you and your gear. You'll appreciate this when it's hot outside. The return air draws to the front of the room, pulling the heat you and your gear give off away from you.

You can see the soffits developed to enclose duct runs. Note in the control room that there are added soffits to maintain the symmetry of the room, the balance. When it comes to treating the room, these can be used for bass traps.

You'll also see that there is a soffit in the corner of the control room to box in the exposed beam in the basement. Again, one is placed on the opposite wall to maintain symmetry.

That beam carries through the main room and creates a dead corner by the iso-booth entrance. The installation of the return air grille in that pocket will assure you air movement to that corner, helping to maintain even temperatures throughout the room.

The beam itself is a pain—a shame you couldn't lose it somehow—but it holds the house up so you live with it. Because it's below the floor joist, it makes it easy for your branch ducts to hide above the ceiling, and you can always mount strip lighting to it for a nice lighting effect.

Learn to use items like these to enhance your room rather than considering them just an eyesore. For ambiance, you can always set up a separate lighting circuit and place some backlighting behind this for the main room. Softly lit rooms can sometimes create the mood you need to get those creative juices flowing when you create your music. Lighting hidden behind beams creates great shadow effects.

By the way, that particular beam had a column located right next to the window into your control room. Your options are to leave it, or add steel flitch plates to either side of the beam and remove it to create an open view of the room.

If you opt for the flitch plate (which this design indicates, you can tell that because you don't see a column in the plan view), then make certain you verify (with a structural engineer) that the column remaining can take the added load because you might have to beef it up if it can't. Also, if you can't get the steel plates into the beam pocket at the foundation, you'll have to verify that the beam itself can take the added load at that location. It's possible that the shear load (the cutting action in a vertical direction at the foundation wall itself) will require an interior column to carry the added load.

DEVELOPING THE DETAILS

OK, you know the design you want to use, you know the room layout, and you have a reflected ceiling plan, so what's the next step?

The next step is to develop some elevations and sections through the rooms at various locations to determine exactly how you are going to build it. Figure 10.8 shows you where you would want to do those in this case.

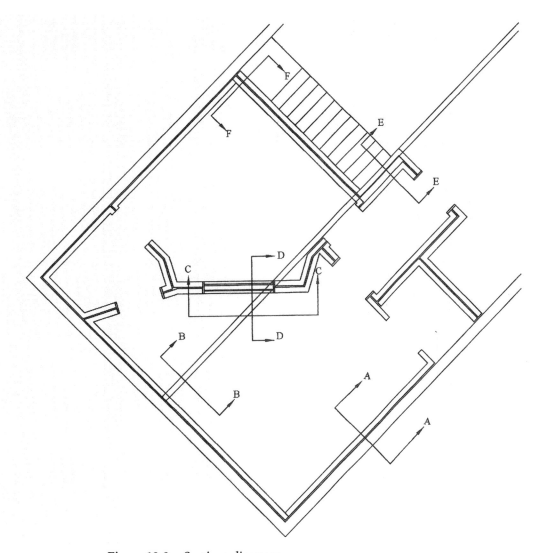

Figure 10.8   Sections directory.

These particular locations were chosen for the following reasons:

Location:

▶ AA—Where you have duct below the ceiling, this will develop a typical soffit detail.

▶ BB—Section through beam in room. You need to deal with this while maintaining isolation.

▶ CC—Framing out the window opening, while maintaining isolation from the beam (and the floor above) is going to be tricky. This will help you see that from this angle.

▶ DD—A second view of that same condition with the window/beam; this time splitting the beam.

▶ EE—Maintaining isolation from the structure above, while dealing with the carrying beam at the stairwell.

▶ FF—This view will develop a typical detail for the areas where duct runs above the ceiling.

You can develop as many of these details for particular areas as you want. Obviously, the more you develop for each different condition, the better off you will be when you begin construction.

These plans and details will also come in handy when you go to the building department in your town to pull a permit for the work. Demonstrating to the building official that you have carefully thought your way through this, and providing him with this level of detail, will go a long way towards helping him understand construction that he's probably not very familiar with, which will help you obtain that permit much more smoothly.

You also have to (based on the existing conditions) make up your mind as to how you want to proceed with construction. Is it going to be a true room within a room—with an independent ceiling and an elevated isolating concrete slab? Or is it going to be walls and ceiling only? Or perhaps a hybrid of techniques.

Some of your decisions might be driven by building codes. For example, if you have 9' ceilings, you can afford quite a bit of vertical construction, while still maintaining the 7' minimum ceiling height proscribed by most building codes. If, on the other hand, you are pressed (vertically) for space, you won't have the same options.

In the case of this particular basement, the existing height to bottom of the floor joist is 7'-6" above the existing concrete slab. For this reason, to maximize ceiling height, the ceiling will be constructed using RC-2 and three layers of 5/8" gypsum board. That would drop your ceiling height to 7'-3 5/8" (1/2" for the RC-2 + 1 7/8" for the three layers of gypsum).

The existing floor joists are 2x10 Hem/Fir #2 construction grade, installed at 16" centers. Out-to-out bearing is 11' 4 1/4", there is 3/4 T&G decking above, with 3/4" oak flooring above that over the live room, and carpet with pad over the control room/iso-booth. The total existing dead load is 7.68 psf above the live room. Seeing as how this is the larger load of the two, you will concern yourself with not exceeding the allowable load for this area.

The space above the studio is split up between living and dining rooms; thus, the required live loads are 40psf.

If you add five layers of 5/8" drywall to the structure (three on the ceiling—two above at the bottom of the plywood deck), with RC-2 on

24" centers—the total added dead load would be 13.08 pounds, for a total dead load of 20.76 psf.

Calculating[1] for a total dead load of 20psf, and increasing the live load to 50psf (for safety's sake) the 2x10 Hem/Fir is capable of a Maximum Horizontal Span of: 12 ft. 10 in. with a minimum bearing length of 0.98 in. required at each end of the member.

If you add one more layer of drywall, for a total of six layers, and added 10 more pounds to the total load calculation, then the joist would still be safe for a span of 12'–0". So your design will be three layers tight to the deck and three layers below RC-2 mounted to the joist. Your wall construction will be 2x4 @ 24" centers, double wall, with three layers of drywall each side, and standard R-13 insulation in each wall cavity.

OK, let's take a moment here to understand why you made the decisions you just did. After all, you're running through this fairly quickly, so you need to take a deep breath and make certain your choices are wise. You looked earlier at what creates isolation, and it's all about mass. Or at least up until the point where flanking takes over. If you need a refresher on this, go back to Chapter 4 and read it through again.

The ceiling/floor assembly will give you pretty good isolation; however, you are very limited in how much weight you can add to this, and you will find that the floor joists themselves are the weak link. This is because they penetrate the three layers of drywall and touch the 3/4" decking. This is never an optimal design, although the drywall does help dramatically. For example, the center frequency of this deck will be around 19.3 Hz, which will help keep your low frequency sounds from penetrating the deck.

Your other weak point here is that the walls are limited at the perimeter, and flanking through the foundation into the structure above will probably be another limiting factor. This is because you are not only going to excite the foundation with transmissions striking it going through the single face wall at its face, but also through the transmissions taking place through the slab. You are also going to have flanking through the slab from room to room within the studio. So you begin with designing your isolation to match the load capacity of the ceiling, and you will have to live with what you have when completed.

As far as the deck goes, you can afford another layer of drywall and can always add another layer to the walls. But until you establish exactly where you are, you are better off waiting until the three layers are up and you can run a few tests to determine whether you need more than you have. No sense in throwing a fourth layer into the mix if you aren't going to need it.

Now that you understand your construction parameters, you can begin to develop your elevations and sections. Figure 10.9 is the developed detail through Section AA. When developing wall sections, one of your

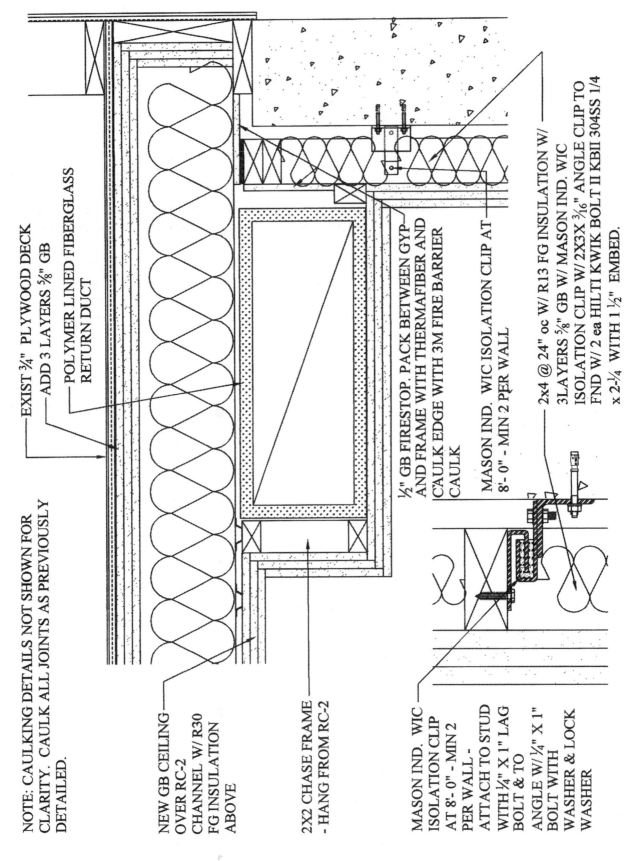

NOTE: CAULKING DETAILS NOT SHOWN FOR CLARITY. CAULK ALL JOINTS AS PREVIOUSLY DETAILED.

EXIST ¾" PLYWOOD DECK ADD 3 LAYERS ⅝" GB

POLYMER LINED FIBERGLASS RETURN DUCT

NEW GB CEILING OVER RC-2 CHANNEL W/ R30 FG INSULATION ABOVE

2X2 CHASE FRAME - HANG FROM RC-2

½" GB FIRESTOP. PACK BETWEEN GYP AND FRAME WITH THERMAFIBER AND CAULK EDGE WITH 3M FIRE BARRIER CAULK

MASON IND. WIC ISOLATION CLIP AT 8'- 0" - MIN 2 PER WALL

MASON IND. WIC ISOLATION CLIP AT 8'- 0" - MIN 2 PER WALL - ATTACH TO STUD WITH ¼" X 1" LAG BOLT & TO

ANGLE W/ ¼" X 1" BOLT WITH WASHER & LOCK WASHER

2x4 @ 24" oc W/ R13 FG INSULATION W/ 3LAYERS ⅝" GB W/ MASON IND. WIC ISOLATION CLIP W/ 2X3X ³⁄₁₆" ANGLE CLIP TO FND W/ 2 ea HILTI KWIK BOLT II KBII 304SS 1/4 x 2-¼ WITH 1½" EMBED.

Figure 10.9   Section "AA" duct chase below ceiling.

biggest concerns has to be how to handle fire-stopping at the top of the wall assemblies. The building official will be looking for this for a very good reason—you would not want a fire that began inside of a wall cavity to be able to spread over your ceilings throughout the various rooms. You always want to compartmentalize your construction to keep a fire from spreading until you can either respond to it or escape from it.

Draw your existing foundation/footing slab and a section through the floor assembly as shown, adding the interior wall and fireblocking, as shown. Note that the ceiling assembly (in this location) is going to end at the inside face of the duct chase. This places the HVAC plenum below the floor joist, located in the cavity between the two isolation assemblies. The chase itself is hung from the RC-2 to maintain isolation from the existing structure.

In order to brace the wall frame, it's important to use isolation clips attached to the structure in some manner. Although the attachment to the resilient channel is an effective means, in this case, it would interfere with the required fireblocking at the top of the wall assembly, so it's easier to attach to the foundation wall as indicated.

Note the gap between the ceiling and the firestop. Although you could place the framing tight to the drywall and achieve the same firestop with just a simple caulk joint (using fire caulk), this would create a short in the isolation system—a direct connection of the two structures. So always design to achieve the two separate goals, which are to stop the spread of fire and never directly connect the two structural elements.

In the case of the beam itself (in the tracking room where it's exposed), it's easy to maintain isolation by utilizing resilient channel from which to hang a soffit. Just make certain to keep the frames free from touching the beam as shown. A half inch of clearance will be more than adequate. You can see this in Figure 10.10

You don't need any structure crossing the bottom of the beam to tie the two sides together because the drywall will serve that purpose. It's better to install the drywall on the bottom of the assembly before the sides, which gives you a chance to verify that the drywall locked the two sides into position without them touching the beam.

These types of frames (floating frames supporting a drywall load) are better when constructed with framing screws rather than nails because the screws have a greater pull-out load capacity than nails do, and you want this to stay up there for a long time without loosening up. Vibration of loosened members, years down the road, could cause noises you do not want to hear in either your rooms or your recordings. So take the extra time here to screw the top and bottom plates to your mini-studs when constructing the side frames.

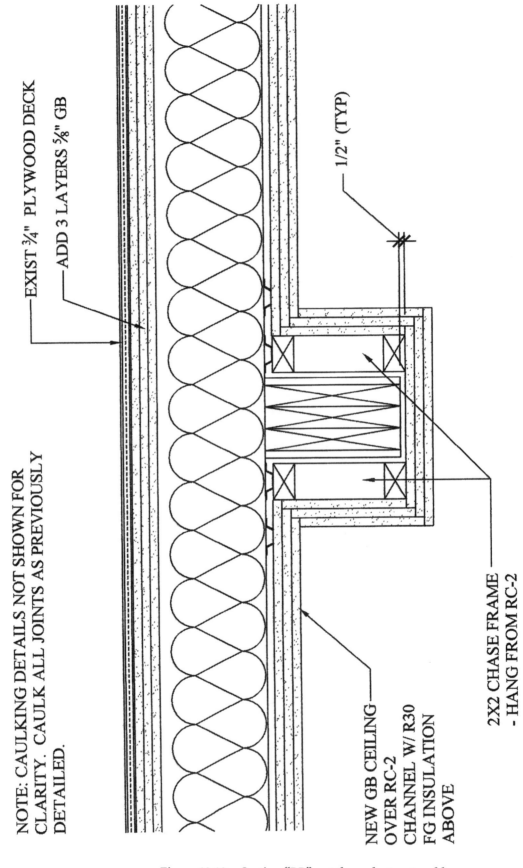

Figure 10.10   Section "BB" cut through structural beam.

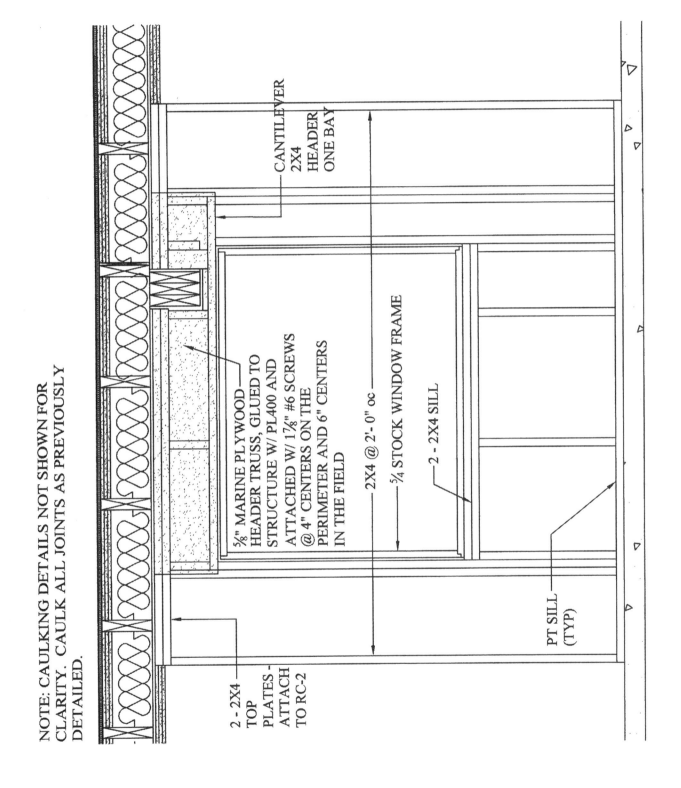

Figure 10.11   Elevation "CC" control room window at beam.

Figure 10.11 shows you how to frame out the window opening into the control room, while maintaining isolation from the beam. Details like this will help you see the difficulties involved with that area. In the case of this window opening, you have the building's carrying beam crossing over the window opening. This not only affects the window height, but also how you go about framing the window, while maintaining a header assembly that will support itself over the years.

In this particular case, it's easiest if you just let the window header (a single 2x4 on the flat) run past the jack studs (on the right-hand side of the window) to the next stud layout as shown. Frame the remainder of the window opening and then create a truss by installing 5/8" plywood attached to the frame.

I know that it might seem to you that the truss will be ineffective with the big chunk of material you have to cut out to accommodate the beam, but that isn't true. First, the header assembly is not really load bearing. (You'll understand that better when you see the next section through that wall.) Second, the cantilever effect created by carrying the header out to the next stud bay goes a long way towards stiffening this up.

Figure 10.12 is another view of that same condition, this time looking through the centerline of the two walls. Note how the two top plates are separated from one another and how the inside wall of the control room never makes contact with the ceiling.

You have effectively designed a slip joint assembly, allowing the beam (and subsequently the floor above) to deflect under various loading conditions without imparting any of that load to the header assembly below. This is why the comment was made that the header is not really load bearing. It only has to support its own weight. All of this work is performed on the main room side of the wall assembly, with the inner wall bracing being provided by the WIC isolator clips attached to that wall.

Note that for this slip joint to work properly, no fasteners are installed connecting the plywood to the uppermost plate. This plate must be free for movement. It is very important that the beam/floor assembly—under loading— does not impart any of that load to the window frame.

This will be a typical detail for all of your interior walls, minus the plywood header. One top plate attaches to the RC, and the other wall attaches to the first one through the use of an iso clip. The only difference is that the remaining carrying walls do not require separated top plates like you used here. They can touch. All of the walls will require the firestop above the lower wall, effectively closing off the gap between the two walls into the ceiling cavity.

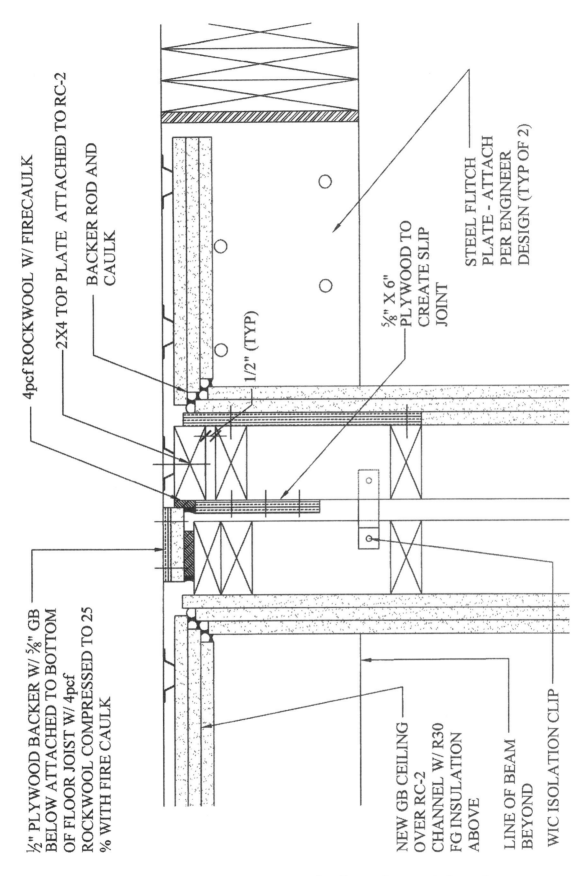

Figure 10.12   Section "DD" control room window at beam.

A comment regarding that. By now you're probably wondering why you don't just carry the ceiling throughout the whole area to begin with and do away with all of these firestops you are going to have to put in. It would be a whole lot easier, right?

The answer is "yes," it would be a whole lot easier, but it would not afford you the same isolation. Connecting the ceilings on both sides of the walls would create another pathway for sound to travel from room to room. So you would decrease your isolation by doing it in that manner. Remember that maximum isolation requires a disconnecting means between rooms. The RC-2 does that for room to room as well as from downstairs to upstairs. The details shown are nice, clean, neat, and provide the isolation you're looking to achieve.

Isolating the air lock from the house structure is as important as dealing with it anywhere else in your studio. Remember that air locks actually give you a slight decrease in wall performance, based on the fact that they create four-leaf systems. This is another item you examined in Chapter 4. However, this is one of those, "Oh well, we live with what we have to live with" deals. Remember, what you can't change, you live with. But just because we have to live with it doesn't mean that you can get sloppy with the details. Plus, the fact that the four-leaf system degrades your isolation makes it even more important.

Take a look at Figure 10.13. It's a cut through the air lock wall adjoining the stairwell.

Note that the wall below the beam is inset 5/8" and attaches directly to the beam. No problem with this direct contact at that location. The outer sheets of drywall lap the beam edge. You should run a bead or two of acoustic sealant behind the drywall to seal it to the beam. There needs to be a way to tie the WIC connector to the other wall (which in this case is too far from the outer wall to make a direct connection between the two). This can be accomplished through the use of a support made from two pieces of 3/4" plywood glued and screwed together. Clip these to the beam using four angle brackets and nail it to the backer you see above the firestop. The firestop should be tight fitting to this support member when installed.

Once again, the inner wall is not tied directly to the existing structure. It's 1/2" below the firestop with the typical detail of compacted 4psf rockwool and a fire-caulk seal.

Focus on the dropped ceiling in this space. It's dropped due to the HVAC supply duct that runs through the air-lock. The first layer of drywall on the wall passes above this ceiling to complete the firestop for the wall cavity. The second and third layers interlock with the drywall on the ceiling, using the standard backer-rod and acoustic caulk detail (which is not shown in this case, just for the sake of clarity). A simple block can be attached (to the side wall) as shown for ceiling connections, although you still have to hang the mid-ceiling supports from the RC-2, as indicated.

Figure 10.13a backs away from this view to give you a better perspective of the entire air lock. Note that the opposite wall is basically a mirror image of the one on the left, as is the wall/ceiling assembly within the closet (where the HVAC return air duct is located). The ceiling is located just 1" above the top of the door in this area to maximize the duct height.

Finally, Figure 10.14 is a section through the area where duct runs above the ceiling. This is a good detail to develop because it also has to deal with the end condition for RC-2 channel, something you haven't looked at previously.

Stop the channel in this condition before the inside face of the wall (1/2" to 3/4" is acceptable). Drop the top of the inner wall 1/2" below the bottom of the joist and install the drywall 1/2" above the bottom of the joist, using blocking as shown (attached to the existing floor joist). Pack the 1' joint between the two surfaces solid with Rockwool; then just caulk the joint between the top of wall and the bottom of the joist with fire-caulk. This is much cleaner to install than if you ran the RC-2 past the wall and used it for attachment (in lieu of the WIC clip). The reason for this is that it's much easier to pack a wide open joint than to pack underneath (and around) the RC-2.

Caulk details for the drywall joints are the typical interlocked drywall with backer rod and acoustic caulk. You have some examples of this in Figure 10.12.

OK, you designed it, you detailed it, you built it, and you're happy with the isolation. Be proud of yourself for paying attention, but you aren't done yet.

This chapter is entitled "Putting It All Together" for a reason. It's going to take you right to the finish line.

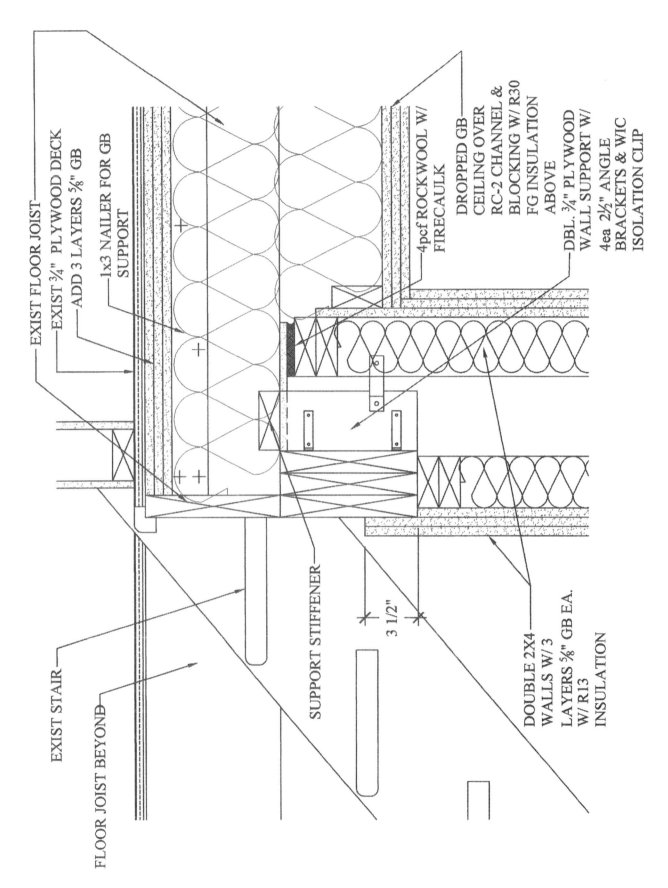

EXIST FLOOR JOIST

EXIST ¾" PLYWOOD DECK
ADD 3 LAYERS ⅝" GB

1x3 NAILER FOR GB
SUPPORT

4pcf ROCKWOOL W/
FIRECAULK

DROPPED GB
CEILING OVER
RC-2 CHANNEL &
BLOCKING W/ R30
FG INSULATION
ABOVE

DBL. ¾" PLYWOOD
WALL SUPPORT W/

4ea 2½" ANGLE
BRACKETS & W/C
ISOLATION CLIP

EXIST STAIR

FLOOR JOIST BEYOND

SUPPORT STIFFENER

3 1/2"

DOUBLE 2X4
WALLS W/ 3
LAYERS ⅝" GB EA.
W/ R13
INSULATION

Figure 10.13   Section "EE" cut through beam at stair.

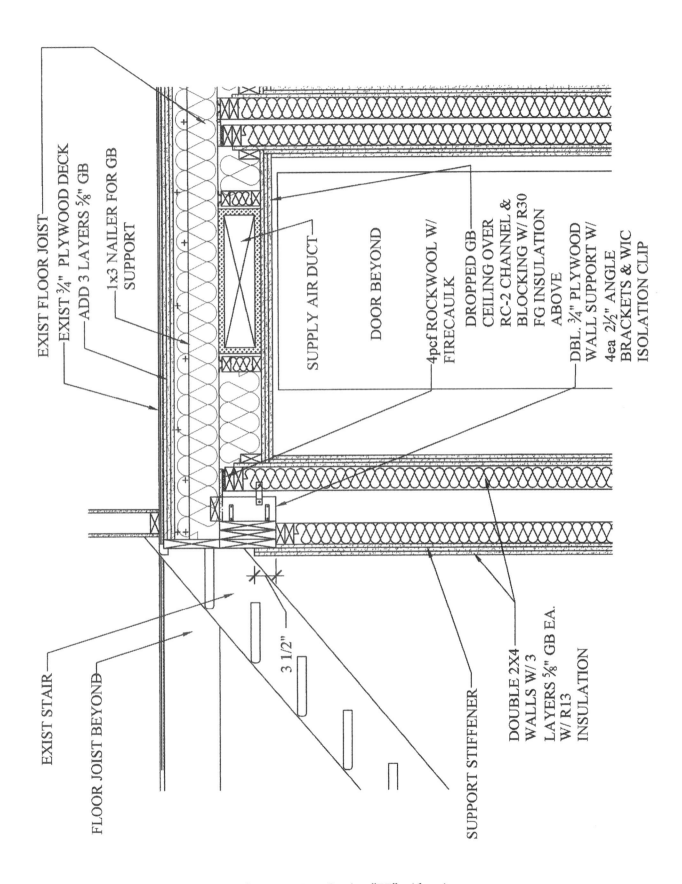

EXIST FLOOR JOIST

EXIST ¾" PLYWOOD DECK
ADD 3 LAYERS ⅝" GB

1x3 NAILER FOR GB
SUPPORT

EXIST STAIR

FLOOR JOIST BEYOND

3 1/2"

SUPPORT STIFFENER

SUPPLY AIR DUCT

DOOR BEYOND

4pcf ROCKWOOL W/
FIRECAULK

DROPPED GB
CEILING OVER
RC-2 CHANNEL &
BLOCKING W/ R30
FG INSULATION
ABOVE

DBL. ¾" PLYWOOD
WALL SUPPORT W/

4ea 2½" ANGLE
BRACKETS & WIC
ISOLATION CLIP

DOUBLE 2X4
WALLS W/ 3
LAYERS ⅝" GB EA.
W/ R13
INSULATION

Figure 10.13a   Section "EE" wider view.

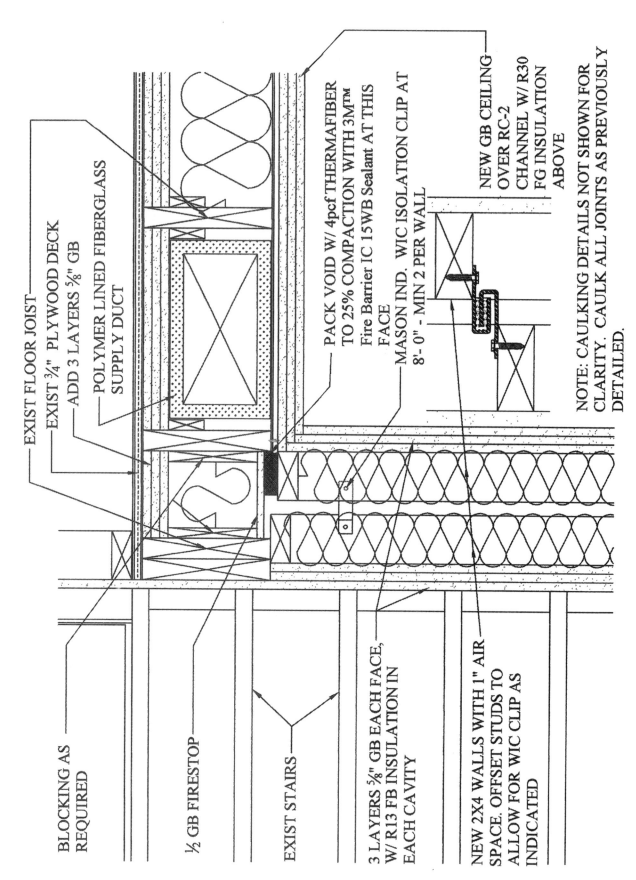

Figure 10.14   Section "FF" cut through duct chase above ceiling.

Labels on figure:

EXIST FLOOR JOIST

EXIST ¾" PLYWOOD DECK ADD 3 LAYERS ⅝" GB

POLYMER LINED FIBERGLASS SUPPLY DUCT

PACK VOID W/ 4pcf THERMAFIBER TO 25% COMPACTION WITH 3M™ Fire Barrier IC 15WB Sealant AT THIS FACE

MASON IND.   WIC ISOLATION CLIP AT 8'- 0" – MIN 2 PER WALL

NEW GB CEILING OVER RC-2 CHANNEL W/ R30 FG INSULATION ABOVE

NOTE: CAULKING DETAILS NOT SHOWN FOR CLARITY. CAULK ALL JOINTS AS PREVIOUSLY DETAILED.

BLOCKING AS REQUIRED

½ GB FIRESTOP

EXIST STAIRS

3 LAYERS ⅝" GB EACH FACE, W/ R13 FB INSULATION IN EACH CAVITY

NEW 2X4 WALLS WITH 1" AIR SPACE. OFFSET STUDS TO ALLOW FOR WIC CLIP AS INDICATED

STUDIO TREATMENTS

You spent quite a bit of time looking at the choices you have for studio treatments in the last chapter. Now it's time to look at where they actually go.

Over the years, there have been several different concepts used for studio treatments. From early studios with near anechoic conditions, to LEDE (Live End Dead End) studios (which became popular after the first LEDE room was constructed by Chips Davis in 1978[2]), everyone in the recording industry has searched for the ever elusive perfect combination of room to treatment ratio. This is a search that continues today.

First a Bit of History

The 1960s: Dead Rooms: Very uncomfortable to work in and almost anechoic in nature.

The 1970s: Rettinger Rooms: The beginnings of the stereo generation, with people developing an interest in what was happening in the room. Good rooms had front walls made from stone and a lot of rear absorption. Raked sidewalls and ceilings helped control flutter echo. Rooms sounded very different from one another, and there were some serious problems with sounds within the spaces as well. An interesting side note here: M. Rettinger was an advocate of reverberant recording studios, utilizing rockwool and rigid glass boards, as well as slat treatments to maintain acoustics, going back into the 1950s[3].

The 1980s: Davis' LEDE Room with Reflection Control: Live End/Dead End really took off in popularity in the 80s. These rooms were really the first real attempt to understand (and deal with) not only room sounds, but psychoacoustics as well. With the front of the room dead (almost anechoic) and the rear end of the room live, Davis, and those who followed him, found a new, fresh approach to studio monitoring environments. The use of reflection control helped to create an environment with better stereo imaging. Using diffusion on the back wall helped to break up room echo, while still maintaining room energy.

The 1990s: ESS (Early Sound Scattering) A design for control rooms where reflections were uniformly random, such that they have no character to impose on the listening space. An ESS control room featured a highly diffusive front end that used diffusers to scatter early reflections. The remainder of the room was absorbent, and it generally used membrane panels for low frequency control. These rooms were pretty live compared to older control rooms. They tended to have a flat frequency response and pretty good stereo imaging.

The 2000s: ? Where it goes from here is anyone's guess.

Beyond History

In the anechoic control room, the goal was for none of the room to affect the sound of the recording, allowing the engineer to hear just exactly what came from the speakers alone. This method of room treatment created a very unnatural environment for the engineer (the human mind is used to hearing sound reflections), one in which the engineer tired rather quickly. This also made it very difficult to determine the amount of reverb to add to any track, as reverb was "eaten up" by the room acoustics.

At the complete opposite of the spectrum, an untreated room creates problems with low frequency modulation (as discussed in Chapter 2) and with higher frequency reflective sounds.

So you have two extremes—and somewhere between the two sits a perfect world. Or perhaps not.

Sound is to the ear, as beauty is to the eye of the beholder. If you did a survey of studio designers around the world and had them list the design they believed created the "best" studio, you would have almost as many different answers as you had designers. There really is no general consensus as to the best studio design (although all would agree that dead (almost anechoic) is undesirable).

So one picks one's path and walks it.

My personal choice leans towards a Reflection Free Zone (RFZ) with plenty of bass trapping. This generally works well with small rooms, which usually do not have the room required for effective diffusion. So with that in mind, let's begin with some basics.

A good friend of mine (Ethan Winer) has a saying that I love: "A corner is a corner is a corner." Let's look at this as it relates to locations for bass trapping. He's absolutely right. You have already found (in Chapter 2) that bass builds up more strongly in corners and most strongly in trihedral corners. You also know by now that the biggest challenge facing you in small rooms is low frequency modal (and non-modal) issues. So where do you start with the treatments you need?

In the corners of the room.

"But Rod," you say, "all of the corners are not available. For example, in the control room (we've been examining in this chapter), the corners by the door and the window into the iso-booth are useless for this purpose."

And in saying this, you're absolutely correct. So let's step outside of the box that locks most people into thinking "wall to wall intersections" when picturing "room corners" and look at this in three dimensions.

Figure 10.15 is a simple cube—could be a cardboard box, could be a room; either way, it has dihedral (two-point) and trihedral (three-point) corners. The numbers placed at various locations with the box indicate where two surface corners are available in the room, with the letters indicating available three corner surfaces.

Figure 10.15
Available corners in a rectangular cube.

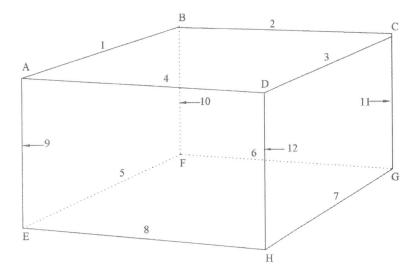

So in a simple cube, you have 12 dihedral corners, plus 8 trihedral corners, available for bass treatments. Now let's take a look at a simple 3D view of the control room you've been dealing with in this chapter. If you examine Figure 10.16, you'll see a total of 19 dihedral corners, plus 10 trihedral corners, available for treatment.

Figure 10.16
Control room corners.

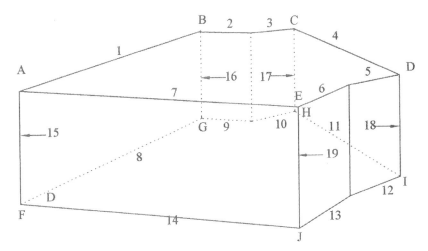

Note that six corners were not included in the list above; these are outside corners, which will not create a buildup of bass frequencies. Only inside corners contribute to this effect. So these corners were not included in either of the two or three face conditions.

Now, in the case of Figure 10.16, you know that there is a duct running below the ceiling, which runs from point A-E on line #7. There is also the beam that runs parallel and in front of line 2, crossing line 4.

However, if you look back at the reflected ceiling plan, you'll see some "balancing soffits" designed to maintain room symmetry, running from points A-B along line 1, and D-E along lines 5 and 6, which are perfect for bass traps.

You would also want to place a bass trap (floor to ceiling) in front of line 15 and add traps behind your speakers at each end of the window from lines 16.5 to 17 (Corner C) and 18 to 18.5 (Corner D).This gives you five locations within the room for bass traps, to begin your treatments. With floor to ceiling and wall-to-wall traps (located at the soffit areas), that's a considerable amount of bass treatments to get you started.

The next recommendation would be to develop a cloud over the room to help handle ceiling reflections. The cloud does not have to cover every inch of the ceiling. It could be installed with a perimeter strip that ran 1'- 6" from the edge of the soffits, creating a coffer effect for the ceiling (which also happens to work with the supply register locations). This is an effective room treatment, and it can also house some shallow, recessed, can-type lighting without the need to penetrate your ceiling. Although treating your ceiling helps you a little bit with low frequencies, it is really helping you much more with problems relating to higher frequency reflections.

You then have to examine your walls from the listening position to complete your RFZ, which means you have to determine your speaker and seating locations.

This is a small control room, and you'd probably be better off with nearfield monitors than anything else, but you'll work your way through that when you're all done building. Layout of listening position isn't all that difficult. You begin by being centered in the room left to right and with your ears sitting 38% of the room depth from the front wall.

Take a look at Figure 10.17 for a moment. It shows you the starting points.

Running a line down the center of the room, from top to bottom, is the first step. Then locate the listening position (38% back), which in this case is 7'-1 1/8" back from the front wall. Step 16" back from here to locate the mic for testing, and then lay out your speakers off this point, using an equilateral triangle. The speaker location ends up centered on the 60° lines, 1'-9 5/8" from the front wall. The location of the speakers (in this case) was specifically determined to allow placement of treatments in the corners behind them. At this point, you can begin room testing (if you desire) or go directly to placement of room treatments.

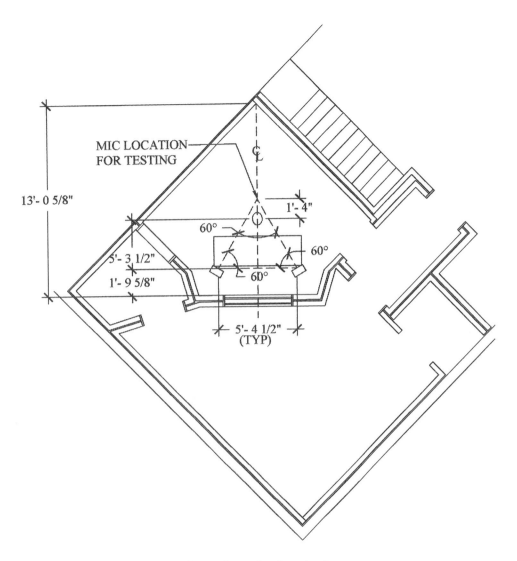

MIC LOCATION
FOR TESTING

13'- 0 5/8"

1'- 4"

60°

60°

60°

5'- 3 1/2"

1'- 9 5/8"

5'- 4 1/2"
(TYP)

Figure 10.17   Seating and speaker location layout.

A personal thought on that—it is my belief (and that of a lot of my peers) that the treatments suggested to you in this book are the treatments required for small rooms (roughly 22% to 25% coverage of total room surface area). Although you can go through the exercise of room testing prior to treatments if you want, you will (99.99% of the time) end up in the same place at the end.

To save you from doing the math:

▶ Floor/ceiling areas are 118.5 sf each.

▶ Wall surfaces total 325.61 sf.

▶ Total surface area in room = 562.61 sf.

▶ Three corner bass traps—6.83' high by 2' in width total 40.98 sf

- ▶ Ceiling cloud totals 38.73 sf.

- ▶ RFZ totals 32 sf.

- ▶ Soffits total 38.42 sf (this include face and bottom of soffit)

- ▶ Total Treated Area = 145.13 sf.

These figures account for 25.79% of the total room surface.

Thus, I would not spend my time testing when I already know the outcome. Having said that, how you proceed is entirely up to you.

It's now time to look at the same floor plan and consider actual trap locations. Let's take a minute to understand the need for an RFZ control room.

One issue with reflected sounds in a listening environment relates to something known as the Haas Effect[4].

An acoustician by the name of Helmut Hass discovered a psychoacoustic effect, which indicated that a listener can hear two identical sounds, from two separate sources, and, if the subsequent arrivals are within roughly 15–25ms of the first, the mind will create the impression that two sounds came from the first source. If the second arrivals are later than this, then the ear hears two distinct sounds. The human mind will disregard the second sound if it arrives later than the outside edge of the Hass Effect. This would be the difference between the mind hearing what it would describe as an echo versus reverb.

However, the European Broadcasting Union (EBU) recommends that levels of reflections earlier than 15 ms relative to the direct sound should be treated to reduce them to at least 10 dB below the direct sound for all frequencies in the range of 1 kHz to 8 kHz[5].

In terms of sound, 15ms of time represents 16.95 feet of travel distance. It's easy to see that in a room as small as this one, it would be virtually impossible to find any place in the room where a reflected sound could not find you within that travel distance. Just to be clear here— these speakers are sitting (in this layout) about 4'-3" away from your head, so the first 4'-3" of reflected travel doesn't affect the time delay—it begins after that.

How you determine where this will take place (which is where you will require treatments) is easy. You simply use a mirror. With you sitting in the listening position and the speakers in place, have a friend walk around the room sliding a mirror along the walls (and ceiling, if you decide not to use a cloud). Anywhere you can see a speaker in the mirror is a first reflection you have to deal with. This includes all walls of the room.

Figure 10.18 shows you where in this room that would be an issue.

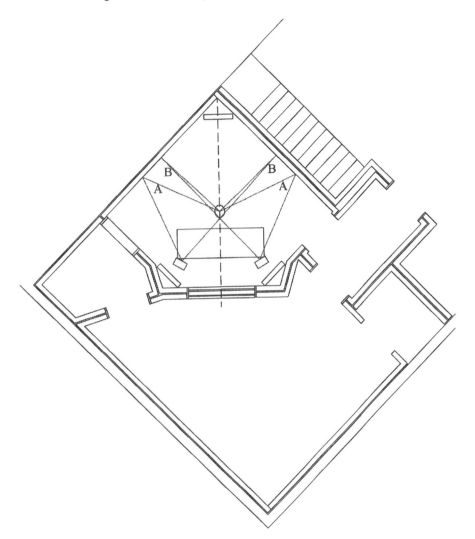

Figure 10.18   Creating an RFZ layout.

In this layout, you can see that there are four locations where the walls are a potential issue (remember that you have already chosen the three corners for bass traps as shown, so any possible reflections from the front two corners are already being dealt with). The total length of travel for line A is 12'-2", while the line B travel distance is 15'-3".

When you deduct the matching travel distance, your remainder is 7'-11" for A and 11' even for B. Both of these numbers are considerably below the 19.95 feet of travel that takes place in the 15ms interval and thus require treatment.

Figure 10.19 shows you the final treatments in place.

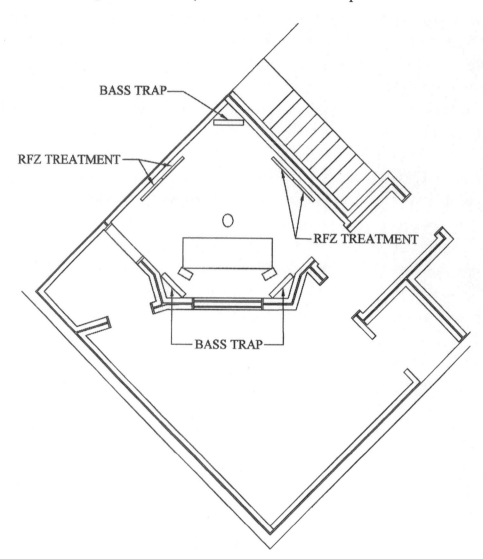

Figure 10.19   Room treatments.

One other thing—understand that creating a reflection free zone is dealing with comb filtering, flutter echo, and other room anomalies.

Final Testing and Adjustments

OK, your room is treated, and you want to know how close it is to what you need it to be. It's time to do some serious testing on it.

So break out your computer, a mic, and turn on your software.

THE UPGRADE TO R+D SOFTWARE

Doug assured me that the R+D package will be fully functional by the time this book hits the market. I've been playing with it throughout the upgrade process and find it becoming everything he said it would be. The following is a breakdown of some of the special features this product will bring to you and your room.

GENERAL FEATURES

The general features and functionality of R+D are listed below.

Frequency Response

▶ Magnitude FFT/bode response

▶ Fractional octave 1oct—0.05 oct smoothing

▶ Psychological response (equivalent bandwidth & constant bandwidth)

Time Response

▶ Impulse response

▶ Band filtered impulse response

▶ Band filtered energy/time curves

Data

▶ SPL average, power response average

▶ Vectorial addition for loudspeakers and DSP based crossover simulation (soon to be released)

Distortion

▶ Multitone with 10 computer optimized frequencies

▶ Flexible two-tone testing

Curve Fitting*

▶ Up to 75 biquadratic filters can be automatically fit to smooth and flatten a frequency response, providing filter estimations for averages, curves, or each measurement individually in the buffers

▶ Flexible user interface for generating large numbers of conventional parametric filters

DSP Xover Emulation*

▶ Emulate digital filters as crossovers with multiple driver systems and measurements providing spatial response information for the optimization of DSP-based equalizers using common filter types for crossover emulation

EQ Emulation

▶ Popular EQs from Behringer are exactly emulated in the software

▶ Behringer DSP 1124 (BFD) currently emulated

- ▶ Standard EQ responses (EQ cookbook/Bristow Johnson) emulation

- ▶ Both standard 1/3 octave and parametric forms included

Data Gathering

- ▶ Hybrid pink filtered MLS for mid/high frequencies

- ▶ Low frequency sweep for frequencies below 250 Hz.

- ▶ De-correlated left and right channel test signals

- ▶ Operates with any standard sound card containing stereo line in and stereo line out connections

- ▶ PSD optimized sweep rate for noisy (hum/cable) background noise when encountered

- ▶ Up to 32 individual measurements can be stored in a file

Hardware Required

- ▶ Microphone/preamp with line level output

- ▶ Windows compatible stereo line in and line out connections

Documentation

- ▶ Standard Windows Help menus

- ▶ SWF files illustrating actual program operation and usage

- ▶ Manual containing detailed information (currently under construction)

Licensing

- ▶ Single user license

- ▶ Commercial license (professional usage) not yet available

- ▶ Basic single user includes all functions except noted *

- ▶ Filter fit license provides functions denoted by * (basic license required for this)

R Future Versions

- ▶ Faster execution times factor of (4–10)

- ▶ Emulation of Behringer DCX2496, DSP2496 and upsampling

- ▶ Special loudspeaker filters for DSP Xover prototyping

▶ RTA operation for setting up non-emulated EQs to the R+D solution

▶ RT/60 Measurements

▶ MIDI link programming of popular EQs

▶ Compressed graphics export

▶ Data import and export

As the above features and capabilities are added, then explanations will be added to this document with an update noted on the Web site.

R+D ENHANCEMENTS

R+D differs from ETF in that it does not provide some measurements. The types of responses and measurements taken in the context of playback systems and room acoustics do not require phase response, as this can be calculated from the magnitude response reliably in minimum phase systems. It is therefore redundant.

It also differs extensively from ETF in the fact that it is a multidimensional tool. Whereas, ETF only gives you the ability to gather and view data, R+D gives you the ability to analyze that data to help determine required pEQ adjustments and speaker tweaks after your room treatments are completed.

Loudspeaker Radiation Pattern

In practical terms, when you set up speakers in your room, the reflected sound should be spectrally balanced with the direct sound. That is one of the goals you tried to achieve with your room treatments. A good loudspeaker is much more likely to give you good sound in a wide variety of environments. But even a bad loudspeaker can sound good in the right environment, *if* the reflections are well balanced with the direct sound, and the loudspeaker has a flat axial response.

Problems arise from the fact that loudspeaker woofers, midranges, and tweeters all radiate sound differently into a room because of their physical size. R+D provides an ETC (energy time curve) response that allows the user to view and differentiate reflected sounds as they originate from any band chosen by the user.

In the measurement below, a two-way loudspeaker is being evaluated in terms of direct and reflected sound. The crossover frequency is 2,000 Hz and the time resolution required is 1 ms. The time resolution of 1 ms requires that we choose a band 1,000 Hz wide to view each driver. One driver operates below 2,000 Hz, so the band 1,000 Hz–2,000 Hz is chosen. The HF driver in this speaker operates above 2,000 Hz, so the band for its ETC curve shall be 2,000 Hz to 3,000 Hz. In evaluating this measurement, we can see how the MF and HF driver perform together in this environment. An ideal case would provide identical looking curves for 1,000 Hz–2,000 Hz (LF driver) and 2,000 Hz–3,000 Hz (HF driver) with both drivers radiating sound identically into the room.

Figure 10.20 is a single measurement with the measurement mic placed at the listening area, while the test signal plays through the left main speaker.

Figure 10.20
ETC showing effect of LF/MF driver and HF driver when operating in a room.

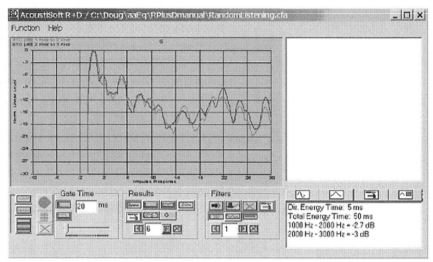

As you can see with the figure above, these components are fairly well balanced—not perfect, but close.

Low Frequency Room Correction

In many cases, after treatment a room will sound good except for a few undamped resonances. If these responses are nulls, then additional treatment will be required to attenuate the nulls. This can be done through the use of narrowband treatments, such as panel traps. However, if the responses in question are slight peaks, then they can be brought under control using precise equalization and optimization for response over the listening area by using R+D.

Remember that you can get to the point where you actually place too much treatment in a room. Oh, there are those out there who would disagree with me, but I stand fast on this—making a room too dead is not a good thing. You want a certain life in a room, so if you can get that couple of a percent there with EQ, then I don't consider this a bad thing.

Electronic solutions work very well over a specified listening area when the listening area is small in comparison to the overall floor area of the room. The SWF video posted on the R+D page at www.acoustisoft.com illustrates a quick and dirty solution using R+D to generate an EQ solution to a (approximately) 150 Hz resonance over a listening area of 3 ft x 2 ft x 8 ft (possible seated listener locations above a long couch). This EQ solution is verified to have a positive effect on the frequency response for almost all mic position measurements within the area.

A basic room measurement consists of taking a few measurements around the listening area within a larger room. A single measurement consists of the mic being in a single spot in the room, while the computer generates a test signal that is played through the speakers and into the room. The test signal plays for two to eight seconds, depending on user settings. The default setting plays for approximately five seconds.

Measurements taken around the listening area are used to set EQ controls to level, but in some difficult situations, this method might not be able to identify modes exactly. Difficult room modes may be identified by placing the mic in a corner with a sub in another corner playing the test signal in subsequent measurements. When dealing with LF modal issues, this makes sense. In fact, if you can place the mic and speaker in opposite trihedral corners, it's even better. Remember that these are the greatest sound pressure levels in the room, and as you smooth those out, the effect is taking place throughout the room.

In the case of room modes, you're looking to identify the room mode as a property of the room. For this reason, your sound system is irrelevant, and it is only the Q and Freq of a room mode you're seeking. Two sets of measurements are ideal for this purpose—one taken in the corners or around the perimeter of a room, and another with the mic placed in random spots within the volume space of a normally seated listener.

In the case of the control room, you may as well focus on your listening position. This is because that's where you are going to be for the vast majority of the time. However, a broader approach is recommended in the tracking room.

In some cases (after treatment), it may be necessary to identify one or two modes that can be found from the listening area making further measurements unnecessary. For this reason, it is recommended that you take 16–32 measurements: 8–16 around the room perimeter and 8–16 around the listening area. The example in Figure 10.21 uses 32 listening room positions and 32 perimeter measurements. This guarantees that enough measurement data has been gathered, and you can proceed to generate, evaluate, and verify an EQ solution without having to go back and take more measurements. The process of taking 64 measurements can take as long as one hour, but this is only recommended for the most complex rooms. In a typical rectangular room, eight measurements around the listening region may be all that are necessary, but you can never have too many measurements.

Figure 10.21
Identified filters to smooth the
region: filters in the bottom window
shown on curve.

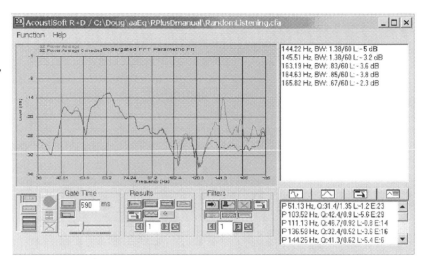

R+D identifies resonances and generates compensation filters for them, using a flexible set of controls found in the Filters frame shown in Figure 10.22. The additional functionality in the Filters frame will only be available to those who purchase the Filter Fit add-on license, in addition to the data-gathering basic license.

The use of the fitting functions is demonstrated in a Flash video that can be found on the Acousti Soft Web site.

In the previous example, you see a set of identified filters that will control the region and give it a smooth response. However, low frequency energy in a room is transmitted through room modes, and damping them all leaves a serious loss of energy. For this reason, only some of the filters from the lower window were actually applied in the emulation equalizer filters (upper window). The filters in the lower window can be viewed in the context of their effect by clicking one of the arrow keys in the filters frame. The effect of the chosen filters on the response, as emulated through BFD or using classic engineering biquadratic filters, can be viewed by pressing the arrow key in the Results frame.

Figure 10.22
Filters chosen to apply: filters in top
emulation window shown.

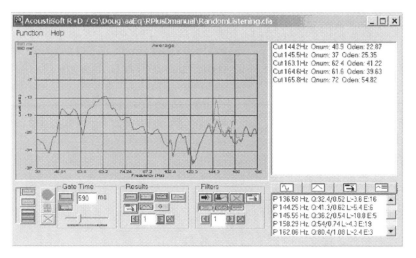

Changing the emulation from BFD filters, to classic biquadratics in the upper window, has no effect on response at frequencies below approximately 1/10 of the sample rate of the emulated equalizer. This is an actual emulation. Therefore, if the filters in the upper window were applied and the results remeasured, this would be exactly the response that would be obtained.

At frequencies of correction above 1/10 of the sampling rate, the EQed curves will look slightly different, depending on the emulation chosen. Different DSP EQs approximate behavior of an analogue EQ a little bit differently (from one another), resulting in a slightly different frequency response resulting from the corrections. Of course, this is irrelevant when the EQ you are using is emulated.

The emulation is then set to the Behringer DSP1124P (BFD) in Figure 10.23, while showing actual biquadratic numbers in Figure 10.22, which are used to design biquadratic sections. Emulation includes a third setting in which parametric controls appear with the customary frequency/Q/Level settings.

Figure 10.23
Same as above, but with Behringer emulation.

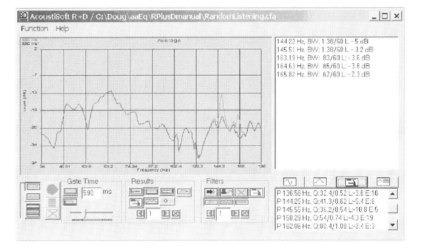

As shown in Figure 10.24, the curve-fitting function was used to identify some additional modes at 46.56, 51.63, and 64.39 Hz. The degree of accuracy in the estimation can be judged by looking at the filtered (bottom) curve, in terms of smoothness.

The resulting correction is not smooth, which means the filters may have some error in them. Fortunately, these filters need to be cut slightly (if at all). Using the above settings would remove most of the low bass energy from the room.

Figure 10.24
Additional modes.

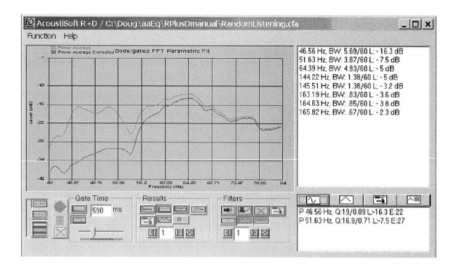

Figure 10.25 is indicative of the extent of the modes prior to adjustment of EQ, while Figure 10.26 indicates the window you will work from to make adjustments.

Figure 10.25
Modes prior to EQ adjustment.

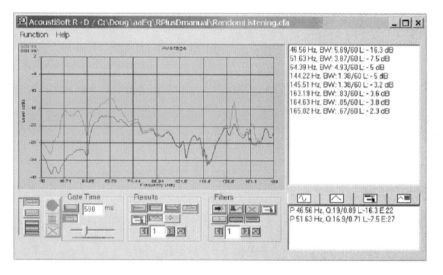

After the desirable EQ filters are found in terms of frequency and Q, the levels need to be set. The eigenvalue control window only appears when a filter being adjusted originated from the Filter Identification Algorithm.

These controls are different from conventional parametrics when being adjusted. Adjusting the level with this control also causes the bandwidth to change. If a parametric control were manually adjusted to control a room mode, Q would have to be adjusted, along with frequency, to maintain a smooth response (i.e., well-controlled time response). This is done automatically in R+D.

Figure 10.26
Adjusting levels.

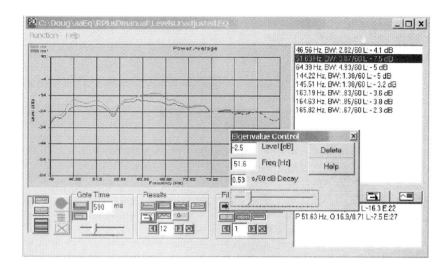

Figure 10.27 is an example of the finished product after a level adjustment has been made at 51.63 Hz. Notice the BW change for the 51.63 Hz resonance as its level is reduced. In Figure 10.25, BW = 3.87/ Level = - 7.5 dB. In Figure 10.27, the level is reduced, and this is accompanied by a change in BW to maintain curve smoothness throughout the adjustment. Note how even with the small adjustment made, the actual extent of modification on the curve is fairly significant.

Figure 10.27
Levels adjusted.

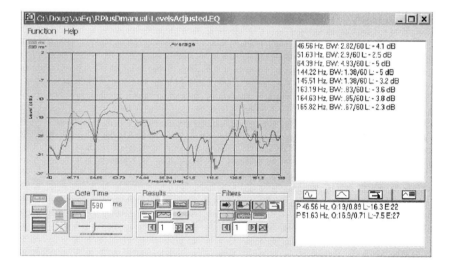

Although the lower modes were not found with perfect accuracy, the amount that was needed to damp them (if any at all) results in a smoother curve and therefore better time response, which means less "room boom" or ringing in the room at these lower frequencies. Some listening positions may contain a dip in the response due to the 140 Hz–160 Hz corrections; however, the dip may hardly be audible where the room ringing was. An example R+D measurement is posted on the Web site and each listener position response can be observed with these EQ settings in place. This is the "listening test" where we see the effect of each filter on each measurement location.

The effect of the filters on the time domain response can be observed by comparing Figures 10.28 and 10.29. There is no information here that was not in the above responses. At each point where a sharp peak is observed in the above resonances, a long decaying portion of the response can be observed in the waterfall plots.

Figure 10.28
Waterfall plot—unfiltered.

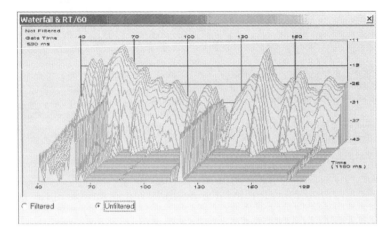

Figure 10.29
Waterfall plot—filtered.

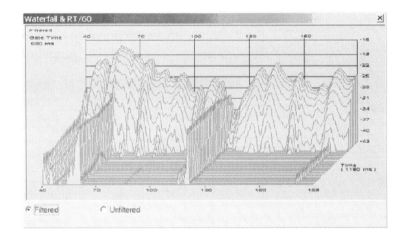

EQ'ing speakers

R+D provides full parametric and graphic EQ emulation to users of the basic data-gathering version of the software. This can be used to make some EQ adjustments for tweaking speakers. This is a difficult thing to do correctly, but can be experimented with. The key is to take lots of measurements both on and off the typical axial response mic positions and make the adjustments with all measurements in mind. After filters are chosen, each individual measured response can be evaluated with the filters. See Figure 10.30.

The applied equalization in this response seems to control two closely spaced resonances; however, given the complexity of loudspeakers, it may be several resonances that comprise these two peaks. In addition to this, the EQ adjustment affects the power response of the loudspeaker, and this cannot be measured without sophisticated facilities and a greater number of microphone measurements.

Figure 10.30
Speaker EQ adjustments.

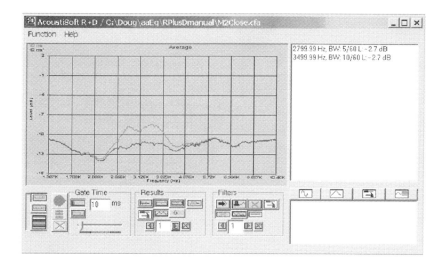

Loudspeaker Simulation with DSP Xovers

This feature is currently under development. This section of the introduction will be updated when it is complete.

Room Damping with Absorbers

R+D offers an efficient and simple way of measuring the effect of absorbers being added to the room to dampen low frequency room modes. This is accomplished by placing a subwoofer in a corner of a room and the measurement mic in another corner, while sound absorbers are successively added. The absorber effect on each individual modal peak is quite evident, and taking successive measurements as absorbers are successively added provides a history of data from which the effect of the absorbers can be seen easily across the frequency range of interest. This is the most informative view of how the absorbers are affecting room response, particularly when compared with viewing waterfall display data. It is also easy to visually compare the effect of an absorber being placed at various locations in the room by using this method. The effect of adding room absorbers can also be easily observed in the filtered response. The history of measurements shown makes it easy to experiment with passive absorber placement.

Data Access and Control

The common settings are accessible from one window. This window allows the user to set the display and functions to the type of measurements being viewed.

In the case of Figure 10.31, the desired setting is the Bode/FFT magnitude response, with a very large gate time (600 ms). This will use enough of the impulse ringing in the measured result to convert to a usable frequency response, and will retain all of the response information necessary to measure room mode behavior. The frequency response shown is the actual frequency response of the system being measured, with no smoothing or averaging applied, when this option is selected.

Figure 10.31
Options set for subwoofer measurements.

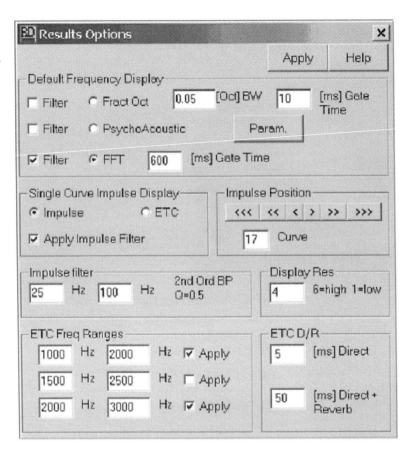

The impulse response can show the effect of room modes in the time domain as a ringing that occurs after the initial impulse. This impulse can be displayed with filters turned on to remove noisy low frequency data. This can be best used when adding absorbers into a room and looking at the effect on the trailing edge of the impulse response. Frequency data below 25 Hz was deemed too noisy. The ETC ranges are irrelevant because the impulse response is chosen as the display type for time data.

In the case of Figure 10.32, a full range frequency response of the system over the listening location is desired. The psychoacoustic response is a better estimate of full range response when compared to the others, although it is not ideal. R+D can smooth frequency response for resolutions between one octave and 1/20 octave.

The ETC curve is the chosen time response view. It is configured to filter the result, as shown with separate bands chosen for the LF/MF driver unit and the HF drive unit. These settings provide a direct comparison of the radiation pattern of the two different drivers into the room.

In this result, curve 8 is observed to start at a slightly earlier time than 8 ms. The impulse can be shifted to the right using these arrows and providing a correct physical measurement of the distance between the speaker and the microphone.

Figure 10.32
Options set for full range measure-
ments.

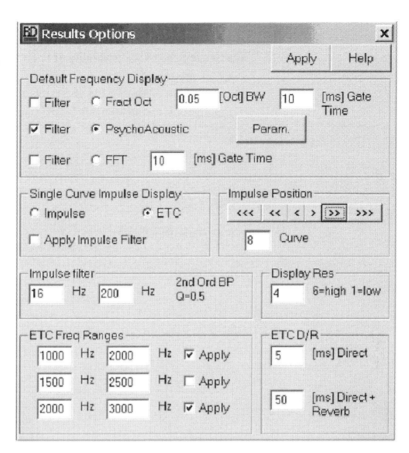

The direct-to-total energy ratio shows the amount of energy that is contained in the first 5 ms of the impulse versus the first 50 ms. This shows how much energy is in the direct response versus the immediate reflections, and it is expressed in dB when ETC curves are viewed.

THE FINISHED PRODUCT
Well, there you go. You have a finished product and can now begin filling it up with gear. You worked long and hard to reach this point, and you deserve the enjoyment your room will bring you over the years.

Enjoy.

Endnotes

[1] Span Calculator used was provided by Washington State University and can be found at "http://timber.ce.wsu.edu/" http://timber.ce.wsu.edu/.

[2] History And Development Of The LEDE Control 1954 (B-5) Room Concept, by Chips Davis and Glenn E. Meeks, presented at the 72nd AES Convention 1982 October 23-27 Anaheim, California

[3] Reverberation Chambers for Broadcasting and Recording Studios*, Michael Rettinger, Journal Of The Audio Engineering Society, January 1957, Volume 5, Number 1.

[4] Helmut Haas's doctorate dissertation presented to the University of Gottingen, Gottingen, Germany as "Über den Einfluss eines Einfachechos auf die Hörsamkeit von Sprache;" translated into English by Dr. Ing. K.P.R. Ehrenberg,

Building Research Station, Watford, Herts., England Library Communication no. 363, December, 1949; reproduced in the United States as "The Influence of a Single Echo on the Audibility of Speech," J. Audio Eng. Soc., Vol. 20 (Mar. 1972), pp. 145-159

[5] Listening conditions for the assessment of sound programme material: monophonic and two–channel stereophonic, EBU Tech. 3276 – 2nd edition, May 1998

CHAPTER 11

Myths and Legends

The Internet is a wonderful source of both information and misinformation. You'll find that a search for a particular item or phrase will return thousands, if not millions, of references. For example, a recent search for the term "Room Acoustics," using a popular search engine, turned up 7,720,000 references in a search only lasting 0.08 seconds.

That's seven million seven hundred and twenty thousand…

Now that is amazing.

Just as amazing is that the vast majority of those references probably contain information that's faulty. Ferreting out what's real and what's false can prove to be troublesome to say the least. For example, the error in the calculation for Helmholtz slot resonators that you were reading about in Chapter 9, not only exists in some obscure Web sites, but also at some universities. How's that for making it tough?

My best suggestion to you, if you want to learn more about acoustics than what you've learned in this book, would be for you to buy some of the excellent books on the subject, such as *The Master Handbook of Acoustics*, by F. Alton Everest.

In addition, there are some excellent Web sites worth visiting, a few of which are hosted by some of the brighter minds in the world. The following are a list of some sites I visit on a regular basis:

▶ http://recording.org

▶ http://forum.studiotips.com

- http://musicplayer.com

- http://www.soundonsound.com

- http://johnlsayers.com

- http://pmiaudio.com

Note that the "studiotips" forum is strictly dedicated to acoustics, and the site from John L. Sayers is devoted to studio acoustics and design. The remaining forums have a fairly wide range of material available relating to many different aspects of the recording world, including recording techniques. Just beware of the "Internet experts," people whose only claim to fame and expertise rests on their ability to post something where everyone in the world can see it.

Some Popular Myths and Legends

What is a myth? The definition that affects us in some manner in acoustics follows:

Main Entry: **myth**
Pronunciation: 'mith
Function: *noun*
Etymology: Greek *mythos*

"A thing having only an imaginary or unverifiable existence."

Let's take a walk through some of the more popular myths relating to sound isolation and acoustic treatments making their way through the Internet today.

FIBERGLASS
Are fiberglass (and glass wool-fiber) products carcinogens? Or are they safe materials to use in home studios?

Well, it all depends on who tells the stories.

Background Information
In the early 1990s, it was announced that fiberglass had been classified as a "possible carcinogen," and that products used in the HVAC industry (such as fiberglass ductboard) could be putting people in danger. This was due to the possibility of small fibers breaking free (from the body of the duct) and entering rooms that were being treated by the HVAC systems. In those rooms, this material could then be taken into the body through the respiratory process and lodge in the lungs. The concern was similar to problems relating to asbestos.

Seeing as how I take the well-being of people very seriously, it was immediately announced that unprotected fiberglass ductboard would no longer be allowed on any project—residential or otherwise—that I was involved with. However, the installation of polymer-lined ductboards would be acceptable. This was due to the polymer lining's ability to hold glass fibers in place.

I followed the track of this investigation throughout the '90s into the present and offer the following from the International Agency for Research on Cancer (IARC):

"Direct contact with fiberglass materials or exposure to airborne fiberglass dust may irritate the skin, eyes, nose and throat. Fiberglass can cause itching due to mechanical irritation from the fibers. This is not an allergic reaction to the material. Breathing fibers may irritate the airways resulting in coughing and a scratchy throat. Some people are sensitive to the fibers, while others are not. Fiberglass insulation packages display cancer warning labels. These labels are required by the U.S. Occupational Safety and Health Administration (OSHA) based on determinations made by the International Agency for Research on Cancer (IARC) and the National Toxicology Program (NTP).

1994—NTP listed fiberglass as "reasonably anticipated to be a human carcinogen" based on animal data.

1998—The American Conference of Governmental Industrial Hygienists reviewed the available literature and concluded glass wool to be "carcinogenic in experimental animals at a relatively high dose, by route(s) of administration, at site(s), of histologic type(s) or by mechanism(s) that are not considered relevant to worker exposures".

1999—OSHA and the manufacturers voluntarily agreed on ways to control workplace exposures to avoid irritation. As a result, OSHA has stated that it does not intend to regulate exposure to fiberglass insulation. The voluntary agreement, known as the Health & Safety Partnership Program, includes a recommended exposure level of 1.0 fiber per cubic centimeter (f/cc) based on an 8-hour workday and provides comprehensive work practices.

2000—The National Academy of Sciences (NAS) reported that epidemiological studies of glass fiber manufacturing workers indicate "glass fibers do not appear to increase the risk of respiratory system cancer." The NAS supported the exposure limit of 1.0 f/cc that has been the industry recommendation since the early 1990s.

2001—The IARC working group revised their previous classification of glass wool being a possible carcinogen. It is currently considered not classifiable as a human carcinogen. Studies done in the past 15 years since the previous report was released, do not provide enough evidence to link this material to any cancer risk." [1]

I also want to reference the following studies, which draw the same conclusions:

Agency for Toxic Substances and Disease Registry. Technical Briefing Paper: Health Effects from Exposure to Fibrous Glass, Rock Wool or Slag Wool. Agency for Toxic Substances and Disease Registry, U.S. Department of Health and Human Services, Atlanta, GA, 2002.

National Toxicology Program. Glasswool in Report on Carcinogens, 9th Edition. U.S. Department of Health and Human Services, National Toxicology Program, Research Triangle Park, NC, 2001.

Man-Made Vitreous Fibres, Special-purpose glass fibres such as E-glass and '475' glass fibres (Group 2B), Refractory ceramic fibres (Group 2B), Insulation glass wool (Group 3), Continuous glass filament (Group 3), Rock (stone) wool (Group 3), Slag wool (Group 3), Vol.: 81 (2002), International Agency for Research on Cancer, World Health Organization, Lyon, France.

The above information notwithstanding, there are still those out there, including Web sites, which would appear to be (otherwise) "legitimate" sources of information, that make serious claims to the contrary. Simply put—they are wrong.

My Advice
So, for you, here is my advice when it comes to fiberglass.

When working with any glass fiber products, wear long-sleeved shirts with the collar and sleeves buttoned. Wear a dust mask and safety goggles.

Under normal conditions, once the glass panels are fabric wrapped, the fibers should be contained within.

When work is completed, use a vacuum cleaner to clean up any stray particles. Do not use a broom to clean up fiberglass dust, as this will raise and redistribute a large amount of particles. If available, a vacuum cleaner with a HEPA filter is the best way to go.

Common sense dictates that you wouldn't want to dump this stuff in your body, but with a little bit of care, it's perfectly safe to work with and have in a home environment.

EGG CRATES AND OTHER GREAT ACOUSTIC TREATMENTS

It's amazing the number of otherwise intelligent people who make comments such as:

"If you want great acoustic treatments for cheap money, use egg crates."

"If you want great acoustic treatments for cheap money, just stick used carpet on your walls."

"If you want great acoustic treatments for cheap money, there's nothing like packing foam, after all—foam is foam."

"If you want great acoustic treatments for cheap money, put some mattresses up against your walls."

(You could fill up a book with comments like these)

Always followed by:

"I know, because I did it, and now my room is perfect."

Let's take a minute and examine these claims that they say work.

Although I have never found any test data for mattresses or packing foam, there is test data for egg crates and carpet. Acoustics First Corporation (formerly Alpha Audio) had egg crates tested at Riverbanks back in 1988, and following are the results.[2]

RIVERBANK ACOUSTICAL LABORATORIES

OF

IIT RESEARCH INSTITUTE

1512 BATAVIA AVENUE
GENEVA, ILLINOIS 60134

REPORT

312/232-0104
FOUNDED 1918 BY
WALLACE CLEMENT SABINE

FOR: Alpha Audio

ON: Egg Crates

Sound Absorption Test
RAL™-A88-80

Page 1 of 4

CONDUCTED: 28 March 1988

TEST METHOD

The test method conformed explicitly with the requirements of the ASTM Standard Test Method for Sound Absorption and Sound Absorption Coefficients by the Reverberation Room Method: ASTM C423-84a and E795-83. Riverbank Acoustical Laboratories has been accredited by the U.S. Department of Commerce, National Bureau of Standards under the National Voluntary Laboratory Accreditation Program (NVLAP) for this test procedure. A description of the measuring technique is available separately. The microphone used was a Bruel & Kjaer serial number 1330658.

DESCRIPTION OF THE SPECIMEN

The test specimen was designated by the client as egg crates. The overall dimensions of the specimen as measured were 2.34 m (92 in.) wide by 2.63 m (103.5 in.) long and nominally 5.1 cm (2 in.) high. The specimen was tested in the laboratory's 292 m^3 (10,311 ft^3) test chamber. The weight of the specimen as measured was 4.5 kg (10.0 lbs) an average of 0.73 kg/m^2 (0.15 lbs/ft^2). The area used in the calculations was 6.14 m^2 (66.1 ft^2). The room temperature at the time of the test was 21°C (69°F) and 61% relative humidity.

PRECONDITIONING

The specimen was held at least 24 hours under the test conditions of 21°C (70°F) and 60% relative humidity.

MOUNTING A

The test specimen was laid directly against the test surface.

RIVERBANK ACOUSTICAL LABORATORIES

OF

1512 BATAVIA AVENUE **GENEVA, ILLINOIS 60134**	**IIT RESEARCH INSTITUTE** **REPORT**	**312/232-0104** **FOUNDED 1918 BY** **WALLACE CLEMENT SABINE**

Alpha Audio

RAL™-A88-80

28 March 1988

Page 2 of 4

TEST RESULTS

1/3 Octave Center Center Frequency (Hz)	Absorption Coefficient	Total Absorption In Sabins	% Of Uncertainty With 95% Confidence Limit
100	0.00	0.02	0.95
** 125	0.01	0.95	0.93
160	0.00	0.00	0.97
200	0.07	4.62	0.96
** 250	0.07	4.90	1.10
315	0.07	4.44	1.08
400	0.13	8.60	1.08
** 500	0.44	29.15	0.78
630	0.73	48.30	0.71
800	0.74	48.64	0.69
** 1000	0.61	40.59	0.70
1250	0.52	34.51	0.68
1600	0.46	30.27	0.74
** 2000	0.48	31.88	0.71
2500	0.58	38.17	0.72
3150	0.59	38.73	0.72
** 4000	0.69	45.38	0.65
5000	0.82	54.14	0.66

NRC = .40

RIVERBANK ACOUSTICAL LABORATORIES

OF

IIT RESEARCH INSTITUTE

**1512 BATAVIA AVENUE
GENEVA, ILLINOIS 60134**

REPORT

**312/232-0104
FOUNDED 1918 BY
WALLACE CLEMENT SABINE**

Alpha Audio

RAL™-A88-80

28 March 1988

Page 3 of 4

TEST RESULTS (con't)

The percentage of uncertainty for the required 95% confidence limits indicated above must fall within the prescribed limits designated in par. 13.2 of ASTM C423-84a. It states that for the absorption of the reverberation room containing the specimen the testing laboratory shall obtain data with less than 4% uncertainty at 125 (hertz) and 2% uncertainty at 250, 500, 1000, 2000, and 4000 (hertz). The method of calculation is described in ASTM STP 15D and outlined in section 13 of the standard.

The noise reduction coefficient (NRC) is the average of the coefficients at 250, 500, 1000, and 2000 Hz, expressed to the nearest integral multiple of 0.05.

Reviewed by Diane C. Perrone   Submitted by Peter E. Straus
Diane C. Perrone   Peter E. Straus
Senior Technician   Senior Technician

RIVERBANK ACOUSTICAL LABORATORIES

OF

1512 BATAVIA AVENUE
GENEVA, ILLINOIS 60134

IIT RESEARCH INSTITUTE

REPORT

312/232-0104
FOUNDED 1918 BY
WALLACE CLEMENT SABINE

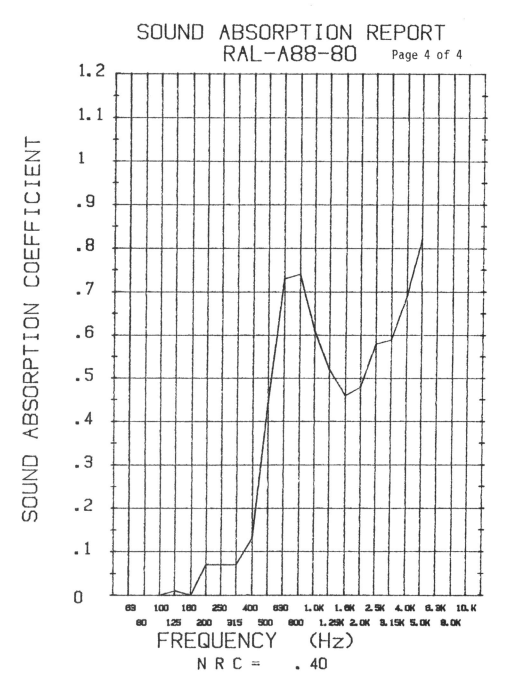

SOUND ABSORPTION REPORT
RAL-A88-80   Page 4 of 4

NRC =   .40

As you can see from the test reports, in the lower frequency ranges in particular, egg crates offer little value for absorption. At best, they can knock down a bit of mid/high frequencies, but this will leave your room muddy in the end.

Figure 11.1 is a side-by-side comparison of the absorption coefficients of egg crates and Auralex 2" Sonomatt Eggcrate style foam.

1/3 Octave Center Center Frequency (Hz)	Egg Crates	Sonomatt	Variance	Variance as Percentage
100	0.00	0.08	0.08	0.00%
** 125	0.01	0.13	0.12	7.69%
160	0.00	0.14	0.14	0.00%
200	0.07	0.2	0.13	35.00%
** 250	0.07	0.27	0.20	25.93%
315	0.07	0.35	0.28	20.00%
400	0.13	0.47	0.34	27.66%
** 500	0.44	0.62	0.18	70.97%
630	0.73	0.75	0.02	97.33%
800	0.74	0.85	0.11	87.06%
** 1000	0.61	0.92	0.31	66.30%
1250	0.52	0.96	0.44	54.17%
1600	0.46	1.01	0.55	45.54%
** 2000	0.48	1.02	0.54	47.06%
2500	0.58	1	0.42	58.00%
3150	0.59	1.02	0.43	57.84%
** 4000	0.69	1.02	0.33	67.65%
5000	0.82	1.06	0.24	77.36%
Mounting	A	A		

**   Values reported as octave-band absorption coefficients in accordance with ASTM C423.

Figure 11.1   Absorption coefficient comparison between egg crates and Auralex Sonomatt.

Note that from 200 Hz and down, egg crates offer little or no value for sound absorption. There was some small value at 250, 315, and 400 Hz, although you would use three to five times as many egg crates to achieve the same value as the Auralex Product. Again, almost no value from 500 through 800 Hz. At 630 Hz, they are almost identical, but then the numbers begin to fall off again—with the Auralex product performing nearly two to four times more efficiently than standard egg crates.

Even more telling is the percentage of confidence in the test results themselves. The last page of the report gives the standard ASTM used at the time of the testing of the egg crates. The requirement for uncertainty at 125 Hz was 4% and was only 2% for 250, 500, 1,000, 2,000, and 4,000 (hertz). The intent of this was to demonstrate that there was a 95% certainty that the test results could be duplicated at this or any other test facility. Yet, the only frequencies that exhibit certainty are the low frequencies, i.e., 125 and 250 Hz. The remaining frequencies fail the repeatability requirements for uncertainty. And you have basically no absorption value at 125 and 250 Hz.

So the myth is put to bed. Even if the uncertainty factor did not come into play, the more material you place on the wall, the more you suck the mids and highs out of the room, leaving the bass modal issues, which you know are the biggest issues in small rooms.

Even if you got all of the egg crates for free, after the cost of treating them so they would be flame retardant, if you compare the total costs per sabins for performance to achieve the results you require, you'll find that this is not an effective means of room treatment.

Oh, one other thing regarding egg crates—the people who tell you how great they are will say that part of the reason they actually work better than test results indicate (this because they can "hear the difference," mind you) is due to the fact that they are diffusors, as well as absorbers.

Well, you've studied the concepts behind diffusors and know that these perfectly symmetrical little egg carriers wouldn't work well for that purpose (they are very narrow in the band they would diffuse based on their geometry), so you can straighten them out about that if they try to sell you on the subject.

CARPETS

Carpet, when placed on the walls of studios, can attenuate mid and some higher frequencies (the same as it will do on a floor), but is (again) not the answer for low frequencies.

This too is coupled with the fact that carpet is not made to be put on walls (with the exception of some Berber carpets that have test data certifying them for that purpose).

Figure 11.2 is from the Carpet and Rug Institute regarding the acoustic value of carpet:[3]

Test Series A-1: Carpet was placed directly on the concrete floor of the test chamber.

TEST A-1 Commercial Carpet Laid Directly on Concrete				
Test Variables	Pile Weight oz/sy	Pile Height Inches	Surface	NRC
Identical construction, different manufacturer	44	0.25	Loop	0.3
	44	0.25	Loop	0.3
	44	0.25	Loop	0.3
Identical construction, different pile surfaces	35	0.175	Loop	0.3
	35	0.175	Cut	0.35
Pile weight/height relationships in cut pile carpet	32	0.562	Cut nylon	0.5
	36	0.43	Cut acrylic	0.5
	43	0.5	Cut wool	0.55
Increasing pile weight/height relationships in woven wool loop pile carpet	44	0.25	Loop	0.3
	66	0.375	Loop	0.4
	88	0.5	Loop	0.4
Increasing pile weight (pile height constant) in tufted loop pile carpet	15	0.25	Loop nylon	0.25
	40	0.25	Loop wool	0.35
	60	0.25	Loop wool	0.3
Varying pile height (pile weight constant) loop pile with regular back		0.125	Loop	0.15
		0.187	Loop	0.2
		0.25	Loop	0.25
		0.437	Loop	0.35
Varying pile height (pile weight constant) loop pile with foam back		0.187	Loop	0.25
		0.25	Loop	0.3
		0.312	Loop	0.35
		0.437	Loop	0.4

Observations: A-1

1. Carpet tested in this program, which were laid directly on concrete, had NRCs ranging between .15 and .55.
2. It was found that when manufacturers met identical specifications, their fabrics have the same NRCs. However, the sound absorption coefficients at individual frequencies varied somewhat.
3. Cut pile carpet, because it provides more "fuzz", provides a greater NRC than loop pile construction in otherwise identical specifications.
4. As pile weight and/or pile height increases in cut pile construction, the NRC may not change substantially.
5. Increasing pile weight while increasing or holding pile height constant in loop pile construction resulted in sound absorption "topping out" because the surface does not change in absorptivity at higher frequencies.
6. Increasing pile height while holding pile weight constant in loop pile fabrics results in improvements in absorption. Loop pile carpets average NRC values of .20 to .35.
7. Foam backed loop construction resulted in an increased NRC value compared to conventional secondary backed carpet.

Page 6 of 8

CRI Technical Bulletin: Acoustical Characteristics of Carpet (0/00)

Figure 11.2   Noise reduction coefficient on carpet.

Note that the NRC (noise reduction coefficient) for carpet is fairly low, especially when you consider that the only carpet you can put on walls is Berber carpet (or at least those Berber carpets that have been tested and approved). Berber carpet comes under the variable heading "increasing pile weight/height relationships in woven wool loop pile carpet." Note that the NRC for this carpet is only 30 to 40 or roughly half that of the Auralex Sonomatt, and you still need to think about ease of installation.

Understanding NRC is easy—you take the average sound absorption coefficient measured at four frequencies: 250, 500, 1,000, and 2,000 Hz expressed to the nearest integral multiple of 0.05. So it's easy to see that you aren't getting any great ratings at those frequencies if your NRC is only 30 to 40.

Next, you need to read this (also from the Carpet and Rug Institute), regarding the placement of carpet on walls:

"Carpet is manufactured for use as a floor covering, and installation on other surfaces, such as walls, is not recommended. Many carpet manufacturers will not assume any liability, real or implied, when carpet is applied on surfaces other than floors."

Interestingly enough, most insurance companies won't assume liability either. If you place carpet on walls, and it is determined that it contributed in any way to a fire, that is a perfect opening for your insurance company to walk away from you.

Once again—no low frequency benefit—and little benefit for what it does provide, especially when you consider the risk at which you are placing yourself.

Packing Foams
We've touched on this earlier in the book. These foams are only to be used for what they are made—shipping packaging. They do not attenuate sound the same way that products made specifically for that purpose do. I don't care what your ears told you—your ears are wrong.

If, after all that's happened with nightclubs and packing foams in recent years, anyone still wants to use these in their room(s), they must be crazy. Once again, your insurance company will drop you like a hot potato, and you can forget about collecting for a fire if that product is installed and contributed to a fire in any way.

Go back to Chapter 9 if you have any questions remaining and re-read the information there relating to foam products.

Mattresses

Yup, some people absolutely swear by these for use in studios as bass traps. They also make claims that they will help you big-time with sound isolation.

First, as you well know by now (having read the book to this point), isolation requires mass, which is sorely lacking in a mattress. Low frequency attenuation requires mass and air, only one part of which is provided by a mattress. Mattresses will treat mid and high frequency transmissions (seem to be seeing a trend here with that), but, once again, the biggest problem in your rooms is going to be LF modal and non-modal activities.

Second, safety is an issue again. Although these won't take to flame quite the same way as packing foam, they will smolder for a long time before a fire actually takes off. You could well have a fire start in a mattress and not know about it for hours.

As always, because the acoustic benefits you might get from the material aren't really helping you where you need it (as well as weighing in the safety factor), don't even bother heading in this direction.

PLEASE BUY OUR SOUNDPROOFING MATERIALS

Beware of companies selling "soundproofing" foams, fiberglass, insulation, etc. There are a fairly large number of companies out there that advertise what are actually sound attenuation products as "soundproofing." Seeing as how they they don't have a clue what their product really is, or how to market it properly, I have serious concerns about whether they produced a product worth purchasing. Let the buyer beware.

The Myth of Soundproofing

A note on the general concept of soundproofing itself, as well as companies that tell you they can soundproof your rooms, homes, etc.

Soundproofing doesn't exist.

Possibly the quietest recording facility in the world is Galaxy Studios located in Belgium. The design is wild and crazy (credit to Eric Desart and Gerrit Vemeir) when you consider that a 100.7dB noise floor is consistent throughout the entire facility. It is said that co-owners Wilfried and Guy Van Baelen are happy to step into one of the studios, close the airtight, concrete-filled door behind them, pull out a starter's pistol (whose report comes in around 125 dB), and fire it. And if you hadn't seen someone pull the trigger, you'd never know it had happened. Understand that this level of isolation had never been accomplished before in any commercial facility.

Interesting thing is—that isn't soundproof, it is just darn quiet, possibly quiet beyond belief, but not soundproof.

For example, a 375 cal. centerfire rifle, with an 18" barrel and a muzzle brake will produce 170 dB upon firing.[4] That would be heard in an adjacent room. (By the way, that would be one uncomfortable rifle to fire without hearing protection since the threshold of pain is 130 dB.)

This doesn't mean that the studio isn't quiet—it just means it isn't soundproof.

Avoid any company trying to sell you "soundproofing." The fact that they even use the term is evidence of their lack of knowledge on the subject.

CLOSE IS GOOD ENOUGH

This is the area where people get caught. And it is a costly mindset for someone trying to achieve isolation.

The details outlined in this book are there for a reason; they ensure that you make it from point "A" to point "B." They are not there to cost you additional monies, but rather to ensure that failures due to the "human factor," and possible deficiencies in materials, do not come back to haunt you in the end.

Thus, in a perfect world, a single layer of acoustic caulk would ensure that there would be no sound leakage through the perimeter of a wall assembly, and yet in here I recommend a caulk joint at each layer of drywall on the edges. The intent of this redundancy is a backup to cover the human factor—or a product deficiency.

Let's examine both of those for a moment.

The Human Factor

Human performance has certain capabilities and limitations that affect the outcome of work produced. When a human being makes an error, he or she will assess the work and make a determination that the error is either acceptable or not acceptable. For example, a piece of drywall cut partly out of square would be typically viewed as being acceptable, whereas a piece of wood trim (intended for a clear finish) not fitting properly would generally be viewed as being not acceptable. These decisions are easy to make, because in one case the drywall joint will be taped over and thus covered up, while the wood trim will be exposed for all to see.

Therein lies part of the problem.

People tend to view things that aren't seen in the finished product as being not quite as important as the finished product itself. I've witnessed this time and time again during my many years in the construction industry. Framing carpenters who believe that framing doesn't have to be cut perfectly square and tight-fitting because it gets covered up and you never see it. Trim carpenters who don't worry about painted trim fitting like it was cut with a razor blade, because the painters can just caulk the joint when they finish it. No one will know or see it in the finished product.

After all, close is good enough.

The fact is, especially in the case of sound isolating construction, nothing could be further from the truth. It's this mentality that is the cause for walls that were designed with a particular isolation in mind to actually have field ratings of 20 dB less or worse. This happens in more cases than one might believe.

But what the heck, close is good enough.

How does one take the human equation out of the picture? Through the use of redundancy. You think "redundancy" because the odds of a person getting sloppy, making a mistake in *exactly* the same location, in the same *exact* manner, in an additional application, are pretty slim. They may very well get sloppy—they may very well make a mistake—but it will not be in the exact same location.

So, having workers stagger the joints in each and every layer of drywall protects you from bad seams. Making them caulk each and every edge of those layers moves any areas of imperfection around the perimeter, with good joint areas protecting weak ones. While we're on the subject of good caulk joints versus weak caulk joints, let's look at the issue of product deficiency. I wish I had a dime for every time I've seen a caulk joint fail. Sometimes, they failed based on sloppy workmanship, and sometimes they failed when the workmanship was perfect.

Product Deficiency

Every product manufactured goes through a QC (Quality Control) process, and all of those QC processes have tolerance ranges, which are the maximum/minimum size, amount of chemical additive, etc. that can be used in the process prior to the product developing a failure. For an engine, it might be the max/min piston diameter vs. the max/min cylinder diameter. So, if the cylinder diameter is below the minimum allowable, then the max diameter piston won't fit within the chamber. By the same token, if the cylinder is over the maximum limit, then the smallest allowable piston might not create enough compression for the engine to operate properly.

The same goes with the chemical compounds that create the bonding capacities with caulk. There are very small variances allowed in the mixing process that will maintain the bonding and curing capacity of the products. But, if the ratios of the mixture are outside of these, the caulk will fail.

So what happens when we take the human factor into consideration with the QC process in these manufacturing plants? Someone in QC decides that an additional 1/1000 of an inch (beyond allowable tolerance) isn't enough of a variance to throw out a run of 10,000 pistons, which end up being installed in some engines where the cylinders were at the maximum allowable tolerance—and you just bought yourself a lemon that never runs right.

In the case of caulk, someone in the QC process decides than an additional 1/1000 of an ounce of a particular chemical (beyond design tolerance) isn't enough of a variance to justify throwing away 10,000 tubes of caulk—and you just bought some tubes that are going to fail.

But what can you expect? After all—close is good enough.

What makes this interesting is that it isn't generally 100% of the run that's out of tolerance. If the tolerance at the beginning of the run were right at the edge when that particular lot was being produced, then maybe only 5 to 8% are out of tolerance. If that were the case, would you throw away stock knowing that anywhere from 92 to 95% of the stock was good? Well, some people in QC would and some wouldn't. (I know this for a fact because my father used to work in QC and forever had people angry with him because he would reject an entire lehr of glass bottles because they slipped over the allowable tolerances. People would say to him, "If 'so and so' had inspected this he would have let it go out, " to which Dad would reply, "Then maybe you should have had him inspect it, but it isn't going out with my stamp on it.")

So you pick up 100 tubes of caulk at your local lumberyard, five cases from that same lot, and anywhere from five to eight tubes are going to have joint failures. Let me clarify this by saying that I am not telling you that for every case of caulk you buy you are going to have five to eight tubes of bad caulk. This is just an example of what could happen with a bad lot that slipped through the QC process.

How does one take product failure out of the equation? Once again (in the case of caulk)—redundancy. If you caulk only one layer of drywall, then any failure of the caulk joint affects you directly. But calking each and every edge of those layers moves any areas of imperfection around the perimeter, with good joint areas protecting weaker ones.

Trust me, invest the money and go the extra mile. It is that commitment to excellence that is going to guarantee success rather than failure.

The Final Word on Myths

The bottom line here is "Beware the acoustical myth."

There are a lot more fallacies and misconceptions in acoustics than could be presented in this chapter. In fact, an entire book could be devoted to the subject, but hopefully, you get the idea.

The examples given in this book are intended to help you avoid some specific problems (or concerns) with your studio design and construction. They are an attempt to illustrate the dangers in believing everything you see or read. Whether it be in a magazine or on some Web site on the Internet, stick with what's tried, true, and tested. You'll never be sorry you did.

Anytime an acoustical myth can be identified and replaced with a little common sense or objective proof, acoustics as a science becomes less mysterious, and one fewer acoustical "truth" will be preached as gospel.

Endnotes

[1] IARC Monographs Programme Re-evaluates Carcinogenic Risks From Airborne Man-Made Vitreous Fibres, Press Release No. 137, 24 October 2001, International Agency for Research on Cancer, World Health Organization, Lyon, France

[2] Reprinted with permission of Acoustics First. Corp.

[3] Reprinted with permission of the Carpet and Rug Institute

[4] Documented by Dr. Krammer, Ph.D., Ball State University, Muncie, Indiana.

CHAPTER 12

Codes, Permits, and Special Needs

I feel the need to spend at least some time with you discussing building codes, permits, inspections, and engineering.

Building Officials

A large number of people I come in contact with who are doing home studio construction tend to view building inspectors as evil ogres bent on stopping them from doing what needs to be done to make their studios right. Nothing could be further from the truth.

Building officials are simply doing their job, which is to ensure that a minimum standard of construction, which has been established to help provide safe buildings for people to occupy, is met.

When you walk into the offices of officials with something totally outside of their experiences, they (rightfully) look very hard at what you propose to do. They probably will require some documentation to assure them that this meets (or exceeds) those standards established in the building codes. They will also perform periodic inspections on the work to ensure that the actual construction meets those same standards.

I have dealt with this for over 30 years, and you would be amazed at the number of times that an inspector notices a code violation on work done by professionals in their field. It could be something as simple as too many wires in an outlet box (which could create heat buildup within that box and cause a fire) to an incorrect nailing pattern used on a shear wall (which could cause a collapse of the building under wind or seismic loads).

I cannot stress enough the importance of these people and the jobs they do, and I recommend that you always pull a permit for any work that you intend to perform.

Structural Analysis of the Proposed Work

I have also found myself alarmed by the number of people who have posted their designs for construction on floors above grade that have not bothered to contact structural engineers to verify that the existing structure could take the additional loads they would be imposing on that structure. By "floors above grade," I'm referring to first floors with basements below, second floors of buildings, etc.

On more than a few occasions, after posting my concerns, I have had the parties contact me and thank me for stressing the need for them to hire an engineer to review their design intent. The engineer assured them that they could *not* do what they wanted and that the structure could *not* carry the additional load.

My insistence that they do this not only saved them a lot of money, but it may have saved a life in the process. One thing about structural collapses, they do not generally give any warning. One moment an overloaded joist is seemingly fine, and the next moment it's gone.

Please do not add structural loads to buildings or cut and remove structural members, without first checking with a structural engineer to verify that you can safely do this. Another thing that you need to understand is that my methods, although tried and true, do not and cannot cover each and every condition that exists in the world. Thus, you really need to consult with professionals in your area (I include building officials in that category) to make certain that you aren't going to damage your structure (at worst), or throw your money away while in the process of constructing your studio.

Let's take a look at a couple of examples to show you how important this really is. Understand that these are not the only times this matters, but rather are indicative of the need in general. One could fill a book with examples and still never scratch the surface of *all* of the problems that could arise.

PROBLEMS RELATING TO THE BEARING CAPACITY OF EARTH
Earth has certain load bearing capacities, which are different from area to area throughout the world, which can't be covered in this book. There are areas of the world where people construct buildings above materials, which are referred to as expansive soils. These expansive soils are considered one type of unsuitable material for load-bearing construction to build on. There are other materials considered unsuitable—for example, earth containing large amounts of vegetation, structures built over old

dump sites, and earth containing large amounts of loamy materials, just to mention a few.

For the purpose of this discussion, though, let's look at expansive soils. Expansive soils are earth generally containing large amounts of clay by volume, which can expand and contract greatly, depending on the levels of the water table in that locale. Often, the elevation of the water table varies by season.

When buildings are built in areas with expansive soils that contain varying water levels, then the structure is generally supported through the use of either piles or caissons. Piles are supports made of either wood, concrete, or steel, which are driven into the ground with a machine called a pile driver. These supports are often driven to bedrock, although they may be designed to support the load strictly through the friction that the earth places on the side surfaces of the pile.

There are then concrete pile caps poured above these piles with a series of concrete grade beams that connect the piles to form the building foundation. In this manner, the piles carry the entire building load, without any transfer of load to the unsuitable soils that surround the building. Figure 12.1 depicts a simple pile foundation.

Caissons are similar to piles, except they are steel reinforced concrete, which is poured on-site. A hole is bored in the earth (often right into the bedrock, which is referred to as a socket for the caisson to sit within), and a reinforcing cage is then lowered into the bored hole where concrete is placed. The remainder of the foundation construction is similar to that which I described for the piles. Figure 12.2 shows a simple caisson foundation.

In the case of homes built above these materials, typically the concrete slabs you see in the basement are floating. The slabs carry no building loads and are designed to float up and down with the movement of the expansive soils beneath. Some of those slabs may float as much as two to three inches between the high points in wet conditions and the low points in dry conditions.

Building a structure on top of these slabs could cause great structural damage to your home during a wet period if the new structure came into contact with the building structure above while lifting. Picture a slab lifting 3" and having the walls resting on it lifting your first floor joists that same 3".

This is a disaster waiting to happen. It is just another reason for getting professionals involved during the design stage of your project to make certain you are not going to perform work that can damage your home or perhaps even destroy it.

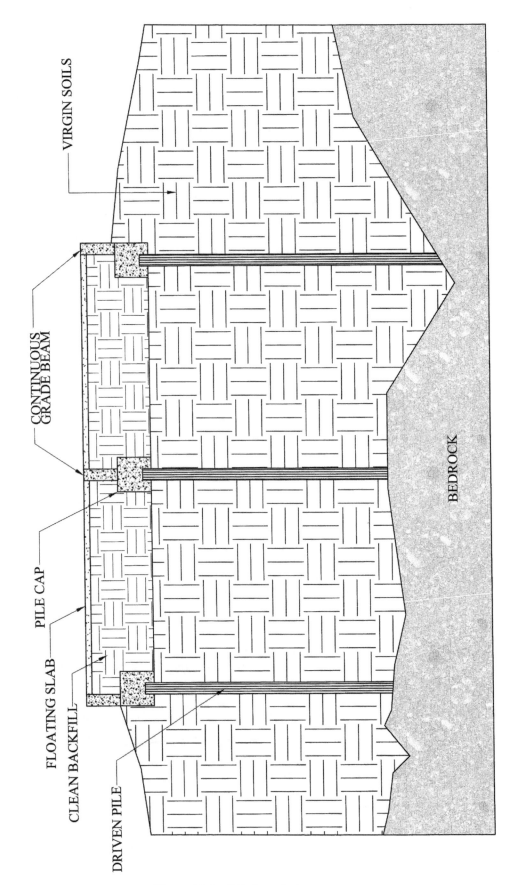

Figure 12.1   Pile foundation.

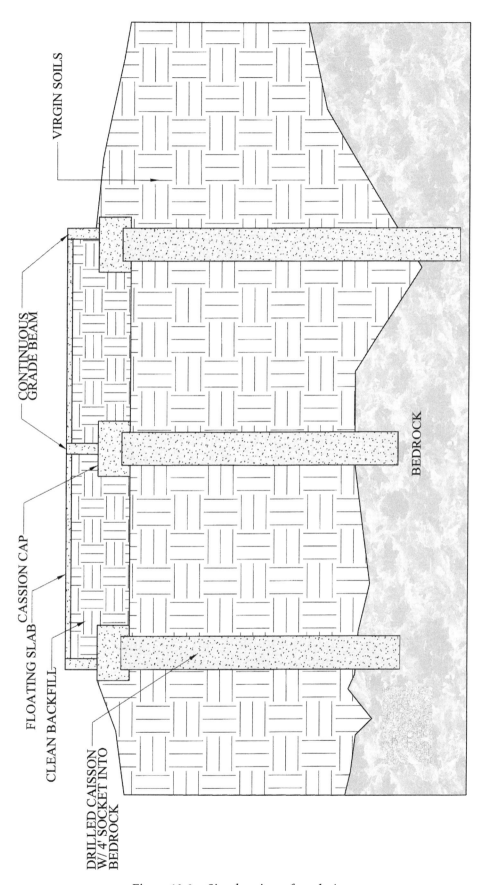

Figure 12.2   Simple caisson foundation.

UNSTABLE CONDITIONS CAUSED BY THE ADDITION OF BEARING WALLS
There are many other ways in which you could damage your home without realizing it. People mistakenly have the impression that bearing walls only exist if they are required to carry a load. Nothing could be further from the truth. Any wall that is built in contact with the joists above it becomes a bearing wall, regardless of whether it needs to be or not.

Floor joists deflect under load conditions and then return to their normal condition when the load is removed. Figure 12.3 shows a floor joist in both conditions. The deflection is exaggerated so that you can see more easily what I'm describing.

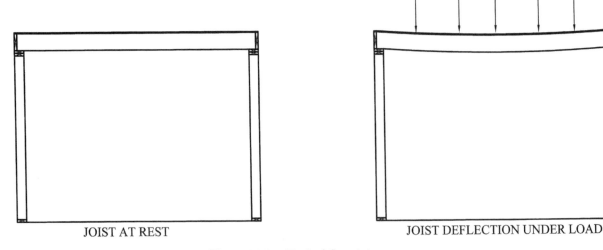

JOIST AT REST   JOIST DEFLECTION UNDER LOAD

Figure 12.3   Typical floor joist.

In the case of simple framing members (i.e., wood floor joists), this generally will not be a problem. However, in the case of floor trusses or composite floor joists, this could be a disaster waiting to happen.

The members of a floor truss are under constant compression and tension from live and dead loads placed upon them. Figure 12.4 shows the forces in play with a simple floor truss.

If you introduce a bearing point beneath them in a location for which the truss was not designed, you could cause a collapse of the truss. Figure 12.5 shows that same floor truss with some new forces in play from a wall introduced below. Introducing a bearing wall in the location indicated in Figure 12.5 causes stresses that could very well collapse the truss. Note that the reaction of the joist (with a wall placed below) is to create a condition where the loading of the web connection is no longer symmetrical.

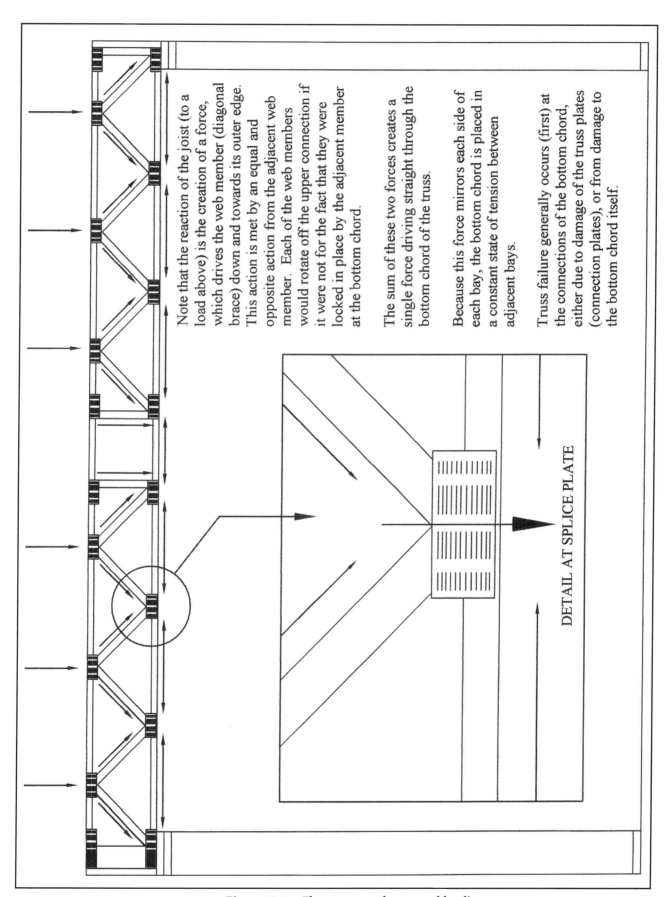

Note that the reaction of the joist (to a load above) is the creation of a force, which drives the web member (diagonal brace) down and towards its outer edge. This action is met by an equal and opposite action from the adjacent web member. Each of the web members would rotate off the upper connection if it were not for the fact that they were locked in place by the adjacent member at the bottom chord.

The sum of these two forces creates a single force driving straight through the bottom chord of the truss.

Because this force mirrors each side of each bay, the bottom chord is placed in a constant state of tension between adjacent bays.

Truss failure generally occurs (first) at the connections of the bottom chord, either due to damage of the truss plates (connection plates), or from damage to the bottom chord itself.

DETAIL AT SPLICE PLATE

Figure 12.4   Floor truss under normal loading.

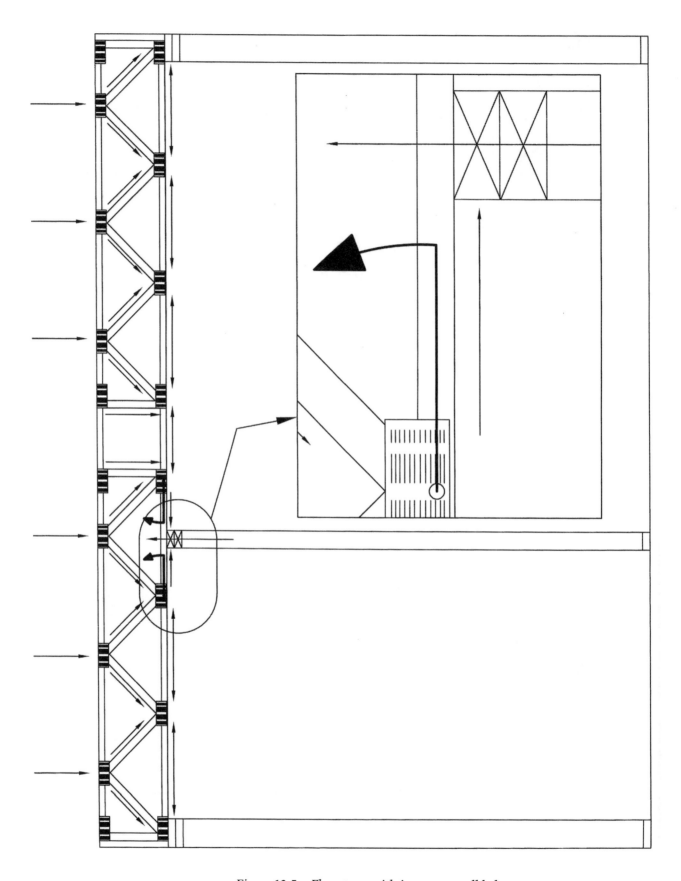

Figure 12.5   Floor truss with improper wall below.

This creates two conditions that can cause truss failure.

The first can be seen in the large scale detail in Figure 12.5. It's the creation of a hinge point located in the bottom chord that centers in the truss plate. This causes a rotational force in the truss plate, which may cause plate failure.

The second condition is the loading on the bottom chord itself. A floor truss is typically constructed using 2x members installed on the flat for the top and bottom chords. The total loading is designed to carry from end to end.

If the truss we see is 20' long and installed on 2' centers, with standard design loading of 10 psf dead load for truss weight and deck loading of the top chord, 10 psf dead load for ceiling, mechanical, and electrical loads on the bottom chord, and 40 psf live load, the total load per truss would be 1,200 pounds. That would mean that 600 pounds of load was transferred to each outside bearing wall.

Introduce a bearing wall in any location along the body of that truss, and you just loaded the bottom chord with 50% of that load. Now we have a 2x member on the flat, and we expect it to carry a load of 600 pounds. Couple the two conditions, and you have a disaster in the making.

In the case of a floor constructed with composite joists, the manufacturers of these joists have very exacting requirements for the installation of their materials. Failure to follow these installation requirements can cause the product to collapse under load.

For example, adding a new wall in a basement, beneath the location of an existing bearing wall above, creates a condition where the load above is transferred through the composite joists to the wall below. These composite joists are not made to transfer that load and may fail by having the web of the joist collapse under the pressure. Figures 12.6 and 12.7 show the before and after conditions described previously.

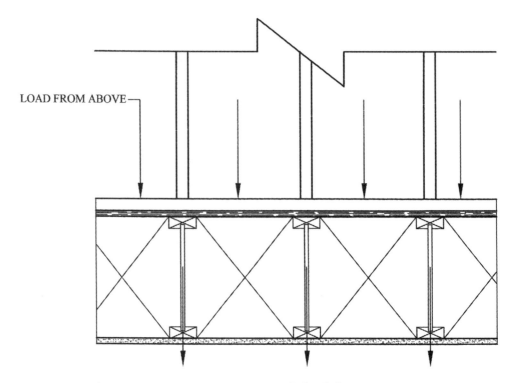

Figure 12.6   Composite joist properly loaded.

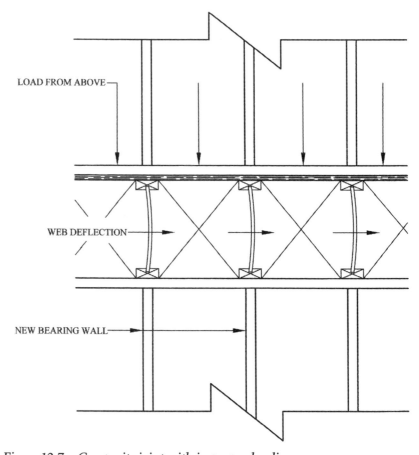

Figure 12.7   Composite joint with improper loading.

In order to install walls safely below floor trusses and composite joists, you need to understand the proper construction techniques involved and then implement them as a part of your work.

Often, you can get this information from the manufacturer (if you can identify them). If not, a structural engineer can determine the forces at work and detail the proper construction techniques required to install the new work safely. Or you can simply install all of your structure in such a manner that it never comes into contact with those members above.

My point here is that there is a lot more to this than just throwing up some walls and building a room. Sometimes, there are variables at work that you know nothing about, so it pays to spend those few extra dollars (for permits and engineering) to make certain everything will be right when you finish your work.

The examples I used above are not just thoughts of mine. They come from real life experiences I've been involved in, and I hope they show you the importance of the message I'm sending you.

Do it right the first time, and you'll never be sorry that you did.

Glossary of Terms

A
. . . .

A-B test—A test between two objects. For example, a test between two different microphones or preamps. For the test to be scientifically valid, levels should be matched, and the tests should be performed in a double-blind controlled environment. *See also* double-blind.

absorption—In acoustics, the reduction in sound pressure levels through the conversion of sound energy to heat captured within an acoustic attenuator. The opposite of reflection.

absorption coefficient—A measurement of sound energy reduction absorbed into or passed through a material. Measurement values range from 0 to 1 (which translates to 0% through 100%) and may vary with any particular material based on frequency and angle of incidence of the sound. This coefficient is typically referred to as sabin units. *See* sabin units.

acoustic impedance—A complex quotient obtained when sound pressure, averaged over a surface, is divided by the velocity of the volume through the surface.

acoustic material—Any material considered in terms of its acoustical attenuating properties. Commonly, a material designed to absorb sound.

acoustics—As used in this book, the study of the physical and psychological properties of sound as relates to isolating construction techniques and attenuation of modal and non-modal activities within a particular space.

AES—Audio Engineering Society.

airborne sound—Sound transmitted through the medium of air.

airflow resistance— The quotient of air pressure difference (steady or alternating state) across a specimen, divided by the volume velocity (steady or alternating state) of airflow through the specimen.

airflow resistivity—The quotient of the specific airflow resistance of a homogeneous material divided by its thickness.

Alcons—The measured percentage of Articulation Loss of Consonants by a listener. A %Alcons of 0 indicates perfect clarity and intelligibility with no loss of consonant understanding; 10% and beyond is increasingly poor intelligibility; 15% is typically the maximum acceptable loss; beyond 15% is unintelligible.

ambience—The acoustic characteristics of a space with regard to reverberation. A room with a lot of reverb is said to be "live"; one without reverb is said to be "dead." Note that the observation of degrees of ambiance is subjective at best, differing from person to person.

ambient noise—All-encompassing sound at a given place, usually a composite of sounds from many sources near and far.

amplitude—The magnitude of an oscillating quantity such as sound pressure. The peak amplitude is the maximum value.

analog—An electrical signal whose frequency and level vary continuously in direct relationship to the signal.

anechoic—Without reverberation.

anechoic chamber—A room designed to suppress sound reflections. Typically used for acoustical measurements.

anti-node—A resonance related to a room mode. An anti-node exists on either side of a node. Anti-nodes create an increase in amplitude, a reinforcement of a particular frequency or range of frequencies

articulation—A quantitative measure of the intelligibility of speech; the percentage of speech items correctly perceived and recorded.

articulation index—A quantitative measure of the intelligibility of speech; the percentage of speech items correctly perceived and recorded. An articulation index of 100% means that all speech can be understood and 0% means that no speech can be understood. Articulation index is calculated from the 1/3 octave band levels between 200 Hz and 6300 Hz center frequencies.

artificial reverberation—Reverberation generated to simulate that of concert halls, etc. This is added to a signal to make it sound more lifelike.

Arithmetic mean sound pressure level—The sum of sound pressure levels, in a particular frequency band, divided by the number of measured levels from different positions, times, or both.

ASA—Acoustical Society of America.

attenuate—To alter the level of an acoustical signal through absorption, diffusion, electronic, or other means.

audible frequency range—The range of sound frequencies heard by a human ear. The audible range typically spans from 20 Hz to 20,000 Hz.

auditory area—The sensory area lying between the thresholds of hearing and pain.

average room absorption coefficient—Total room absorption in sabins, divided by total room surface area in consistent units of measurement.

average sound pressure level in a room—Ten times the logarithm of the ratio of the space and time average of squared sound pressure to the squared reference sound pressure, the space average being taken over the total volume of the room, except for the regions of the room where the direct field of the source and the near field of the boundaries are of significance. Unit: decibel (dB).

A-weighting—The A-weighting curve is a wide bandpass filter centered at 2.5 kHz, with ~20dB attenuation at 100 Hz, and ~10dB attenuation at 20 kHz. It exhibits heavily roll-off at the low end, and a less aggressive roll-off on higher frequencies. This rating is the inverse of the 40-phon equal-loudness of the Fletcher-Munson Curve.

axial mode—Room resonances associated pairs of parallel or non-parallel walls or ceiling/floor.

B

background noise—Existing noise within a space, from sources unrelated to a particular sound, or sounds, that are the object of interest.

bandwidth—The frequency range of a system. Generally specified by establishing an upper and lower frequency range, i.e., 20–20,000 Hz plus or minus 4dB.

bass—The range of audible frequencies below 250 Hz.

boomy—A listening term that refers to excessive bass response.

bright—A listening term, which generally refers to upper frequency energy.

broadband noise—A wideband spectrum consisting of frequency components, no one of which is individually dominant.

C

cavity—A space between the surfaces of walls, ceilings, floors, etc., where insulation is typically installed.

characteristic impedance of the medium—The specific normal acoustic impedance at a point in a plane wave in a free field.

clipping—A type of distortion that occurs when an amplifier is driven into an overload condition. A "clipped waveform" generally contains an excess of high-frequency energy.

coherence—A listening term that refers to how well integrated the sound of a system is.

coloration—A listening term that refers to adding to a sound, something that was not in the original sound. Coloration can be a factor of room characteristics, a signal imparted by the gear being utilized in the sound reproduction, or a combination of the two.

comb filter—A distortion produced by combining an acoustical signal with a delayed replica of itself. The result is constructive and destructive interference, which results in a series of peaks and nulls introduced into the frequency response.

compression—The portion of a sound wave in which molecules are pushed together, forming a region with higher-than-normal atmospheric pressure. Acoustic compression (within a room or space) can be caused by room modes, as well as non-modal activity.

critical band—Frequency components within a narrow bandwidth that mask a given tone. Critical band varies with different frequencies, but is commonly found between 1/6 and 1/3 octaves.

critical distance—The distance from a sound source at which direct sound and reverberant sound are at the same level.

critical frequency—The frequency below the separating point where standing waves will cause significant room modes.

cutoff frequency—The frequency of a sound attenuator above which the normal incidence sound absorption coefficient is most effective.

C-weighting—A weighting curve designed into filters for equipment measuring sound output levels. The C-curve is "flat," with -3 dB corners at 31.5 Hz and 8 kHz, respectively. It is intended to loosely correspond to how people perceive sound at higher volume levels.

cycles per second—The frequency of a wave measured in Hertz (Hz).

D

damp—To cause a loss or dissipation of the oscillatory or vibrational energy of a signal or object. In the case of a membrane (e.g., a wall surface, the face of a panel trap, etc.), the placement of insulation touching the inner face of the membrane will create this effect.

dB—*See* decibel.

dB (A)—*See* A-weighting

dB (C)—*See* C-weighting

decay rate—As relates to airborne sound, the rate of decrease of the level of vibratory acceleration, velocity, or displacement, measured after the initial excitation has ceased.

decibel (dB)—A unit used to measure the amplitude of sound. A measure of sound intensity as a function of power ratio, with the difference in decibels between two sounds being given by $dB=10 \log 10(P1/P2)$, where P1 and P2 are the power levels of the two sounds. The faintest audible sound, corresponding to a sound pressure of about 0.0002 dyne per sq cm, is arbitrarily assigned a value of 0 dB.

diaphragm (also diaphragmatic)—As used in this book, room surfaces or diaphragmatic sound attenuators (panel traps), which vibrate in response to sound.

diffraction—A change in the direction of sound energy in the area of a boundary discontinuity, such as the edge of a reflective or absorptive surface.

diffuse field—An environment in which sound pressure levels are the same throughout and the flow of energy is equally probable in all directions.

digital—A converted numerical representation of an analog signal.

distortion—As used in this book, an undesired change in the waveform of a signal.

double-blind—A testing procedure, as relates to recording equipment, designed to eliminate biased results, in which the identity of the equipment is concealed from both administrators and subjects until after the study is completed.

E
. . . .

echo—A reflected sound that arrives at the ear long enough after the original sound so that it is clearly defined as a separate image.

Early Early Sound (EES)—Sound travels faster through a dense material than through the air. Thus, it is possible for a sound to reach a microphone through a building structure before reaching it through the air.

EFC—Energy-frequency curve.

EFTC—Energy-frequency-time curve.

equal loudness contour—For all audible frequencies, a contour representing a constant amplitude.

ETC—Energy-time curve.

extension—The extent of the range of frequencies that a device can reproduce accurately.

F
. . . .

far field—That part of the sound field in which the decrease in sound pressure is inverse in relation to the distance from the source. This corresponds to a reduction of 6dB for every doubling of distance. *See also* inverse-square law.

FFT—Fast Fourier Transform.

field sound transmission class, FSTC—Sound transmission class calculated in accordance with ASTM E 413.

field transmission loss, FTL—Sound transmission loss measured in accordance with ASTM E336

flame spread—The time it takes for flame to spread, measured in accordance with a variety of standards based on the use of the materials involved.

flanking transmission—Transmission of sound, from the source to a receiving location, through a structural path other than the one anticipated.

Fletcher-Munson Curve—Equal-loudness contours indicating sound pressure levels (measured in decibels), over the range of audible frequencies, that are perceived as being of equal loudness. (Measured by Fletcher and Munson at Bell Labs in 1933).

flutter echo—A distinctive ringing sound caused by echoes bouncing back and forth between hard parallel surfaces following a percussive sound.

Fourier analysis—The application of the Fourier transform to a signal to determine its spectrum.

free field—Any environment in which a sound wave may travel in all directions without obstructions or reflections.

frequency—As used in this book, the number of waves (pressure peaks) that travel a distance in one second measured in Hertz (Hz).

frequency response—As used in this book, the frequency within the human hearing range, roughly 20 Hz to 20 kHz.

FTC—Frequency-time curve.

fundamental—The lowest frequency of a complex tone.

fusion zone—A term evolving from misinterpretations of the Haas effect. It implies that all sounds arriving (at the human ear) within an interval of time (ranging from about 20 to 50 milliseconds) are fused into a single sound. Simplistic at best, totally wrong at worst, this does not take into account that within these time limits there are several levels of clearly distinguishable characteristics, including spaciousness, timbre change, image shift, multiple sound images, and, at large delays, echoes that can color the sounds to create a separateness between them.

G

grating, diffraction—A series of minute, parallel lines used to change the direction of a sound wave.

grating, reflection phase—A diffuser of sound energy using the principle of diffraction grating.

H

Haas effect—A psychoacoustic effect, also referred to as *precedence effect*. If a listener hears two identical sounds (i.e., identical soundwaves of the same intensity) from two separate sources, then the source that is closer to the listener appears to be the only source of the sound. The level of the delayed signal may be up to 10dB higher than the direct signal before disturbing the localization effect.

hard room—A room in which the surfaces are very reflective.

harmonics—Tones at frequencies that are multiples of a fundamental tone. These are further characterized as either "even-order" or "odd-order" harmonics. Even order harmonics (second, fourth, sixth, etc.) are even octaves above the fundamental tone. Odd order harmonics (thirds, fifths, sevenths, etc.) are simple multiples of the fundamental, which may or may not produce pleasant overtones.

hertz—A measurement unit of frequency in cycles per second.

Helmholtz resonator—A tuned sound absorber.

I

imaging—The effect created by a stereo system that provides a three-dimensional re-creation of the sound recorded.

impulse—As regards acoustics, a short signal containing a "spike" input that sharply rises from zero and as abruptly decays back to zero.

impulse response—The response of a system to a short signal containing a "spike" input that sharply rises from zero and as abruptly decays back to zero. Impulse response measured in a room will indicate any series of reflections (from walls, etc.) of the direct response.

in phase—When two periodic waves of the same frequency synchronize, they are said to be "in phase." Signals in phase boost one another in amplitude.

initial time-delay gap—The span of time between the arrival of a direct sound and the first reflection of that sound.

interference—The combining of two or more signals in either a constructive or destructive manner.

inverse-square law—Under far/free field conditions, the effect that mandates a sound pressure level decrease of 6dB for each (and every) doubling of the distance.

isolate—To reduce sound vibrations from passing through a structure or assembly.

J
. . . .

JASA—Journal of the Acoustical Society of America.

JAES—Journal of the Audio Engineering Society.

K
. . . .

KHz—1,000 Hz.

L
. . . .

law of the first wave front—*See* Hass Effect

LEDE—*See* Live End Dead End.

Live End Dead End—An acoustical treatment plan for control rooms in which the front end is highly absorbent and the rear of the room is reflective and diffusive.

M
. . . .

masking—The amount (or the process) by which the threshold of audibility for one sound is raised by the presence of another (masking) sound.

mass law—Simply, the greater mass a sound wave has to move to create vibration transfer, the greater the reduction of noise energy. Mass law dictates that for every doubling of mass, a 6dB increase in sound isolation will occur.

mean free path—Relating to sound waves in an enclosure, the average distance traveled between successive reflections, generally measured in relation to reverberation time (RT60).

millisecond (ms)—One thousandth of a second.

mode—A resonance based on a room's dimension, coinciding with the length of a particular frequency. *See also* axial mode, tangential mode, and oblique mode.

modal resonance—*See* mode.

N
. . . .

NAB—National Association of Broadcasters.

near field—The sound field located between the source and the far field. The near field exists under optimal conditions at distances less than four times the largest sound source dimension.

node—The opposite of an anti-node. When standing waves occur, there are positions in space relative to the wave, called nodes, at which there is no movement at all. The wave interferes with itself to create this instance of opposition (e.g., a wave reflecting off a wall and back into its own path). Nodes are spaced one-half wavelength apart. Nodes cause a decrease in amplitude or (if perfectly out of phase) a full cancellation of the signal.

NRC—The abbreviation for Noise Reduction Coefficient. A specification used to indicate the effectiveness of acoustic absorption materials. It is arrived at by averaging the sabin absorption coefficients of a material in the octave bands between 125 Hz to 4 kHz. The greater the number, the more sound is absorbed.

null—A minimum pressure region in a room or space.

O
. . . .

oblique mode—A room mode involving all six surfaces, i.e., the four walls, ceiling, and floor.

octave—A doubling or halving of frequency.

P

passive absorber—A sound attenuator that dissipates sound energy as heat through absorption.

PFC—Phase-frequency curve.

phase cancellation—An occurrence when two signals of the same frequency are out of phase with each other, resulting in a net reduction in the overall level of the combined signal. If two identical signals are 180 degrees out of phase, they will completely cancel one another if combined.

phon—A unit of perceived loudness, a subjective measure of the strength (not intensity) of a sound. At a frequency of 1 kHz, 1 phon is defined to be equal to 1dB of sound pressure level above the nominal threshold of hearing.

pink noise—Random noise produced with equal energy per octave.

plenum—A large (typically), absorbent-lined duct through which conditioned air is routed. Plenums are generally used as a supply (or return) connection for multiple branch ducts.

psychoacoustics—The study of the effect of the human auditory system and brain as it relates to acoustics.

pure tone—A tone without harmonics.

R

random noise—A noise signal, commonly used in measurements, which has constantly shifting amplitude, phase, and a uniform distribution of energy.

rarefaction—The portion of a sound wave in which molecules are spread apart, an expansion of the sound pressure field. The opposite of compression.

reactance—The opposition to the flow of electricity posed by capacitors and inductors.

reactive absorber—A sound absorber, such as the Helmholtz resonator, which involves the effects of mass and compliance as well as resistance.

receiving room—As relates to acoustical measurements, the space in which sound transmitted from a source room is measured.

reflection—As relates to sound, a return of residual sound, after striking a surface within a room or space. Reflection in low frequencies does not truly exist in the sense of ray tracing. Higher frequencies will display off a surface, although the strongest signal will be returned based on the theory that the angle of reflection equals the angle of incidence

reflection-phase grating—A sound diffuser using the principle of diffraction grating.

resonance—The tendency of a mechanical or electrical system to vibrate or oscillate at a certain frequency when excited by an external source, and to keep oscillating after the source is removed.

resonant frequency—The frequency at which resonance occurs.

reverb—The remainder of sound that exists in a room after the source of the sound has stopped.

RFZ—Reflection-free zone.

room mode—The normal modes of vibration of an enclosed space. *See* mode.

RT60—Reverberation time measured as the time required for a reduction of sound pressure levels by 60dB.

S

Sabine—Wallace Sabine, the originator of the Sabine reverberation equation.

sabin unit—A unit of acoustic absorption equivalent to the absorption by one square foot of a surface that absorbs all incident sound.

sound absorption—The property possessed by materials, objects, and structures, such as rooms of absorbing sound energy, measured in sabin units.

sound absorption coefficient—The absorptive properties of a material, in a specified frequency band, measured as outlined in ASTM C423; again, typically measured as sabin units.

sound pressure level (SPL)—Ten times the logarithm of the ratio of the time-mean-square pressure of a sound, in a stated frequency band or with a stated frequency weighting measured as a decibel (dB).

sound transmission class, STC—A single number rating, calculated in accordance with ASTM E 413, using values of sound transmission loss. STC ratings are calculated based on the frequency range of human speech.

sound transmission loss, TL—A measurement of the reduction in sound level when sound passes through a partition, floor, or ceiling assembly.

standing wave—A low frequency resonance condition, within an enclosed space, in which sound waves traveling in one direction interact with those traveling in the opposite direction, resulting in a stable condition exhibiting a series of localized peaks and nulls.

structure-borne noise—Transmission of sound through structural members in a building.

T

T60—*See* RT60.

tangential mode—A room mode produced by reflections off four of the six surfaces of the room.

TDS—Time-delay spectrometry.

TEF—Time, energy, frequency.

tuning frequency—The resonant frequency of a tuned sound attenuator.

U

ultrasonic frequency—The frequency range that exists and is higher than the nominal frequency range of human hearing, measures as hertz (Hz).

V

vibration—Oscillation of a parameter that defines the motion of a mechanical system.

vibration isolation—A reduction in the ability of a structural system to transmit vibration in response to mechanical excitation, attained through the use of a resilient coupling or any other manner of decoupling of separated structural assemblies.

W
· ·

watt—A measurement unit of electrical or acoustical power.

wavelength—The distance a sound wave travels to complete one cycle. The wavelength of any frequency is found (in the simplest sense) by dividing the speed of sound by the frequency.

white noise (ANS)—Noise with a continuous frequency spectrum and with equal power per unit of bandwidth.

white noise—Random noise with equal energy per frequency.

Online Tools

Folks, you were promised from the very start of this book that you would not have to do any real math in order to build your studio. As I worked my way through the book, I realized that this would be more difficult than I imagined unless you were provided with the tools you needed to accomplish this.

We tussled with this one, toying with the idea of a CD insert in the back of the book, but ended up deciding to go the route of a series of online tools. I believe this is a better choice for a variety of reasons, not the least of which is the ability to upgrade these as time permits or to add features when necessary.

The tools provided were written by me (the author), Brian Ravnaas, the head of engineering at Audio Alloy, and Jeff D. Szymanski, PE, who was (until very recently) the head of engineering at Auralex Acoustics.

My personal thanks to both Brian and Jeff for their efforts in this regard. They constantly give of themselves at Internet Web sites to help people understand acoustics more clearly. Their assistance in putting together the toolkit for this book just shows again their devotion to both the field of acoustics and to you, the readers.

The toolkit includes the following files:

▶ Panel Absorber.xls, called "Panel Absorber" on the Web site. A simple calculator for a narrowband panel trap, written by the author.

▶ Fmsm_calc_RG(2).xls, called "Fmsm Calculator" on the Web site. A calculator to determine the Mass Air Mass Frequency of various wall assemblies you might consider constructing, written by Brian Ravnaas.

▶ OC 703-705.xls, called "Absorption Coefficients" for OC 703/705 on the Web site. Simply a spreadsheet of the Owens Corning 703/705 line of rigid insulation for use with some of the toolbox tools. Please build on this for your use. Provided by the author.

▶ TLmodeler_mini_RG_(2).xls, called "TL Mini Modeler" on the Web site. A neat little tool for the analysis of Transmission Loss data in wall assemblies, written by Brian Ravnaas.

▶ helpTLmodeler_mini[2].pdf, called "TM Mini Modeler Help File" on the Web site. A help file for use with the above mentioned tool.

▶ sabin - RT60 calculator.xls, called "Sabin - RT60 Calculator" on the Web site. A simple calculator to enable you to determine your future room's RT60 empty, as well as when you install treatments. A good tool for budgeting purposes, written by the author.

▶ HVAC Calculator.xls, called "HVAC Calculator" on the Web site. A calculator to determine sensible and latent HVAC loads in your studio, written by the author.

▶ Quadratic Diffusor.xls, called "Quadratic Diffusor" on the Web site. A calculator for "Well Type Quadratic Diffusors," ranging to prime 31. Includes a side view and inverted 3D view of your diffusor, written by the author.

▶ resonance_toolbox(2).xls, called "Resonance Toolbox" on the Web site. This is a great little tool by Brian Ravnaas that calculates single panel isolation values based on mass law, and also includes a modulus and critical frequency calculator for free panels, a bound panel resonance calculator, and a multi-layer panel stiffness calculator.

▶ Helmholtz Calculator.xls, called "Helmholtz Calculator" on the Web site. A simple calculator for slat-type Helmholtz traps, written by the author.

▶ Room Mode Calculator.xls, called "Room Mode Calculator" on the Web site. Written by Jeff D. Szymanski, PE, this is probably the best room mode calculator I have ever worked with. If you want to calculate it, this tool gives it all to you.

These tools can be located at the Thomson download site: www.courseptr.com/downloads.

Or at the author's Web site: http://rodssoundsolutions.com/Outside.html.

Index

M

magnetic weather-stripping, door construction, 97
main room design, 3–4
MAM (Mass Air Mass) systems, 33
Manley company, 1
manufactured doors, 98
manufactured room treatments
  AudioTile features, 188
  Auralex product test data, 198, 200–204
  B22 ProPanels, 196
  B24 ProPanels, 196–197
  discussed, 185–186
  GIK Acoustics product line
    discussed, 219
    GIK 242 panels, 216–217
    GIK 244 panels, 216
    product data, 218–219
  LENRD Bass Trap, 193–194
  RealTraps product line
    discussed, 204
    GoboTraps, 209–210
    MicroTraps, 208–209
    MiniTraps, 205–207
    MondoTraps, 208
    product test data, 212–215
    room kits, 211
    SoffitTraps, 210
    stands, 211
  SpaceArray diffusors, 187
  SpaceCouple treatment, 188
  Studiofoam acoustic panels, 189–193
  TruTraps Genesis system, 194–195
  Venus Bass Trap, 195
  VersaTile absorption, 195–196
manufactured units, window construction, 92
mass
  Mass Law, 35
  sound isolation, 35–37
Mass Air Mass (MAM) systems, 33
Mass Spring Mass (MSM) system, 45
material location considerations, wall construction, 54
mattresses as bass traps, myths and legends, 286
M-Audio company, 2
Maximum Length Sequence (MLS), 141
medium-sized rooms, 25
members, defined, 11
meters, sound level, 34
mic combinations, room design considerations, 3
MicroTraps, 208–209

mid/high bass absorbers, 182
mini-split air conditioning systems, 124
MiniTraps, 205–207
MLS (Maximum Length Sequence), 141
modal analysis, room modes, 24–25
modes. See room modes
MondoTraps, 208
MSM (Mass Spring Mass) system, 45
multipurpose rooms, 226–227

N

neutral feed flowing, electrical considerations, 99
Newton's Cradle example, 17
nodes, 17
noise, electrical, 103–107
non-modal waves
  back wall interference, 20–21
  SBIR (speaker boundary interference response), 21

O

oblique room modes, 27–28
outlets, polarity checking, 109
Owens Corning fiberglass panels, 170–171

P

P1324 Quadratic Residue Diffuser kit, 184–185
Packaged Terminal Air Conditioner (PTAC) unit, 132
packing foams as sound absorption, myths and legends, 285
partition supports, 78
people factor, HVAC systems and room design criteria, 113–114
Percussion/Rhythm room, room design, 4–5
permits, planning and design, 238
pianos, string room design, 5
planning and design, 221
  air locks, isolating from house structure, 246
  building codes, 238
  dead load, 238
  details, development, 236–238
  fire-safing, 241
  HVAC system, 246–247
  permits, 238
  sections directory, 237–238
  wall sections, 239, 241
  window construction, 244
plexiglass, window construction, 85
polarity checkers, 109
portable air conditioning systems, 126

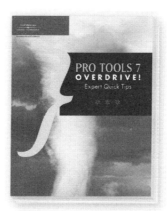

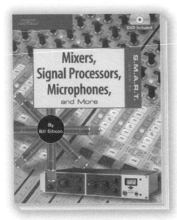
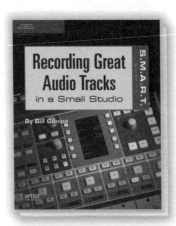

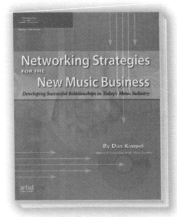